ROUTLEDGE LIBRARY EDITIONS:
BRITISH SOCIOLOGICAL
ASSOCIATION

Volume 5

SOCIAL CHANGE
AND POLITICAL
TRANSFORMATION

SOCIAL CHANGE AND POLITICAL TRANSFORMATION

Edited by
CHRIS ROOTES AND HOWARD DAVIS

LONDON AND NEW YORK

First published in 1994 by UCL Press

This edition first published in 2018
by Routledge
2 Park Square, Milton Park, Abingdon, Oxon OX14 4RN

and by Routledge
711 Third Avenue, New York, NY 10017

Routledge is an imprint of the Taylor & Francis Group, an informa business

© 1994 Chris Rootes, Howard Davies and contributors

All rights reserved. No part of this book may be reprinted or reproduced or utilised in any form or by any electronic, mechanical, or other means, now known or hereafter invented, including photocopying and recording, or in any information storage or retrieval system, without permission in writing from the publishers.

Trademark notice: Product or corporate names may be trademarks or registered trademarks, and are used only for identification and explanation without intent to infringe.

British Library Cataloguing in Publication Data
A catalogue record for this book is available from the British Library

ISBN: 978-1-138-49942-3 (Set)
ISBN: 978-1-351-01463-2 (Set) (ebk)
ISBN: 978-0-8153-4838-2 (Volume 5) (hbk)
ISBN: 978-0-8153-4840-5 (Volume 5) (pbk)
ISBN: 978-1-351-16720-8 (Volume 5) (ebk)

Publisher's Note
The publisher has gone to great lengths to ensure the quality of this reprint but points out that some imperfections in the original copies may be apparent.

Disclaimer
The publisher has made every effort to trace copyright holders and would welcome correspondence from those they have been unable to trace.

Social Change and Political Transformation

Edited by
Chris Rootes & Howard Davis
University of Kent at Canterbury

© Chris Rootes, Howard Davis and contributors 1994

This book is copyright under the Berne Convention.
No reproduction without permission.
All right reserved.

First published in 1994 by UCL Press

UCL Press Limited
University College London
Gower Street
London WC1E 6BT

The name of University College London (UCL) is a registered trade mark
used by UCL Press with the consent of the owner.

ISBN:
1-85728-147-0 HB
1-85728-148-9 PB

British Library Cataloguing in Publication Data.
A catalogue record for this book is available from the British Library.

Typeset in Baskerville.
Printed and bound by
Biddles Ltd., Guildford and King's Lynn, England.

Contents

Contributors	vii
Acknowledgments	ix

Introduction   1
Chris Rootes

1 European countries in a post-national era   13
  Alain Touraine

2 The European Community   27
  regime-building and institutionalization of criteria for rationality
  Rainer Lepsius

3 Harmonization and the art of European government   39
  Andrew Barry

4 Theses on a post-military Europe   55
  conscription, citizenship and militarism after the Cold War
  Martin Shaw

5 Changing attitudes in the European Community   72
  Sheena Ashford and Loek Halman

6 Support for new social movements in five western
  European countries   86
  Dieter Fuchs and Dieter Rucht

CONTENTS

7 Environmentalism in Europe: an east–west comparison 112
Petr Jehlicka

8 Order, crisis and social movements in the transition from
state socialism 132
Nick Manning

9 Intellectuals and democratization in Hungary 149
András Bozóki

10 State and society in Poland 176
Mira Marody

11 Some thoughts on trust, collective identity, and the
transition from state socialism 188
Adam Seligman

Index 203

Contributors

Sheena Ashford is a Research Fellow at QQSE, University of Sheffield.

Andrew Barry is a Lecturer in the Department of Sociology at Goldsmiths College, University of London.

András Bozóki is Associate Professor in Political Sociology in the Faculty of Law and Government, Eötvös University of Budapest, and a Fellow of the Central European University in Budapest.

Howard Davis is a Reader in Sociology at the University of Kent at Canterbury.

Dieter Fuchs and *Dieter Rucht* are researchers at the Wissenschaftszentrum Berlin für Sozialforschung.

Petr Jehlicka is a research student at Fitzwilliam College and in the Global Security Programme, Faculty of Social and Political Sciences, University of Cambridge. He was previously a member of the Institute of Geography at the Czechoslovak Academy of Sciences in Prague.

Loek Halman is a Research Fellow at IVA, Institute for Social Research, Tilburg University, The Netherlands.

Rainer Lepsius is a Professor in the Institute of Sociology, University of Heidelberg, and co-editor of the *Kölner Zeitschrift für Soziologie*.

Nick Manning is a Reader in Social Policy at the University of Kent at Canterbury.

Mira Marody is a Professor in the Institute of Sociology at the University of Warsaw.

Chris Rootes is a Lecturer in Sociology and Director of the Centre for the Study of Social and Political Movements at the University of Kent at Canterbury.

CONTRIBUTORS

Adam Seligman is an Assistant Professor of Sociology at the New School for Social Research, New York. During 1991–2 he was a Fulbright Fellow at Eötvös University of Budapest.

Martin Shaw is Reader in Political and International Sociology at the University of Hull.

Alain Touraine is Director of CADIS, the Centre for Sociological Analysis and Intervention, at the Ecole des Hautes Etudes en Sciences Sociales, Paris.

Acknowledgements

We are indebted to Nicola Kerry, Nicola Cooper and Yvonne Latham for their help with the word-processing, to Katy Pickvance for her assistance with the translation of Chapter 9, and to Nick Dalziel, until recently Publications Officer of the British Sociological Association, for his help in securing the publication of this and its companion volume.

Introduction

Chris Rootes

In 1989, when we first proposed the theme "A New Europe?" for the 1992 Annual Conference of the British Sociological Association, the Berlin wall had just fallen, talk of "our common European home" began to seem more than merely wishful thinking, and western Europe was being encouraged eagerly to anticipate 1992, when the completion of the Single European Market would bring real substance to the promise of the European Community (EC). We wanted to bring Europe to the top of the agenda of British sociology because we believed, as we believe still, in the desirability of cross-nationally comparative sociological research, but also because we considered that some of the enthusiasm for European integration was indiscriminate and needed, as a corrective, a stiff dose of critical sociological analysis. We imagined then that we should be writing this amidst a wave of euphoria about the New Europe taking shape before our eyes, and that we should be orchestrating pinpricks of dissent against the excesses of Eurohype and internationalist fervour.

Alas not so. The Europe in which we write is an altogether more sombre place than we could have imagined: the European Community seems at times to be in danger of unravelling under the impact of continuing difficulties surrounding ratification of the Maastricht Treaty, the recurrent crises of the Exchange Rate Mechanism (ERM), and the consequences of the European recession; the post-communist states of eastern Europe, their economies in tatters, appear to teeter from crisis to the edge of catastrophe; a war of a savagery not seen in Europe for more than a generation rages in what used to be Yugoslavia and threatens to overflow into the rest of the Balkans; resurgent nationalism threatens the security of ethnic minorities and the exclusion of refugees and asylum-seekers. What we imagined would be the unfashionable scepticism of our contributors in the face of euphoria about

INTRODUCTION

Europe's golden future seems more in tune with the tenor of the times than we could have anticipated. Indeed, there is such widespread disenchantment with the vision of a Europe united, peaceful and prosperous from the Atlantic to the Urals that we are in danger of losing sight of what has been achieved.

In view of the recent changes in both western and eastern Europe, it seems opportune to reconsider the question of convergence among European societies. The sociological discussion of convergence has centred around the debate stimulated by Clark Kerr and his colleagues (Kerr et al. 1960) over the extent to which a "logic of industrialism" was producing such changes in all industrialized societies as amounted to their convergence upon a model of "pluralistic industrialism". Assessment of the extent to which such long-term processes of change in technology, organization and values are at the root of recent developments is obscured by the more obvious rôle played by the interventions of political elites: the expansion and deepening of the EC was and is a deliberate political project of "enlightened" political elites determined to put Europe's war-torn past behind it and to consolidate liberal democracy and prosperity; in the East, the transition from state-socialism is variously represented as the triumph of reforming elites dismayed by the inefficiencies and corruption of state-socialist systems, or as the product of the loss of belief by communist elites in their own competence and fitness to rule. Secular tendencies associated with the "logic of industrialism" have undoubtedly played a part in the background to and the outcomes of these processes, but any account that did not give primacy to the rôle of political will (or the loss of it) would be seriously inadequate.

The European Community:
integration, regime-building, harmonization

For Alain Touraine, European integration is entirely desirable because it offers the prospect of the development of new forms of institutional mediation between an increasingly globalized mass culture and the particularities of the locally rooted lives of individuals and groups. The crisis of the national state is that, increasingly, consequential decisions are taken and loyalties reside elsewhere. The construction of a politically integrated European Community is the best hope of preserving national, regional and individual identities that would otherwise be threatened by the clash between the globalizing tendencies of mass culture on the one hand and defensive nationalism and ethnic exclusivity on the other. If defence and monetary policy, which can

INTEGRATION, REGIME-BUILDING, HARMONIZATION

no longer be effectively conducted at the level of the national state, were transferred to the EC, national parliaments and governments would be freed to focus attention upon social questions and mediation between globalizing forces and local, regional and minority cultures.

Such are the peculiarities of national languages, customs and histories that it is unlikely that the EC will develop as a kind of super-nation-state, or even a federal state resembling the United States; whatever the shared interests, the dynamism of national cultures will ensure that the EC remains something looser than a nation-state. In that respect, and in the opportunities it offers for the development of new forms of political mediation, the EC is a unique and uniquely encouraging political project. The crucial need now is to recognize the nature of the crises of national states, to understand the process of de-nationalization that is under way, and to enhance the hitherto relatively neglected *political integration* of the EC to ensure that the best of the possibilities it offers are realized and so to avoid the nationalist backlash that would otherwise be likely to come from peoples buffeted by globalizing forces over which they have no control and in the face of which they feel defenceless. The promise and the challenge of European integration is to build a new, European identity that will not replace but supplement existing national identities and that will make Europeans less anxious to cling to exclusionary national and ethnic identities whose existing political representations are less and less effective in protecting their interests in the modern world.

The main problem with the positive construction Touraine puts upon the development of the EC is that, however encouragingly it might serve as a beacon of hope and a pointer to the ways in which the EC *should* develop, it does not accord very well with the ways it *has* developed thus far. The EC has long ceased, in fact if not in popular perception, to be the European *Economic* Community, but it is nevertheless the case that its most conspicuous successes to date have been in the realm of economic harmonization; in the forging and implementation of common foreign policies, even in respect of trade, the record is distinctly patchy, and there is as yet no coherent EC defence policy, let alone an integrated EC defence institution.

When Touraine talks about European integration, it is clear that he is talking principally about the integration of the EC. But, as Rainer Lepsius points out, since 1989 European integration has also had another and larger meaning – the integration into the Western state system of the newly post-communist states of central and eastern Europe. However, this challenge arises at a time when the EC, overburdened as it is by the problems of integrating the economies and societies of the existing 12 members and antici-

3

INTRODUCTION

pating the accession of perhaps another six Scandinavian and central European states, is in no position on its own to accomplish the rescue that the economic and political shipwreck of eastern Europe seems to require.

It is perhaps because of its very novelty not only that so much of the business of the EC remains unfinished, but that the development of EC law and administration has far outrun the development of mechanisms for effective democratic control. The original vision of the signatories of the Treaty of Rome – that the political integration of Europe should be achieved by the integration of European economies – has, so far as western Europe is concerned, substantially been realized with the completion of the Single Market, but the nature of the political entity so produced is still remarkably ill defined.

Lepsius urges us to be clear-headed about what is going on, and insists that we should be properly conscious of the fact that there are *choices* to be made about what sort of regime the EC becomes. It is not enough for Europeans to proceed unreflectively, comfortable in the belief that they are on an escalator that will, somehow, someday, deliver them into the golden meadows of a unified Europe; they must *choose* where they want to go and the means appropriate to getting there. Lepsius, then, ends, like Touraine, with a plea to put the politics back into European integration.

Without denying the need for political choice, Andrew Barry argues that the process of harmonization so central to the development of the EC is not simply an economic, much less a "neo-liberal" project. It has precedents in the attempts of the nation-builders of the 19th century to secure "the government of men by means of the administration of things", but its object is to provide the conditions for the exercise of government in an enlarged economic and social space without any parallel increase in the size of the central state. If it can be represented as an attempt by elites to gain greater control, it can equally well be represented as a necessary condition of the rational decision-making most of us would claim to desire; it is a matter of political choice which areas – economic, social, environmental or whatever – should be subjected to harmonization, and the object may equally well be equality among consumers or workers as among producers or traders. Within the EC, harmonization proceeds from a recognition of the weakness of national political institutions to which Touraine refers, and aims "to provide the conditions under which it is possible to know and to regulate" the effects and development of the inter-dependence that modern conditions impose. In other words, far from being part of some ghastly plot to subject Europeans to the rationality of the market, or even, as Lepsius suggests, the unreflective application of the principles of economic rationality to ever wider realms,

INTEGRATION, REGIME-BUILDING, HARMONIZATION

harmonization is no more and no less than the necessary condition of effective government by whatever party and for whatever ends might be chosen. Who the political actors capable of making and implementing such choices might be, is a question that remains to be answered.

As Martin Shaw reminds us, Europe as it now exists has been shaped by war and military rivalry; indeed, to a great extent, the modern European state system is a distinctly martial accomplishment. Paradoxically, the beginning of the Cold War stimulated the development of a framework of co-operation that has made war between major European states increasingly improbable. The novelty of a post-war Europe, Shaw argues, requires sociologists to challenge the separation of international relations from social theory and to recognize the transnational rôle of social movements. The revival of nationalism need not lead to a resurgence of military conflict, and military service is likely to lose the close connection with citizenship that, in continental Europe, it has had until now. As armies become increasingly professionalized and as other dimensions of European political integration proceed, so the visibility of discernably national armed forces will recede, and European troops are likely to see action only as participants in international peace-keeping and "policing operations". Indeed, especially in the light of what is widely perceived to have been an inadequate EC response to the conflicts in Yugoslavia, their ability to do so is a fundamental test of the credibility of European integration. Nevertheless, despite the occurrence of small and bloody wars even within Europe, the existing level of military co-operation is itself no mean achievement in a continent where, little more than a generation ago, over 20 million people perished in five years of total war, and where the long peace from 1945 to 1989 was achieved only by the balance of terror between Cold War rivals.

The pacification and increasing political integration of Europe might be supposed to correspond to a convergence among the attitudes of the citizens of European states. But, as Sheena Ashford and Loek Halman show, when data from the European Values Surveys of 1981 and 1990 are compared, the picture that emerges is complex. Evidence of the continuation, indeed the strengthening, of traditional values regarding the family and parenting co-exists with striking testimony to increased liberalism and individualism in sexual matters and a marked decline of formal religious practice if not of belief, but there is little evidence of convergence in attitudes and some of increased *dissimilarities* among the citizens of EC states.

Modest declines in national pride (and a decline in the differences among states in this respect) are accompanied by increased aspirations for social

INTRODUCTION

change. Consistent with this is the even more striking increase in the proportions of citizens of EC states who say they have signed or might sign a petition, and who have participated or might participate in lawful demonstrations. European publics, which have become more individualist in the course of a decade, appear also to have become considerably more participatory in their dispositions towards politics. Although the European Values Surveys do not provide longitudinal data on support for social and political movements, it does appear from the 1990 survey that there are very high levels of support throughout the Community for the ecology and human rights movements, and rather less and less cross-nationally consistent support for the women's movement.

This lack of longitudinal evidence in the European Values Surveys is partially remedied by the Eurobarometer data analyzed by Dieter Fuchs and Dieter Rucht. Contrary to what some commentators have suggested, and despite an apparent decline in the levels of actual social movement mobilization (as environmentalists, in particular, have moved from direct action to campaigning?), the evidence examined by Fuchs and Rucht suggests that the *potential* level of mobilization in support of anti-nuclear, peace and, especially, ecology movements is high and rising. At least as interesting, however, is the finding that, when cross-national comparisons are considered, the pattern of support for and opposition to the new social movements varies quite idiosyncratically from country to country. Once again, we are reminded that the histories, cultures and politics even of the major western European societies are different and that the consequences of those differences are enduring.

If the paucity of longitudinal data on support for social and political movements is readily explained by the difficulty of securing funding for its collection, the data analyzed by Fuchs and Rucht amply demonstrate the methodological problems that attend cross-nationally comparative survey research, particularly on questions such as these. Although awareness of the problems has improved the quality of regularly repeated cross-national surveys such as Eurobarometer, there are inherent difficulties in ensuring the comparability of questions that must be administered to respondents in their native languages and in ensuring equivalencies of meaning in different societies with different histories, cultures and political systems, and where the salience of movements and political issues changes according to nationally specific timetables. As a result, the quantitative data yielded by such surveys are most appropriately treated, as they are in this volume, as impressionistic, qualitative and approximate, and not as material amenable to rigorous statistical analysis.

INTEGRATION, REGIME-BUILDING, HARMONIZATION

Even so, the interpretation of such evidence as demonstrating the existence of a high potential for social movement mobilization should be treated with caution. This is, after all, evidence of attitudes or, at best, of professed dispositions to act, rather than of action itself, and it is unlikely that such dispositions will be straightforwardly translated into action (Rootes 1981). Indeed, the evidence Ashford and Halman present of near universal "support" for the ecology and human rights movements sits uncomfortably with the rather more modest proportions prepared to countenance taking even so undemanding an action as signing a petition. Fuchs and Rucht are aware of this problem, and count as part of the "mobilization potential" of a movement only those who both approve of it and claim to be prepared to act in support of it, but it remains likely that there will be substantial and variable differences between "mobilization potential" so measured and the social and political profiles of actual mobilizations. Nevertheless, taking the evidence of the European Values Surveys and the Eurobarometer together, there is nothing to support the contention that the "new politics" of social and political movements and unorthodox political parties is a merely temporary enthusiasm. Moreover, despite the fact that the latest waves of these surveys were conducted at or near the peak of the recent surge in environmental concern, the very high levels of professed support for ecology movements suggest that the issues they raise will continue to play an important rôle in the politics of western European countries for some time to come.

Petr Jehlicka's discussion of environmentalism in both western and eastern Europe serves to remind us not only of the diversity of levels of environmental awareness and mobilization across Europe, but of the stages of development through which environmental consciousness has passed in those countries where it now appears most developed. The initial impetus to environmental consciousness came from people's perceptions of the deterioration of their own immediate environments, and was only later transmuted into awareness of and concern with global environmental problems. Fuchs and Rucht suggest that ecologism is strongest in the most "modern" European societies, but as Jehlicka points out, these are also the western European countries that suffer the worst pollution; they are also countries that share certain elements of political culture and that are, in particular, unusually decentralized and regionalized. If people in the Germanic "core" of western Europe have now largely completed the journey to global environmental awareness, those of the southern periphery are still at the stage of "personal complaint" environmentalism, and in eastern Europe, where environmental degradation is greater even than in central western Europe, even that level

INTRODUCTION

of environmental concern has come to take a back seat to anxieties about the economy and employment.

The transformation of central and eastern Europe

The rôle of environmental movements in the emerging opposition to communist rule in central and eastern Europe has often been remarked. Jehlicka argues that environmental movements assumed so prominent a rôle partly because the environmental degradation that occurred under state-socialist regimes was so catastrophic, but partly too because "green was a protective colour" for more fundamental opposition to communist domination. It was possible to mobilize under the banner of environmental concern protests that, couched in more overtly political terms, would have been vigorously repressed. But, despite the continuing environmental catastrophe, green politics was quickly eclipsed as the transition from state-socialism was accomplished, environmental activists became politicians in various of the emergent political parties, and the public became increasingly preoccupied with economic survival.

The rôle of environmental movements is one of the themes taken up by Nick Manning in his wide-ranging discussion of the crisis and transition in eastern Europe but, whatever their importance as vehicles for the mobilization of opposition in the latter stages of state-socialist regimes, environmental movements are upstaged by intellectuals who, whether as elites increasingly central to the functioning of state-socialism or as critics crucial to the stimulation and co-ordination of the opposition, emerge as the key actors in the process of transition, particularly as the "revolutions" of eastern Europe were more characterized by the collapse of ruling elites than by the mobilization of popular challenges to their rule.

The rôle of intellectuals is examined in greater detail by András Bozóki. It is particularly appropriate that Bozóki's analysis should focus on the Hungarian case, because it was Hungarian experience that informed the most celebrated account of the rôle of the intelligentsia in state-socialist societies, Konrád and Szelényi's *The Intellectuals on the Road to Class Power* (1979). As Bozóki demonstrates, Konrád and Szelényi's characterization of the intelligentsia as an emergent class "on the road to power" was plausible at the time they wrote, in the post-Stalinist period of the mid-1970s, but it obscured latent divisions within the intelligentsia that were to come increasingly to the fore as communist power faltered and as the beginnings of a pluralistic civil society began to develop.

THE TRANSFORMATION OF CENTRAL AND EASTERN EUROPE

The rôle of intellectuals and the intelligentsia was indeed crucial in the transition period – in easing the communist regime's path to reform, in devising the constitutional, administrative and political arrangements of the post-communist state, and in staffing the newly formed (or revived) non-communist political parties – but the very fact of their having played such a prominent political rôle in the transition saddled intellectuals with such conflicts of identity and rôle as have made it difficult for them to find a congenial and responsible place in the democratic civil society that has resulted. Although some intellectuals have happily shed the inhibitions of the clerisy for the rôle of politician, others are more influenced by a variety of traditional intellectual reservations about democratic politics (see, e.g., Linz 1978, 48). The increasingly strident nationalism of some "popular" intellectuals raises fears that Hungary will fall victim both to "ethnic cleansing" and to wars to recover territory and population lost (to Romania in particular) in the aftermath of the First World War. On the other hand, nostalgia for the politics of social movements inhibits more modern and reformist intellectuals from playing an effective and constructive rôle.

Mira Marody and Adam Seligman point out some of the obstacles that lie in the way of social, economic and political change in post-communist societies, let alone their effective integration with those of the West. As Marody argues, the habits of thought and action into which people were socialized during 40 years of state-socialism cannot be shed overnight; yet, until they *are* shed, the promises of capitalism and liberal democracy will remain unfulfilled. Moreover, as Seligman observes, the absence of trust that plagues these societies is not simply a product of 40 years of subordination to autocratic communist elites, but is rooted in the fact that most of these societies are still barely modern in the sense that patterns of loyalty and trust are still fundamentally those of rural societies suspicious of strangers and especially of urban cosmopolitans and gypsies and other ethnic minorities.

If the evidence from Hungary is to be believed, the collapse of communism has made matters not better but worse. In the early 1980s, disillusion with state-socialism may have been widespread but it was not total or universal; if the collapse of communism destroyed what remaining trust Hungarians had in the institutions of the old regime, it did not automatically generate trust in the institutions of the new one, with the result that in 1990 the only institution Hungarians trusted more than in 1982 was the Church. In such circumstances, it is hardly surprising that the "civil-familial privatism" that Habermas (1976) believed to be so central to the crisis tendencies of "late" capitalism is much more marked in Hungary (the only post-commu-

INTRODUCTION

nist society for which we have survey data) than it is anywhere in western Europe.

The evidence and arguments marshalled by Marody and Seligman scarcely inspire confidence in prospects for the stabilization of democracy in central and eastern Europe. However, both Seligman and Bozóki refer to a case that does give grounds for hope – the Budapest taxi-drivers' blockade of 1990. Despite the fact that protest was directed against the government, it was remarkable in that it was not anti-democratic, it attracted public support on the basis that it challenged allegedly incipient authoritarianism on the part of the government, and it produced a negotiated settlement that testified to a degree of restraint and flexibility that augurs well for the prospects for democratic politics in Hungary. Although it is only right and proper that we should be reminded of the difficulties that stand in the way of stable liberal democracy in central and eastern Europe, it is difficult not to be impressed by the extent to which democracy has, so far and so often, been responsibly accepted by people who have no practical or even historical experience to prepare them for democratic politics.

This, perhaps, is the final vindication of Kerr et al.; whatever the discontents of an extremely painful period of economic and social reconstruction, and however much the advent of liberal democracy has disappointed the highest hopes held for it, there is little sign of widespread enthusiasm in central and eastern Europe for any alternative; it is as if the peoples of central and eastern Europe have, like those of the western half of the continent, accepted with resignation that "pluralistic industrialism", with all its imperfections, is their common fate.

Too much is yet unsettled in central and eastern Europe for anyone confidently to predict the course or outcome of developments now in train. There remains the possibility that divergent futures lie ahead, even that a "third way" may yet be fashioned between an unpalatable capitalism and a discredited socialism, but even if central and eastern Europe does continue along the road on which it presently appears to be set, there is no reason to suppose that its progress will be smooth or uneventful. As several of the contributors to this volume observe, what most distinguishes the democratization of central and eastern Europe from that of southern Europe is that in the latter the systemic transformation was only political, whereas in the former it is simultaneously political, economic and social.

But it is not only central and eastern Europe that may yet confound the prophets of pluralistic industrialism. To predict that further integration and enhanced toleration of and autonomy for minorities remains the most probable future for western Europe is to wager that governments and citizens alike will *choose* such a future. There remains the possibility, however remote, that the forces of extremist nationalism and the far right will fashion an altogether less attractive outcome. It is some comfort that, despite the persistence of the Front National in France and the electoral successes of the Republikaner in Germany, the survey evidence suggests that the great majority of western Europeans remain attached to the political culture of pluralistic liberal democracy.

Implications for sociology

When we set about organizing the conference at which versions of these chapters were first presented, we were motivated by the conviction that sociologists had paid too little attention to Europe. We were concerned to encourage work that compared British and European experience across a wide range of social issues, and some of the fruits of such comparative research are presented in this and its companion volume. We were particularly concerned to make amends for sociologists neglect of the European Community, and to that end we invited the two plenary speakers – Alain Touraine and Rainer Lepsius – whose contributions are published here. Touraine and Lepsius demonstrate very effectively that the theoretical traditions of sociology have much to offer in the analysis of European integration, just as other contributions show the value of cross-nationally comparative empirical research. We hope that the chapters in this book will stimulate more interest among sociologists in what is a unique social and political experiment of the most far-reaching significance.

Sociologists have been quicker to recognize the importance of the great natural experiment being conducted in the eastern half of the continent. Not only is a great deal of research now under way, but consideration of the problems of the transformation of eastern Europe has revivified sociological thinking in the West. Issues such as trust, civil society, democracy, and political culture, which had slipped from the mainstream of sociological debate, have been rescued from obscurity. It is particularly encouraging that, as the contributions to this volume testify, central and eastern European sociologists are themselves contributing as equals to this debate. Stimulated by new issues and by conversation with new colleagues, it is not only European societies that are being reconstructed but European sociology as well.

References

Habermas, J. 1976. *Legitimation crisis*. London: Heinemann.

Kerr, C., T. Dunlop, F. Harbison, C. A. Mayers 1960. *Industrialism and industrial man*. Cambridge, Mass.: Harvard University Press.

Linz, J. 1978. *Crisis, Breakdown and re-equilibration*. Vol. I of J. Linz & A. Stepan (eds) *The breakdown of democratic regimes*. Baltimore & London: The Johns Hopkins University Press.

Rootes, C. A. 1981. On the future of protest politics in western democracies: a critique of Barnes, Kaase et al. *Political Action*. *European Journal of Political Research* **9**, 421–32.

Chapter 1

European countries in a post-national era[1]

Alain Touraine

I

European integration may not appear an exciting topic for a sociologist to address. For many people, this integration is just one more step towards an open world market and makes intra-European wars or protectionist barriers obsolete; for others, it means the loss of political and cultural independence of European nations and the subordination of political and social institutions to arbitrary decisions made by markets or bureaucrats. But both arguments, positive and negative, are so general and so unable to demonstrate the errors of the opposite stance that we don't trust them. We consider them, on the contrary, as ideologies that rationalize precise but limited interests or as historical intuitions that can have extremely important effects but, instead of offering explanations of actual behaviour, need themselves to be explained. The reason for our uneasiness when we speak about Europe is that it is an indirect way of speaking about something else or, more precisely, about the opposite of European integration, namely our national states. The political process in which we are participating is much less the construction of a European state than the partial de-nationalization of European countries or their entrance into a postnational era. If this idea is accepted, a reflection on European integration becomes an interrogation of the positive or negative effects of this integration on the countries that are undergoing this process of de-nationalization for reasons that have less to do with European institutional integration than with the formation of superpowers during the Cold War and with the diffusion of an internationalized but American-centred mass culture.

In our Western tradition, the political expression of modernity is the nation state. Like modern society, according to Parsons' sociology, it is a com-

EUROPEAN COUNTRIES IN A POST-NATIONAL ERA

plex system oriented towards rational action and one in which subsystems fulfil specific functions. In it, cultural values, institutionalized norms and motivations correspond to one another, at least in principle – "in principle" because traditions, ascribed statuses and irrational behaviour are in fact never eliminated. Countries such as Britain and France, beyond their differences, have been and still are strong national states, so strong that for the other country's citizens, their economic, political or cultural institutions appear to be first of all national and specific, even if they express common values or general processes.

Integrated Europe is not going to fit with this political type of organization; it is not going to be a big new nation-state. Partly because its main components are real nation states, it is impossible to imagine the creation of a European culture corresponding to a European economy and to European policies. On the contrary, it appears that Europe has many different faces. It is an economic unit with customs barriers, processes of internal redistribution and, in the near future, possibly a common currency. But at the same time, the European Community has a very limited political decision making capacity, and its parliament almost none; it is, moreover, culturally highly diverse and fragmented, even if the English language – which is actually a world language more than a European one – tends to be used everywhere as a *lingua franca*. Socially, it is true that the heterogeneity of western Europe has decreased with the rapid improvement of the situation of countries such as Spain or Portugal, but there are still striking differences among the immigration policies and the very definitions of nationality in Britain, Germany and France, not to mention Greece, as well as between union memberships in Belgium and Spain or between northern and southern countries' fiscal policies.

To become European does not mean an English or a French man or woman adding a new broader identification to his or her former national identity; rather, it means combining a weakened citizenship with participation in a multiplied community in which economic organization, political institutions and cultural production do not correspond to one another. Nobody can imagine, within the next 20 years, a strongly integrated Europe. Jacques Delors recently estimated that the Community's budget should represent approximately five per cent of each nation's budget, and he insisted that social security systems as well as educational institutions should remain national.

No nation is simultaneously so deeply diversified culturally, yet so open economically to international trade, and yet so weakly developed in its po-

EUROPEAN COUNTRIES IN A POST-NATIONAL ERA

litical institutions, as is the European Community. European society is not likely to become either a federal or a confederal state, and will for a long period of time be called a "community", a vague notion that does not correspond to common cultural values. In many ways, Europe is today less united and specific than it used to be during centuries when Christianity created a cultural community and when intra European wars defined a European political system strengthened by marriages and alliances. Today few, if any, cultural products are European. They are produced by the so called Western world and most of them by the United States, which is the main exporter of cultural goods and habits, or by individual nations.

It is not true that European construction has reached a point of no return. Negative attitudes are growing, and the ratification of the Maastricht agreements will not be easy in some countries. Few people are openly anti-European, but anti-Europeans have more intelligently defended the idea of a free trade zone, which would prevent Europe from acquiring a political or even an economic decision making capacity comparable to that of Japan or the United States. No economic argument is sufficient to defend European integration. Economic argument generally favours open world trade of the sort advocated in the GATT (the General Agreement on Tariffs and Trade) by third world countries and the United States, and opposed by the European Community. It seems essential to introduce social and political arguments, that is, a sociological analysis, to defend or oppose European political integration. And such a sociological analysis must begin with an analysis of the forms and meaning of the present crisis of national states, the process of de-nationalization that so profoundly transforms the lives of the European countries that created the nation state and that is an exception in a world where new nations are constantly being created and where national consciousness and nationalism are strong almost everywhere.

We must, then, conclude that European integration has to be analyzed not in itself but in terms of its effects on European nations that are suffering a process of de-nationalization.

II

The most important aspect of this process is the dissociation between mass production and the diffusion of material and cultural goods on the one hand, and the cultural meanings that are created by memory, education, self image and the material presence of the past in landscape, monuments and language on the other. The new Europe is becoming "postmodern", if this

EUROPEAN COUNTRIES IN A POST-NATIONAL ERA

expression is taken to mean such a separation between signs and meanings, objects and subjectivity, market and values. Systems and actors no longer correspond to one another. We could speak of future Europe as of present-day Switzerland, a country in which people live at the world level and at a local level more than at a national level. Germans often defend the image of their country as a world economic power made up of autonomous *Länder*, and people who dream of a new *Mitteleuropa* describe it not as a national state but as a collection of European *Länder*, such as Croatia, Bohemia or Baden Württemberg, partly unified by the predominant rôle of German companies, which can very well operate in English.

Many people will object here that the United States, in a parallel way, is at the same time the core of the world mass consumption and mass communication culture and a loose federation of communities that are more eager to define their specificity than their participation in a national society. Nevertheless, in the present period of time, the United States acts as a strong nation state that is widely recognized as the only hegemonic power at the world level and where national consciousness and pride are strong. If we add that international trade plays a limited rôle in a country whose internal market is huge, we see that the dissociation between mass culture, political power and social attitudes is much more limited in the United States than in most European countries. Only Europeans can imagine their future as one defined by a growing participation in world trade associated with a tendency of national cultures to protect themselves in a more and more aggressive way and of political institutions to remain weak and deprived of democratic legitimation.

III

If we are interested in assessing the strength or weaknesses of such a Europe, we probably have to conclude that its future will be rapidly to disintegrate; that is, to be reduced to a zone of free trade while one or several European nation states, if they are able by themselves to play an international rôle, will use this free trade zone to enhance their competitiveness with Japan or the United States. Such a trilateral system, which would most probably include Germany, would limit the importance of Europe. But if I mentioned the fragility of such a loosely integrated Europe, it was first of all to underline the fragility of a society whose political system is not able to hold together an internationalized economic activity and a particularistic cultural life. A postnational society is doomed to be politically weak and unstable.

EUROPEAN COUNTRIES IN A POST-NATIONAL ERA

In a post-national society, the control exerted by institutions, democratic or administrative, on social, economic and cultural life, decreases both because their power is more limited and because the distance between worldwide production, consumption or communication centres and private experience increases so much that the two universes part from each other. In this type of society, people participate in flows of money, information and decisions, but these activities are not easily transformed into value orientations. To use Riesman's famous expressions, "inner directedness" is not substituted by "other directedness" but lives side by side with it. Moreover, the larger the gap between the two universes, the more inner directedness is oriented by cultural heritage or by psychological impulses.

If it is true that national society was the political expression of modernity, at least in its first phase, when it meant trade, enforced laws and bureaucratic authority, post-national societies appear with the passage from a modernity that was limited to the world of production to a wider modernity that penetrates the worlds of consumption and communication. Because mass consumption is based on the central rôle of consumers' demands, which are not rational, rationality becomes purely instrumental so that complex technologies and management methods can be used to satisfy either fun activities or racist propaganda as well as the progress of productivity. In a classical industrial society, production methods and workers' or consumers' behaviour were supposed to be similar, and education methods emphasized the necessity of subordinating passions to reason and immediate need satisfaction to deferred gratification. Reason was supposed to be both a principle of economic and social organization and a general pattern of behaviour. Modern society meant hard work and saving as much as domination of nature by science and technology.

In our new cultural environment, production is no longer oriented by objective or substantive rationality but by an instrument of rationality that serves the satisfaction of needs that are themselves more and more defined in terms of liberation of desires, impulses, needs, and dreams, and in terms of social status and mobility. From a society of production to a society of consumption and communication, the link between culture, society and personality disappears. The Weberian image of modernity corresponded to a merchant or proto industrial society more than to a mass production society, and is very far from present-day mass culture. In France, young people say, when they enjoy themselves, that they "burst out" (*ils s'éclatent*). The expression is quite accurate. Pleasure means suppression not only of external social controls but of internalized repressive control. The decay of the

17

EUROPEAN COUNTRIES IN A POST-NATIONAL ERA

classical concept of "I" opens the way to the separation of two opposite definitions of personality. The first one is the self, which is defined by social expectations, and more precisely built by social agencies, political or administrative. Michel Foucault has given many examples of the construction of the self by institutions. But on the other side, personality is replaced by the effort of the individual to be an actor, that is to transform his or her social environment. This "I" – this effort to be an actor – is not defined by a content but rather as a movement for itself (*pour soi*) and, more concretely, as a resistance against the transformation of the individual into self by central social and cultural agencies.

We are here very far from the classical idea that personality is built by internalization of social norms, by the learned capacity to participate in collective rational activities. I defend here the opposite view, according to which the subject is created by individual or collective resistance to the pressure of institutions that either try to increase their own control of the behaviour of social actors or just intend to transform behaviour into participation in economic, political or informational markets. Instead of speaking of a necessary correspondence between institutions and motivations, which should be created by socialization agencies, I speak of a conflict between two logics: the logic of the system and the logic of the actor. The actor is not the result of a socialization process but of the capacity of individuals or groups to resist their reduction to market-oriented demands.

You may wonder what the relationship is between these ideas and a discussion about Europe. The relation is a very direct one.

Europe was a continent of nation states in which culture, society and personality were tightly intertwined. We are entering, we have already entered, a world in which mass culture and personality are so deeply separated that social and political institutions are weakened and seem to be empty, to have no influence over either the economy or individual behaviour. We no longer behave according to social rôles, as citizens or workers, as we used to, especially in France and Britain, where the concept and the reality of the nation state were created.

To speak of society meant speaking of national societies in which social and political institutions worked out the integration of actors into society. Now legal and political institutions are largely replaced by markets, and social rôles by creativity, and, according to Giddens, by reflexivity. Society is no longer national, and the actor is no longer a citizen or a worker. Internationalization of markets on the one hand, reflexive individualism and what I call the process of subjectivation on the other, are not complementary as-

EUROPEAN COUNTRIES IN A POST-NATIONAL ERA

pects of a national society. They do not belong to a social system, they are independent and in many ways conflicting universes. It is obviously difficult for European countries that have been nation states *par excellence* to adjust themselves to this post-national era, to the growing separation between system and actors and to the fundamental crisis of the concepts and agencies of institutionalization and socialization.

IV

Before responding to these difficulties, we must make clear that a complete separation between the inner world and the outer world, between system and actors, is likely to have pathological consequences. If individuals and groups are defined only by their impulses or by their cultural heritage, that is, by their differences, there is no possible communication among them and no social life is possible, except one based on segregation and aggression. At the same time, a mass society is not just one worldwide open market. If it is not controlled by political institutions, it is a battlefield in which the most powerful impose their interests on weaker countries or individuals. In many ways, the postmodern and post-national world would be heading back to the state of nature as it was defined by Hobbes. On one side, the defence of identity can be reduced to extreme differentialism, if not to racism; on the other, a consumer-oriented society can give full power to central institutions over atomized consumers.

These dangers make it clear that the growing separation between mass society and individual subjects must be compensated by the creation of new social and political mediations. Each of the two universes tends to exclude the other. Markets can be instruments not of need satisfaction, but of accumulation of power and resources; cultural specificity can be transformed into the opposite of personal freedom, into rejection of the other. My view is that this growing separation is positive inasmuch as society recognizes that its life is based on the conflict between two value orientations: maximizing the circulation of commodities, money and information on the one hand; maximizing the control of actors, individual or collective, over their social or material environment, on the other. This conflict between efficiency and freedom must be institutionalized and limited. If not, the negative tendencies will prevail and the world will be dominated by a deadly war between world trade or military centres and fundamentalist individuals or groups.

The recent triumph of the American empire over the Soviet empire induced many people, including some political philosophers, to think that the

EUROPEAN COUNTRIES IN A POST-NATIONAL ERA

period of basic conflicts and fundamental choices was over, that the whole world agrees today on the superiority and necessity of a market economy, political democracy and secularization. My view is just the opposite. Past conflicts were limited, even class struggles were limited, because social adversaries shared common value orientations and fought only against the social use of cultural resources and values that were accepted by all. Entrepreneurs and organized labour, for example, accepted the positive value of industry, science and progress, but each camp identified itself with them and denounced their opponent as an obstacle to rationalization and progress. Today, on the contrary, the opposition between market and identity, instrumental rationality and subjectivation, can be complete and the conflict between them can become both cultural and social, so that compromises become more difficult. Conflicts are actually replaced by total rejection of the other, and competition or class conflict by exclusion or by religious wars. Each national society tends to be internally divided: on one side are people and institutions defending the economic superiority of the market, and oriented by rational interest and technological efficiency, and on the other are individuals or groups that oppose this view in the name either of individualism or of a national or religious tradition. The liberal view attracts many people in both rich and poor countries; the individualist and the culturalist points of view are equally present in all parts of the world.

Our world is not one world. It is almost completely divided between two contradictory views. The advantage of rich countries is that they offer limited free territories to individual freedom and to cultural minorities, even if these are often closed into ghettos, while in poor countries, which feel threatened by exogenous change, defence of cultural traditions can easily be transformed into fundamentalist or assimilationist regimes.

I can now formulate my question in a more precise way: is Europe going to be a continent of extreme separation between mass culture and personal identity or, on the contrary, because of its history as a continent of national states, will it be a region of limited decay of this type of political organization? Or is Europe going to be an area of new institutional mediations, strong or weak, between markets and identities? When I say "strong", I mean able to institutionalize the conflict between these forces; when I say "weak", I mean unable to overcome the juxtaposition of mass consumption and isolated individual or group, that is to say, the separation between social behaviour and cultural meaning.

These problems are not entirely new. They are actually a more general expression of what was considered as a central debate in industrial society.

EUROPEAN COUNTRIES IN A POST-NATIONAL ERA

Here already the separation between mass production and the personal freedom of creativity was visible. And the institutional response to what was called class struggle was industrial democracy and, more precisely, collective bargaining and labour laws. But, as I have said, in industrial society, the rupture between system and actors was far from being complete. Today, on the contrary, common values can disappear and social conflict be replaced by a contradiction between mass culture and counter culture, national, religious, local or sexual, or extreme moral individualism.

V

The most "national" European countries undergo with great anxiety their passage to the post-national era. Many of their citizens are afraid of losing their identity, of being "invaded" by foreign cultures. Britain and France present opposite solutions to the integration of immigrants, but I am more impressed by the similarity of their problems than by the differences between the solutions they implement. In the past, both countries were open to immigrants and refugees and both had great confidence in their capacity to integrate newcomers into a culture and a society that considered itself to be the best expression of universal values. Both feel strongly that their international influence is declining, and they react negatively to the presence of immigrants, who are supposedly unwilling to be integrated and who persist in defending their cultural differences. This negative reaction takes mainly social expression in Britain and political expression in France, but this important difference does not prevent the two countries living through with equally great difficulties the crises of their national states. In a more general way, beyond the obvious contrast between the pro European attitude of French governments and the frequently anti European postures of the British, the similarity of reactions in the two countries is visible. Both countries want to defend their specificity; the French believe they can achieve this goal by maintaining a certain leadership in the construction of Europe, the British by limiting the power of the European Commission, but it is superficial to define the French attitude as pro European and the British one as anti European.

The resistance to Europe was apparently more limited in countries such as Italy and Germany where cultural and political unity have long been dissociated, as *Deutschtum* and *Deutschland* were, but a reunified Germany has great difficulties, like Britain and France, in finding a working compromise between national and post-national political organization. In Germany and

Italy, the rejection of hungry foreigners is growing, and xenophobia is finding new political expression. In all countries, the defence of national identity has more negative than positive consequences, and creates in many cases a dangerous fear that transforms Europe into a fortress that feels threatened by barbarian crowds.

It is easy today to observe that resistance to the dissociation of the components of a national society has serious negative consequences. But does it have positive consequences as well? I am convinced it is possible, because national political institutions, precisely because they are weaker than in the past, instead of imposing an integrative pattern on all aspects of social life, can offer the necessary mediations between a globalized economy and cultural identities. This is the process through which European countries can transform their possible disintegration into a good chance to create a healthy combination of cultural diversity and mass consumption or communication.

European political integration, by transferring important elements of national sovereignty to Brussels, gives new opportunities to national political systems to act as go betweens, elaborating compromises between economic competitiveness and individual freedom or minority rights; while, on the contrary, defensive nationalism tries to impose the image of a culturally and socially homogeneous nation that no longer corresponds to the situation, and leaves less and less autonomy to the political system, which is subordinated to what is called "national interest" or, to put it more directly, international competitiveness or military influence.

In a situation when we can no longer concentrate all aspects of our social and cultural life at the national level, European construction offers us the chance to live simultaneously at various levels of political and social organization; if we don't use it, we will be torn between universalism and particularism or close ourselves into a desperado nationalism.

There is no contradiction between national identity, European integration, and minority or regional rights; on the contrary, the combination of these three levels is the best way to integrate the internationalization of mass production and mass consumption with the defence of individual and collective actors who at the same time defend a memory, a cultural heritage, and try to enhance personal freedom and creativity. This point of view has direct consequences for sociologists. More often than we think, we are part of a cultural and political tradition more than its observers and analysts. We must learn more and more to separate various levels of the phenomena we study instead of exploring them too spontaneously as part of national life.

The transformation I have just mentioned represents a dangerous

EUROPEAN COUNTRIES IN A POST-NATIONAL ERA

challenge for our political institutions, but it can also give them new strength.

In most countries, our political systems have been weakened first because they correspond to old social problems, so that parties' representativeness has been eroded, but even more because the state, as executive power, imposes its rule on parliament. If the main attributes of the state – monetary policy and defence – are transferred to the European Community, our political systems and, more concretely, our parliaments, will be more able to respond to social demands and will concentrate on their rôle of making compatible competitive participation in the world economy and the respect of cultural diversity. Because such a diversification of political organization could result from European integration, Europe could very well represent a more advanced type of political system than the United States. The United States so strongly dominates the mass consumption and mass communication world networks that it often tends to identify mass culture with the American way of life and to create moral majorities that exclude minorities and deviants. At the same time, United States' society accepts more easily than most European countries an extreme separation between mass culture and local or specific communities, a dualization that is made dangerous by an extreme liberalism that has lowered the level of many public services and contributed to the crisis of political parties, especially the Democrats. Japan, on the other hand, is such a strong national society and one that mobilizes its resources for economic success that it will be a long time before Japan accepts a certain dissociation between rationalization and subjectivation, between economic efficiency and individual freedom.

It would, in any case, be as meaningless for European countries to defend their traditional attributes as national societies as to dream of a new European nation state, federal or not. It would even be a mistake only to look for a well balanced co-ordination of European integration and national identity; the three aspects of cultural and political change I have just described – world economic integration, subject-centred culture and new forms of representative democracy – cannot be separated from one another. National specificity will be defined not by a cultural "essence" or tradition but by institutional processes, by the ways of combining, in education as well as in social security systems, economic constraints and social demands, national integration and minority rights, reason and memory, technology and imagination. The British political tradition, both at the parliamentary level and in all aspects of public life, should find here a new field of application as much as the French tradition of intellectual and political debates.

EUROPEAN COUNTRIES IN A POST-NATIONAL ERA

The main danger for Europe would be to abandon the state social interventionism that characterizes most European countries and to let society be reduced to a series of loosely connected markets. It is true that social democracy has been progressively transformed into neo corporatism. Liberals – in the European sense of the word – are right to oppose the necessity of free trade to the temptation of economic and social protectionism. But social democracy, which belongs to industrial society, must be replaced by a new mechanism of political debate and social integration. Labour problems are certainly still very important, but new problems appear, more cultural than economic, more national than social, in the narrow sense of the word. The most difficult problem of our society is to maintain or permit communication among people and groups who defend their identity and their difference but, at the same time, are active in a technological world. Women, ethnic groups and most of what we call minorities are actively involved in a search for such a combination. Civil society should not be another name for economic system but for a network of social communication that recognizes both universalism and particularism and gives more opportunities to individual initiative or expression and to personal freedom. Instead of just protecting old industries and underdeveloped regions, we must imagine new definitions of national unity, of social equality, and of the relationship between minorities and majority.

VI

My conclusion is that European integration is positive if it helps to create a high degree of differentiation in our public life, protecting us both from a narrow and defensive nationalism and from a wider and wider gap between local traditions and world mass culture, between rich "cosmopolitans", a national middle class, and poor "locals". What should be considered as a priority? A reconstruction of political institutions, a growing participation in mass consumption and mass communication, or the growth and acceptance of moral individualism? In other words, should the process of creating a new European society start from the top, from the bottom, or from an intermediate level? The question is a traditional one but the answer cannot be found in past experience. The idea that has been repeatedly expressed in these pages is that the defence of the traditional concept of the nation state is hopeless and that, behind nationalist myths, the growing dissociation between a world mass market and social or personal consciousness will be accelerated by the lack of new policies of social integration. That leads me

EUROPEAN COUNTRIES IN A POST-NATIONAL ERA

to think that we must give high priority to the construction of a European decision making capacity. The Maastricht meeting achieved only partly positive results. Monetary unity is now a real possibility, but political and military integration is lagging behind. My suggestion is that only an increasing political integration will permit the transformation of the European national states into political systems, whose main task will be to invent new forms of cultural and social integration in a context where an internationalized mass culture and personal or collective identities are more and more distant and disconnected from one another. It is only when these two upper layers of our public life have been transformed that it will be possible to lower the level of cultural control in our society and to increase the autonomy of individual life and of minority groups without unleashing a nationalist backlash.

These suggestions are not strong arguments for accelerating European integration, but their aim is not to influence policy-makers; it is to describe the historical context in which we face some very real problems, among which I want, summing up previous remarks, to mention two, the most difficult ones to solve.

The first is the aggressive nationalistic rejection of processes of change that are interpreted as external threats: new immigrants who supposedly cannot be integrated; loss of national identity; and even loss of democratic control over technocratic or bureaucratic decisions. In each case, real problems are pinpointed but a dangerous feeling of impotency is spreading, which leads to exclusion or irrational fear.

The second is the crisis of representative democracy, of the capacity of political institutions and parties to represent social demands and to transform them into political programmes. Social life is reduced to the market and citizens to consumers. Social movements are disappearing and unions have lost a large part of their strength, except when they have been accepted as participants in the economic decision making system. Private life and world markets exist side by side but without any social and political mediation. Intellectual debates, whose function is to relate values to concrete historical options, disappear in a world that is both internationalized and sectarian, where the circulation of goods is intensified but the separation of private and public life is increased.

I do not pretend that European integration is a solution to all these problems; but I do contend that it is an important instrument for the reconstruction of our public life, by creating a clear-cut differentiation between a European state, national political societies, and a more and more diversified and individualized social life.

EUROPEAN COUNTRIES IN A POST-NATIONAL ERA

European integration is the best way for European countries to avoid the separation between economic activities and cultural values that is a major threat in post-national societies. It opposes this separation by transforming national states, deprived of a large part of their sovereignty, into open democratic social systems and by enlarging public space to make it able to combine worldwide consumer behaviour with personal or collective identity and freedom.

Note

1. This is the revised and edited text of a plenary address delivered to the 1992 Annual Conference of the British Sociological Association.

Chapter 2

The European Community
*regime-building and institutionalization
of criteria for rationality[1]*

Rainer Lepsius

When I first came to England in 1951 and stepped off a boat at Harwich, there was a gentleman shouting "British passports please! British passports please!", and those holding British passports quickly proceeded through Customs and were sitting on the train to Liverpool Street, while the rest, all those bloody foreigners, were standing on a drizzling, cold day, waiting endlessly to pass through Customs. When I arrive in England today, I follow the sign at the airport that says "EC Countries and Nationals" and I proceed very quickly and at the same speed as Britons through Customs. This tremendous development is not peculiar to the European Community, and many such developments would have taken place without it, but the founding of the EC has given a special drive and a special importance to European integration. Since 1989, however, the meaning of European integration has changed; now we mean the integration of the former Soviet bloc countries into the Western economic and political system. The EC has become what it always was – a Western European community. We need, then, to distinguish between a number of processes of European integration, one directed towards the integration of the eastern European countries, and another, the consolidation and further development of the European Community itself.

A number of countries have already made applications to be admitted to the EC. All these procedures have been postponed until the Single Market is achieved, but it is very likely that by 1995, or perhaps two or three years later, the present 12 member states will have grown to about 18, possibly 20, members embracing all of western, southern, northern and a substantial part of eastern Europe. This puts the existing EC under enormous pressure, and at the moment it is not at all clear what might be the consequences of this external pressure to accommodate the demands of the eastern European

THE EUROPEAN COMMUNITY

countries and the enlargement of the Community to include the Scandinavian and central European countries.

What is, however, clear is that the economic as well as the political potential of the EC will be totally overburdened by the urgent demands of European integration. It is quite impossible for the European Community to take on the enormous task of stabilizing the former Soviet bloc economically, not to say politically. Recent proposals for the G7 meetings clearly indicate that without the intensive co-operation of the United States and to a lesser degree Canada and, of course, Japan, this enormous task will not be achieved. The European Community finds itself internationally in a limited position, similar to the one that prevailed during the Soviet period when the EC could not defend itself without the United States. The EC today is unable to master the consequences of the dissolution of the Soviet empire without the United States and Japan. I want to stress this at the beginning. Sometimes one gets the impression that discussion about the further development of the EC overestimates the potential of the Community in international affairs, and its capabilities in relation to global problems. The EC will be a regime alongside others, an entity within a network of other regimes. The Conference on Security and Cooperation in Europe at present embraces 51 states, and it may become a sub-entity of the United Nations for the northern hemisphere, eventually developing its own security council and peace-keeping forces. The Conference of the G7 members might then be enlarged in order to co-ordinate economic development, primarily in the northern hemisphere. It appears likely that the next major task in which the EC will be involved will be the reorganization of the northern hemisphere, not only in terms of its economic stability, but also in terms of its ecological performance. In other words, if the integration of the former Soviet bloc is to be achieved, the northern hemisphere will emerge as the site of a separate regime-building process alongside, outside, and above the EC.

The European Community is completing the first stage of its development as envisaged in the founding Treaties of Rome in 1957. At the end of 1992, it completed the so-called Single Market, a goal that was set more than 30 years ago. It is, however, exactly at this moment confronted with mounting external conflicts and internal pressures. In the present economic and social situation, the plan for European currency union and the European Central Bank meets growing opposition, particularly in Germany, even though it was the Germans who were most keen to promote this idea a couple of years ago. Times change quickly, and so do preferences and political goals.

28

REGIME-BUILDING AND CRITERIA FOR RATIONALITY

The goal of European political union, reaffirmed at the summit meeting at Maastricht in December 1991, is unclear in form and content. No clear sketch nor even proposals are on the table to suggest what the political union will be and in what categories it will develop. The old regime of the EC is quite often regarded as out-dated, but it is still the basis of the present existence of the Community and of its very vital and successful activities. The regime of the reformed EC will face the dual problem of not yet decided boundaries and not yet conceptualized internal order. The EC has reached a critical moment.

After periods of stagnation, periods of what some have called Europe's sclerosis, the EC has shown remarkable vitality and efficiency in recent years. The completion of the Single Market and the simultaneous integration of the southern European member states (Portugal, Spain, and Greece) is an enormous success. The basic institutional structure has in general remained unchanged since its foundation, despite the fact that the number of member states has grown from 6 to 12. Numerous decisive actions have been taken; any country that joined the Community now would have to adopt at least 1400 legal provisions that have accumulated over the past 30 years.

The Community has not only proved to be effective and efficient, it has also secured inter-governmental consensus in its major decision-making processes, and it enjoys substantial popular support among the populations of the member countries. If we leave aside Britain and Denmark, the attitudes of the populations of the Community countries show overwhelming support for the European integration process as conducted by the EC. This development is without precedent, and as such it deserves much more attention than it generally receives, particularly from the social sciences and sociology. It is a development that, in terms of institution-building and in terms of effectiveness in regulating public affairs, is paralleled only by the development of the nation-state in the 19th century.

Inventiveness and success can be related to a specific and, I think, interesting process of what I call differentiation of criteria of rationality. When Max Weber asked "Why is it that the Occident develops differently by comparison with the Orient?", he advanced his famous thesis of the rationalization process. He did not believe that the West became rational while the East remained irrational, bound by magical practices, unable to calculate causes and effects. What he was interested in was a much more specific problem, not the contradictions nor the distinctions between rationality and irrationality or a-rationality. Weber tried to grasp the character of the occidental rationalization process as he saw it by asking three more precise questions: first,

"What spheres of life are affected by rationalization?"; secondly, "To what degree and in what direction are these spheres of life rationalized?"; and thirdly, "What constellations are formed by the lesser or more rationalized spheres of life as they co-exist at any given historical moment? And what will be the effects caused by such constellations on policy, culture, the conduct of the lives of individuals, and the structure of societies?"

The direction and degree of rationalization is, in Weber's view, defined by a process of differentiation of objectives and particularly by the establishment of rules, procedures, and criteria by which actions to achieve such objectives become calculable and accountable. If such standards of rationality are to become socially effective, they have to be institutionalized, which means that they have to become generally accepted as appropriate when dealing with a given problem in a given situation. As an arena of action becomes internally homogeneous, people acting in this arena will adopt the same criteria for defining problems, for the seeking of solutions, and for the acceptance of the means to solve problems. They regard these criteria as appropriate for the issue, and legitimate. Others are excluded; they are considered as irrelevant for the issue or irrelevant and not appropriate for the context in which action is to be taken. Accordingly, only certain consequences and contingencies of actions are accepted as caused by such actions as are institutionalized under these principles of rationality, while others are externalized: the consequences have to be dealt with not by those who made the decisions, but have to be faced by other social contexts, entities, spheres of action, individuals, and organizations. To give an example: for Weber, modern rational capitalism is not the effect of an internal drive of men to become richer and richer and to exploit others as far as possible but, rather, modern rational capitalism rests upon the differentiation of the arena of actions, out of the general social context, in which particular criteria of economic actions are legitimately applied, namely the calculability of economic returns in regard to economic investment. If this becomes the major criterion of economic decision-making, then the context in which this behaviour is executed must be fairly well differentiated from other contexts. This, in Weberian language, means the firm as an entity has to be differentiated from the household because within a household quite other norms prevail, other solidarity values are apparent, and a pure calculation of investment and return is not possible because of the non-specialized diffuseness of the moral obligations within the social context of the household. If, from a Weberian perspective, capitalism was to be introduced in terms of rational modern capitalism, then the precondition of it was the sharp distinction between arenas of ac-

REGIME-BUILDING AND CRITERIA FOR RATIONALITY

tion and the exclusion of certain consequences from the economic arena, the externalization of consequences to other arenas, to individuals who have to adjust, and to other solidarity units that have to cope with social problems caused by capitalistic behaviour.

If we take this as a starting point and look at the EC, and if, as I suggest, the particularly innovative and successful development of the Community, particularly since the mid-1980s, can be analyzed in terms of the specific way in which criteria of rationality became institutionalized, then we have to look at those institutionalization processes as they occurred in the Community. The goal was the achievement of a common single greater market in western Europe by abolishing barriers between the member states. This goal, already set in 1951, and then enshrined in the European Economic Community in 1958, was legitimated by a belief, just as everything that is regarded as legitimate rests on a belief. The belief in this case was that the greater market would produce greater competition and innovation by competition, and thereby also greater productivity. Greater productivity would in turn lead to enhanced welfare production and this would serve all members, be they collectivities or individuals. So the goal of the Single Market was constructed in the expectation that it would produce effects that everybody could enjoy. However, the goal of the common market was isolated from other goals from the very beginning: isolated, for example, from the goal of defence and security; isolated from welfare state goals; isolated from goals in terms of cultural identity, participatory self-determination, and others one could imagine. The EC was specialized in the pursuit of one goal, while other objectives were kept outside the realm of the Community institution. The North Atlantic Treaty Organization has been particularly important; it upheld, and upholds even today, all questions related to European security or west European security or North Atlantic and, today, northern hemisphere military problems and security issues.

The goal of the common market was further operationalized. It was operationalized by the so-called "four liberties". The four liberties – the freedom of the transfer of goods, services, capital and individuals across the boundaries of the member states – are the guiding principles of EC policy. Such criteria of rationality as expressed by the four liberties could be fairly well isolated from the political traffic of the member societies as long as their implementation consisted in regulations: de-regulation of national norms hindering the free traffic of goods, services, capital, and persons; re-regulation of some new common standards and the conditions by which the members mutually have to accept different national standards of member coun-

THE EUROPEAN COMMUNITY

tries. Such a policy does not cost much money, and it does not interfere in the organizational structure of conflict formation and interest mediation of the various member countries. Segmental de-regulation in a rather limited technical economic realm did not cause any major break-up or re-shuffling in the basic political and social fabric of the member states. The adaptation to new regulations was left to the member states and the individuals or firms that were competing in the common market. Initially, these effects were small and the adaptive capacities were great. There was also no need for explicit legitimation by direct parliamentary control, as the activity was technically reduced and, as I have already said, it did not interfere in the basic social and political fabric of the member states. Interest groups and governments participated in decision-making to the full extent of their interests, either in their capacity as interest groups to influence the provisions made by the Commission in Brussels or, in the case of governments, in their capacity to make the final decisions in the Council of Ministers. The EC could work without a parliament. The national systems of conflict articulation and conflict resolution continued to operate within the usual national contexts. Only certain economic interests were co-ordinated, and these were interests that were already highly organized and vertically distinguished from other interests within the national systems.

The success of the EC rested in its initial phase on criteria of rationality for decision-making that were highly instrumental, generally accepted, well insulated from other fields of policy, and operationalized in terms on which agreement could be found. The organizational pattern of the Community and the criteria of rationality were mutually well adjusted. The originality of the EC rests in its construction as an innovative regime of supra-national character. It is integrating its members by legal norms; law enacted by the Community is directly applicable in the member countries and affects every single citizen of the member states. This law is sanctioned by the European Court, the decisions of which directly govern the rulings of the courts of the member states as well. By having the interference and the interventions of the Community covered by legal instruments and sanctioned by the rulings of the European Court, the entire implementation of the policy of the European Community was covered under a specialized legal frame and executed via the national courts and nationally adopted and accepted legal norms, without interference from the political systems, parliaments, or supreme courts of the member nation states. So in a way, by using legal norms, the implementation of the EC was invisible and was covered by the general acceptance of law customary in the member states themselves.

REGIME-BUILDING AND CRITERIA FOR RATIONALITY

What was enacted in those 30 years is practically irreversible. This is basically because none of the member states has the right to reorganize the already agreed-upon regulations. Only by unanimity among the member states, or by a majority, if it is an issue that can be decided by a majority vote, can any given regulation be altered. It is not like the situation in a parliamentary democracy in which you might have another government from time to time, and the government can order new laws or reorganize certain areas; here you have a situation in which no single country, its national parliament or courts, can unilaterally alter what has been agreed upon during the formative years of the Community.

The institutional structure of the EC has placed the Commission in a central position. The Commission is not the government; it is less and more at the same time. The Commission is not only the agency with the sole right to make any proposition for a decision that has later to be taken by the Council of Ministers; it is also an organization with the capacity to control the implementation of its decisions by the national governments. The Commission therefore has a veto power in so far as, without the consent of the Commission, no proposals can be taken to the Council of Ministers, despite the fact that the Council of Ministers are the sovereigns, or the representatives of the sovereign parties, to the whole treaty arrangements. It is as if, in a parliamentary democracy, the parliament was never in a position itself to initiate proposals but was allowed only to vote upon proposals that had been made by the government. Thus decision-making capacity is to a large degree concentrated, not formally but in practice, within the Commission. The Commission also has, by its ability to appeal to the European Court, an independent weapon to guarantee the implementation of its decisions, independent of the governments that are the members that cast their votes on the original decision. The greater the output of decisions, the more the members lose their competence to regulate fields or issues that have already been regulated by the Community, and this despite the fact that they are the only ones who have the right to make a decision in the Community. Integration within the structure of the EC is therefore primarily achieved by legal regulations and, secondly, by a cumulative process of visibility of law.

This has led to a quite fantastic and unexpected growth in the activities of the Community and its success. It is interesting that the Commission itself has deliberately played a low-key rôle. It calls itself the "European Community", and nobody knows what the Community is; it has deliberately taken a term with which no clear conception can be associated. The Commission continually refrains from defining itself, whether in respect of its

33

nature or its future development, and thereby discourages any systematic analysis of the Community as it exists. The Community is no longer even willing to call itself a supra-national organization; it merely justifies itself in terms of technical efficiency and functional necessity. It has often been stressed that the very limited rôle of the European Parliament, which is actually nothing more than an advisory council, does not conform to democratic norms, but it is not so much democratic legitimation which is missing as, rather, parliamentary control. Neither the European Parliament nor the national parliaments directly controls the Commission or the representatives of governments in the Council.

Having achieved the goal of the Single Market, the EC has come to the end of its first stage. The cumulative character of its activities has led to increasing interference in other policy fields, albeit still under the rule of the Community's original criteria of rationality. To extend the homogeneity of conditions of equal opportunities in the common market, the European Community is continuously ruling on a great number of other issues: ecological standards of industrial products, equality standards of national tax systems, quotas of television programmes, social security methods, educational compatibilities, local regional development schemes, programmes to fight unemployment, and so on. The realm of competence is continuously extended; the problem definition and the objectives, however, remain under the guidance of the old criteria of rationality, namely, the advancement of the homogeneity of market conditions and equal opportunities for competition within the Single Market.

We can observe the drifting apart of the realm of competence on the one side and the criteria of rationality on the other. This causes repercussions in the organizational structure and in the general acceptance of the policy of the Community. This drifting apart is aggravated by the fact that there is a high inter-dependency between policy fields, and ambitions to enlarge the competence of the EC can always be justified in terms of this inter-dependence. At present, and since the summit meeting in Maastricht in December 1991, a new stage in the development of the European Community is intended, namely the development of the European currency union by 1996 or 1999, or whichever year one takes to be decisive. At the same time, the Community's competence in respect of environmental, social, and cultural issues is being enlarged. In the long run, it seems that political union is the final goal. The more competence the Commission or the Community acquires, the more the regulations of the Community will interfere in other fields of politics, and the less it can secure its own legitimacy on the basis of the rather pure criteria by which it was justified in its first 30 years, namely the establishment of a common market, and the promises that were believed to go along with the enlargement of the market.

Functionally, there is no limit to the process of economic unification. Quite evidently there are many fields that could or should become homogenized in order to establish truly equal conditions. Homogenization of national monetary systems, fiscal policies and national subsidies policies is functionally plausible, but if this is achieved the governments of the member states lose, perhaps for the first time, the means to conduct independent policies of structural development of their economies and social subsidies to soften the repercussions of economic development.

The capacity of national governments to adjust to the implementation of EC decisions will at the same time decrease. If this is the case, the externalization of the contingencies of European policy will no longer function as it has until now. If externalization of contingencies is severely limited, there are two consequences. First, the criteria of rationality that have until now governed the EC will no longer be legitimated and upheld; those criteria will have to be mixed with and mediated by other criteria of rationality and will thereby lose their homogeneity in problem definition, problem solving, and in facilitating instrumental consensus over divergent interests. Secondly, the relative isolation of the economic criteria of rationality will be saved and the capacity of mediation of interests and divergent criteria of rationality strengthened, but in another institutional context. This would mean either that the EC would lose its internal basis in terms of rather homogeneous criteria of rationality, or that internal basis would remain, in which case it would have to be mediated by other institutional structures.

In response to this situation, much attention is paid to the organizational analysis of the EC, and many of the reform proposals deal with the further development of its organizational structure. There are tendencies to develop the institutional structure by analogy with the principle of parliamentary democracy of the nation-states. Thus it is envisaged that the competence of the European Parliament will be extended to such a degree that it will perform the functions of a real parliament, namely legislation in an unrestricted and ultimate sense, while the Commission will be parliamentarized and will behave like a government in a parliamentary democracy, the Council of Ministers being transformed into a second chamber of representatives of the member states, possibly along the lines of the German Bundesrat. Such a vision is influenced by the image and the experience of the development of the nation-state in western Europe or the United States of America in the 19th century. However, the more fundamental question is not so much whether the parliament should decide this or that, how many representatives it should have, what the rules of representation for the different member states will be, but rather "What spheres of life do we want, to what degree, and in what direction, to become rationalized under what criteria?". Regime-building in this perspective is always the institutionalization of criteria of rationality. Any institutionalizations are institutionalizations of criteria of rationality. They cause liberty, and conflicts, because by the very differentiation of the contexts of society, culture and the life-chances of the individual, conflicts must arise and are not the fault of one type of institutionalization or another, but the consequence of *any* type of institutional differentiation.

The questions with which we are concerned are: "To what degree do we want to institutionalize divergent criteria of rationality?", "How great should be their relative capacities to overrule other criteria of rationality?", "What conflicts do we want to become institutionalized?" and, "By what procedures do we want to resolve or mediate these conflicts?". Let me dramatize the situation for a moment, and come back to Max Weber once again. He was concerned with the problem, "What type of human being do we want to become?". The self-domestication of humankind is a continuous task. We know what decisive repercussions institutional provisions and organizational matters have for the conduct of the lives of individuals as well as collectivities, economically, politically, culturally, and of course also morally, in terms of the self-identity of an individual. We have only to recollect the experiences of Nazi-dominated Germany and the Stalinist period in eastern Europe to see what enormous consequences a specific type of institutionalization of criteria of rationality can have. The less they are differentiated, the less any accountability for a decision can be constructed; the more they become mixed, fused, the more they become manipulated. Therefore, in a way, the liberal credo is also combined with the strategy of differentiation of criteria of rationality, of accepting the conflicts that arise out of these differentiation processes, and the will, the voluntary decision, to have a situation in which, by differentiation of criteria of rationality, there is accountability and there is a conflict between divergent, equally valuable, equally morally acceptable, ultimate goals of the society.

The European Community is at the crossroads. The decisions taken in the remaining years of this century will be decisive not only for the operation of the Community as an organizational entity, but necessarily also in terms of the nature of the traditional political fabric of the European states, the total fabric of interest articulation and interest mediation as developed

REGIME-BUILDING AND CRITERIA FOR RATIONALITY

during the 19th and 20th centuries in those states, the solidarity norms that are established and, not least, the amount of participation in decision-making. If western Europe and the enlarged Community were to be imagined as a super-nation-state according to the model of the nation-states of the 19th century, it would necessarily mean a highly centralized bureaucratic structure in which participatory elements would decline. The idea that there might be some sort of subsidiary regulation, or some sort of independence or participatory realm for the regions, is, to my mind, totally mistaken because what the nation-state cannot secure, the regions will never obtain, namely an independent capacity to define the rules of the game in conflict with the manner in which those rules are defined at the European level.

The demands for participation, cultural and social autonomy, and mediation of divergent criteria of rationality have, however, to be related to economic rationalization. The less we cut down on the economic performance of society, then the higher the demands we make in terms of ecology and international relations, and the less we are able to cut down on the rationality of economic decision-making. If it does not look plausible to interpose some mediation between divergent calls on the highly centralized level of the EC with all its necessary restrictions on communication, representation, and participation, the Community should not even aim at becoming the integrative centre of west European societies and cultures. It might be enough to strengthen and uphold the frame of an economic union, and it will become more and more difficult to do so.

Of course, there will be strains and conflicts even in this limited realm of competence, but the institutionalization of conflict is a value equal to the institutionalization of functional efficiency, as long as we know for what reasons and objectives we want conflict. The institutionalization of competition in the market is an institutionalization of conflict, and there may be good reasons to institutionalize competition in conflict, not only between suppliers, but also between nations, religions, regions, cultures, professions, belief systems, and styles of life. However, if we make a decision to institutionalize such conflicts, we always have to keep in mind that with the institutionalization of conflict we have also to provide the mediating capacities, the mediating procedures, by which those institutionalized conflicts uphold divergent criteria of rationality in the process of self-domestication of humankind. This we should want; what we do not want are disruptive and destructive conflicts that do not advance the self-domestication of humankind.

THE EUROPEAN COMMUNITY

Note

1. This is an edited transcript of a plenary address delivered to the 1992 Annual Conference of the British Sociological Association.

Chapter 3

Harmonization and the art of European government

Andrew Barry

The mid-1980s saw a qualitative shift in the importance of the European Community in European political and economic life. At the beginning of the 1980s it appeared that the EC had stagnated, permanently enmeshed in a series of protracted intergovernmental disputes, particularly in relation to the problems of Britain's budgetary contribution. Of the main areas of EC policy, the Common Agricultural Policy absorbed an excessive proportion of the Community's budget, its technology policy was oriented primarily to the increasingly irrelevant technology of nuclear power, and its regional policy was little more than a mechanism for redistributing small amounts of tax revenue between the richer and poorer regions of the Community. At the same time, institutionally, the European Parliament was an irrelevance, and the actions of the Commission were very effectively constrained by the exercise of the veto in the Council of Ministers (George 1985).

By 1987–88 this situation had changed dramatically. The passing of the Single European Act of 1987 freed up the institutional process, enabling the Commission to initiate policies in a wide range of areas within which it had hitherto been blocked by the Council of Ministers. At the same time, Jacques Delors' proposal that the Community should work towards the formation of a Single European Market by the end of 1992 provided the focus and the rationale for such initiatives (Ross 1992, 57–63).

Some commentators have interpreted the changes in the European Community in the mid-1980s as a result of the broader dominance of neo-liberal economic thought during this period, and a belief in the impossibility of any narrowly national programme of economic restructuring. According to John Grahl and Paul Teague, in an interpretation that draws extensively on "regulation theory":

> The market completion programme at the same time accelerates the dissolution of national economies as distinct objects of control, thus excluding any repetition of the French experiment [of 1981–83], and redefines the European Community in purely market terms as a huge field for the free play of private interests, increasingly open to global trade and investment flows and only minimally supervised by the tiny apparatus of the EC commission. (Grahl & Teague 1989, 34)

This assessment of the meaning of "1992" is one that, in part, mirrors the UK government's own vision of the European Community. Since late 1988 the Department of Trade and Industry (DTI) has sought to promote what it perceives to be the virtues and challenges of the Single Market, promoting seminars, running a "1992 hotline" and disseminating information to industry. "Europe", as the DTI has put it, "is open for business". The possible implications for social policy or science policy have been largely ignored.

While the official rhetoric attempts to construct an idea of a dynamic European entrepreneurial culture, the reality of the Single Market programme is much more mundane. In practice, the years up to 1992 saw a seemingly never ending succession of directives and programmes, emanating from the Commission, recommending or demanding action in areas ranging from toy safety to accounting procedures. In this context, the uncomprehending British media confined themselves to covering only the most humorous examples of such directives. While such policy initiatives took many different forms, they were unified by a commitment to what the Commission has called "harmonization".

The idea of harmonization appears to have a straightforward rôle in the UK government's vision of 1992. Different technical regulations and expert practices in different member states mean that it is often quite difficult for companies to operate across frontiers. Alan Sugar, for example, has grumbled that exports of fax machines by his firm, Amstrad, are frustrated by the diversity of technical regulations operating across Europe. Breaking down these national systems of bureaucratic regulation, the government argues, will enable British and other national capitals to compete on equal terms across the Community and so benefit from the same scale of home market available to their American and Japanese rivals. In practice, as Grahl and Teague point out, the Single Market programme may simply reinforce the dominance of multinational capital in European markets rather than enable small and medium-sized firms to compete successfully within a larger market.

GOVERNMENT, HARMONIZATION, AND VISUALIZATION

While the idea of "1992" as a neo-liberal project appears plausible, there are two significant difficulties with understanding it entirely in such terms. First, it is clear that, after some initial suspicion of the Community's programme, labour organizations in Europe have come to support the broad development of that programme. In Britain, Delors' speech to the Trades Union Congress (TUC) in 1988 was significant in shifting the political balance in this respect. In Laclau and Mouffe's terms, ideas of "Europe" and the "Single Market" have been articulated with notions of social justice and workers' rights (the Social Charter) (Laclau & Mouffe 1985, 113). If "1992" is really a neo-liberal programme on a continental scale, then we would need to understand why such traditionally anti liberal economic actors have accepted the basic framework of the programme. Second, while the Single Market programme aims to break down barriers to trade between member states, it cannot straightforwardly be understood as a process of deregulation. Rather, the process of harmonization has involved the development of new forms of regulation at a European level, whether in relation to questions of competition, environmental safety, or professional practices.

In the light of these remarks, I want to argue that harmonization, far from being simply part of a neo-liberal economic project, is of much more general significance for European political and economic life. In making this argument I draw, in particular, on Foucault's analysis of the art of government ("governmentality") and Bruno Latour's work in the sociology of science and technology.

Government, harmonization, and visualization

Michel Foucault has traced the history of thought on what he calls "the art of government" (Foucault 1979). For Foucault, an art, or rationality, of government can be understood as a manner of thinking "about the nature of the practice of government capable of making some form of that activity thinkable and practicable both to its practitioners and to those upon whom it was practised" (Gordon 1991, 3). In his account, the 18th and early 19th centuries saw the emergence of a new conception of the art of government that involved a transformation in the understanding of the proper relation between knowledge and government. This transformation is particularly associated with the writings of liberal political economists such as Adam Smith. For liberal political economy, the state was limited in its capacity to know and control the economic and social life of the nation. Yet at the same time, liberal government was argued to depend upon the use of knowledge by both the state and individual economic actors. Liberal government, in other words, depends upon the self governing activities of individual actors, as well as an evaluation of their own limitations on the part of state institutions.

While there have been many insightful accounts of the importance of knowledge in the development of the modern nation state (e.g. Giddens 1985, Ch. 7; Dandeker 1990), for my purposes Foucault's characterization of the modern liberal art of government has a number of advantages as a way of thinking about the significance of harmonization. First, Foucault's account does not itself seek to provide a theory of the state, but instead seeks to examine the development of a certain way of governing that exists both within state and non-state institutions. As Foucault suggests, his analysis does not demonstrate the growth of state control or bureaucratization (the *étatization* of society) but rather, what he calls "the governmentalization of the state" (Foucault 1979, 103; Rose & Miller 1992). This perspective is important because, as we shall see, harmonization does not involve any substantial increase in the scale of state activity, but does seek to provide the conditions for the exercise of government. Secondly, Foucault's account is helpful in indicating the significance of knowledge in the exercise of government. Knowledge, for Foucault, is not narrowly understood as a means of surveillance or control but rather as the means by which state institutions and non-state actors seek to regulate their own activities and to understand their position within a complex politico economic situation. Seen in this light, I argue, harmonization is a process designed to establish a particular territory as a knowable and governable economic and social space.

It is possible to trace a long history of attempts to harmonize technical procedures and measurements. Standard measures of length, of weight and capacity, for example, were increasingly used from the late medieval period onwards in England for the purposes of trade and taxation (Conner 1987). However, it was only in the late 18th century that the importance of technical standards was recognized by political theorists. For the French republican government of the 1790s, the development of a metric system was recognized to have an important rôle in enabling them to unify a political and economic space in a common interest. Prior to its introduction, France, along with other European countries, possessed hundreds of local systems of measurement. Without any common system it was literally impossible to know the extent of the wealth of different regions of the republic and therefore to implement any uniform system of taxation. In effect, then, such local systems served to protect regional power bases from the intrusions of the centre.

GOVERNMENT, HARMONIZATION, AND VISUALIZATION

An extensive programme of standardization was, however, established at a national and international level only in the 19th century. This occurred in three areas, and was intimately linked to the consolidation of a form of government based upon the use of knowledge.

First, there was the development and standardization of various measurements and other forms of representation that have been increasingly used to visualize and assess the state of an industry, a nation, or an empire (Porter 1986). As Ian Hacking has noted, the 19th century saw a veritable "avalanche of printed numbers" (Hacking 1990). Many of these measurements were linked to the emergence of political economy as a discipline, which was central to the exercise of government from the 19th century onwards (Foucault 1979: 20). Such measurements included indicators of savings, of investments, of outputs, and of the balance of trade. But there were also measurements and representations of the demography of populations, of the mental health and degeneracy of the urban poor (Pick 1990; Hacking 1990), of hygiene (Latour 1988) and of the state of the nation's factories. And there was also an increasing concern with the subject of measurement and representation in the natural sciences, whether in relation to the uses and varieties of plants or to the mineral resources of imperial territories. It was only in the late 19th century that the natural sciences became primarily understood as sciences of measurement (Wise & Smith 1986; Schaffer 1991). Lord Kelvin, in a now famous address on "electrical units of measurement", laid out what he was to call "a philosophy of measurement". His claims should be read a part of a broader programme to establish measurement as the important principle of scientific work rather than as a statement of the essential character of science. According to Kelvin:

> In physical science a first essential step in the direction of learning is to find the principles of numerical reckoning and methods for practicably measuring some quality connected with it. I often say that when you can measure what you are speaking about, and when you can express it in numbers, you can know something about it.
>
> (Thomson 1883, quoted in Smith & Wise 1989)

If there was a massive growth in the number of measurements made in the 19th century, such measurements cannot be thought of as straightforward empirical facts. Nor were they simply the social constructions of specific scientific paradigms or discursive formations. Rather, such measurements were constituted through the use of specific devices and practices of

HARMONIZATION AND THE ART OF EUROPEAN GOVERNMENT

measurement. Following Bruno Latour I shall call such devices and practices "inscription technologies" (Latour 1987). Many important inscription technologies were developed or institutionalized during the late 19th century. These technologies included many important laboratory procedures, photographic techniques (Tagg 1988), and fieldwork and survey methods.

While there was growth in the number and range of measurements and other forms of representation in the late 19th and early 20th centuries, this growth was accompanied by the development of standard forms of measurement practice and standard techniques of calculation. These developments were intimately linked to the emergence of university laboratories and departments, which sought to inculcate the discipline of following standard procedures and to encourage the adoption of attitudes of precision, patience, and rigour (e.g. Gooday 1990).

The importance of standards to understanding the relations between knowledge, inscription technologies and government should not be underestimated. Without standards, inscriptions made at different times and places cannot readily be compared. With the development of standard processes of inscription, it became possible to compare and combine inscriptions made at different times and in different places (Latour 1987). Comparisons, for example, could be made concerning the levels of urban poverty in different neighbourhoods, or of the natural resources of different colonies or of the mortality of different populations (Hacking 1990), and accurate calculations could be made concerning the rate of growth of populations or the efficiency of different methods of generating power.

The standardization of inscription technologies was, then, an important process. Within the context of a standard it became possible to constitute an object of knowledge that was extended in either time or space. Thus it became possible to constitute the population, the economy, or the territory of a nation or empire as an object of knowledge and, therefore, as the object of government based upon knowledge.

The second broad way in which the harmonization of technologies was intimately linked with the government of space was in long-distance communication. Michel Foucault noted, for example, how at the beginning of the 19th century what he called the chief "engineers of space" were the civil engineers from the Ecole des Ponts et des Chaussées (Foucault 1986). A similar title could be given to the physicists and electrical and telegraph engineers who in the latter half of the 19th century established the imperial communications networks. As the British telegraph engineer, Charles Bright, argued:

GOVERNMENT, HARMONIZATION, AND VISUALIZATION

> A perfect and completely organized system of telegraphic communication is, in these days, a matter of supreme importance to the welfare and security of any large and populous state. To the British Empire, owing to the enormous distances which separate its different units, such a means of cohesion and easy access is more essential than any other. (Bright 1914, 134)

If the security of nation and empire depended upon reliable and fast forms of long-distance communication, then the possibility of such communication depended upon the harmonization of measurements and procedures. Standard procedures in astronomical measurement defined the position of stars for naval navigation (Schaffer 1988), and electrical measurements and standards enabled British laboratories to regulate the properties of cables hundreds of kilometres out in the Atlantic Ocean (Wise & Smith 1986). The laboratory disciplines encouraged by standard measurement practices were the basis of reliable procedures in telegraph engineering (Schaffer 1991); electrical instruments and procedures developed in London, Cambridge, and Glasgow provided the standards against which the rest of the Imperial telegraph network could be assessed, and towards which the procedures of telegraph engineers had to be adjusted. During the same period, in 1884, Greenwich was defined as the world centre for the measurement of space and time (Howse 1980). British laboratories became centres for measurements of the speed and energy of information transmitted along the telegraphic cable. Together, Greenwich and the electrical laboratories provided the basis, in principle, for calculating the exact spatial and temporal co-ordinates of any event in the world.

Much later, in the 1920s, measurements of electrical reception enabled Marconi to define the conditions for short-wave transmission; and this allowed others to suggest the kinds of procedures required by skilled radio operators to ensure the most effective use of their equipment. In brief, effective long distance communication required both standard measurements of the properties of objects and the management and disciplined training of operatives and engineers who could be relied upon to carry out their work at a long distance from the centre. As Max Weber remarked, it is perhaps not surprising that the telegraph industry in the late 19th century was one of the first industries (along with the railway) to develop a bureaucratic management structure (Weber 1922; Chandler 1977). To achieve long-distance communication thus requires the standardization of both objects and practices.

HARMONIZATION AND THE ART OF EUROPEAN GOVERNMENT

The third area in which there was a programme of harmonization in the late 19th and early 20th centuries was in manufacturing technologies. David Noble has traced the links between the emergence of a demand for new standards of quality and compatibility to the development of science-based and corporate industry in America. As Noble argues, "never before had there been such a demand for controls in production, for uniformity, precision, reproducibility, and predictability, as there was in the electrical and chemical industries" (Noble 1977, 70).

In the United States, technical standards were both an instrument and a result of monopolistic industrial competition. They were of central importance to the early development of firms such as Eastman Kodak, Bell, and Edison, for example. However, although standardization was a market strategy it was also enthusiastically promoted by the emerging engineering profession, not only in the USA, but in Germany, and to a lesser extent in Britain and France. The drive towards standardization was part of a more general movement on the part of professional engineers to establish their position within the emerging hierarchical structures of corporate industry (Lash & Urry 1987, 173), but it was also represented as a development absolutely necessary for national economic prosperity. Around the turn of the century, standards laboratories such as the Physikalische Technische Reichsanstalt in Berlin and the National Physical Laboratory in Teddington were established to provide benchmarks against which the quality and accuracy of national industrial products could be measured and improved.

Industrial standards should not be thought of narrowly as ways of regulating the properties of objects simply in order to provide the conditions for mass production. They were also perceived to be linked to the development of a new discipline and moral order in the workshop, the factory, and the laboratory (Schaffer 1988). The adoption of standards required training, organization and a recognition of the importance of accuracy. In effect, the regulation of the properties of objects provided one of the means for the regulation of individual practices. Standards were not just the objects of government but the agents of government. To paraphrase Saint Simon, standardization involved "the government of men through the administration of things". Arguing for the formation of a National Bureau of Standards, one US businessman suggested:

> We are the victims of looseness in our methods; of too much looseness in our ideas; of too of much of that sort of spirit; born of our rapid development, perhaps, of a disregard or a lack of comprehen-

EUROPE AND TECHNOLOGY

sion of the binding sanction of accuracy in every relation of life . . .
Nothing can dignify this government more than to be the patron
of and establisher of absolutely correct scientific standards and such
legislation as will hold our people to faithfully regard and absolutely
obey the requirements of law in adhesion to those true and correct
standards.

(Quoted in Noble 1977, 75)

Standardization was, then, a process orchestrated primarily at a national
level. National standards were established either through the monopoly position of public or private industries or through the direction of professional
organizations. If the late 19th and early 20th centuries can be characterized
as a period of "organized capitalism" (Lash & Urry 1987), then the programme of standardization had an important rôle to play in the national and
international organization of economic life.

Europe and technology

While notions of measurement, precision and standards acquired particular political and cultural prominence in the late 19th and early 20th centuries, by the 1950s and 1960s their political visibility had undoubtedly declined. To be sure, standardization activities still continued throughout
industry and within specifically designated state laboratories, but they were
no longer perceived to have such a central importance in solving the economic and cultural problems of the era. They were taken for granted or
ignored. As late as 1980 the UK government's Advisory Council on Applied
Research and Development (ACARD) regarded the work of preparing and
negotiating technical standards as tedious, unattractive and with apparently
little commercial value (ACARD 1980, 37). It is a reflection of this attitude that
international standards bodies such as the International Telephone and
Telegraph Consultative Committee (CCITT) and the International Standards
Organization (ISO) have attracted little interest from social scientists.

If the idea of standards declined in importance in the post-war period,
ideas of "science and technology" acquired renewed political and cultural
significance. In the USA, in France, in Britain, and elsewhere, vast resources
were devoted to the development of new "high technologies" based on advanced research in "basic science" (Ronayne 1984). At the centre of these
new research and development programmes were the new technologies of

47

space exploration and nuclear power. In Europe, collaborative programmes were established in order to develop specific high technology artefacts (computers, satellites, nuclear reactors, etc.). The aim of such programmes was in part to share scarce technological resources, in part to counter the perceived danger of American technological hegemony, and in part to use technological collaboration as a driving force and a symbol for further European integration (Pavitt 1971/72). In effect, the launchers and reactors of the European programmes were seen by governments somehow to embody the process of the political integration of Europe and its opposition to American dominance.

The technological and political success of these early European technological programmes was extremely mixed. The failure of many was a failure, in part, to recognize that building a technological system is not a narrow problem of designing a piece of hardware, but also a social and economic problem of creating and meeting human needs, of constructing a market (Callon 1987). This failure is not surprising. In the context of the then prevailing orthodoxy within Western governments, it was assumed that "high technology" would create its own new markets simply by virtue of being advanced. By the early 1980s many of the high technology projects initiated in the 1960s had either been abandoned or remained as reminders to Euro sceptics of the follies of European collaboration. One of the few successes of the period, the Ariane satellite launcher, had, in effect, become a largely French project.

In the absence of any emphasis on standards and harmonization in the 1960s and '70s, the central importance of "harmonization" within the European Community of the late 1980s and 1990s is remarkable. In what follows I want to indicate the significant similarities as well as the differences between the contemporary project of European harmonization and the various nationally centred projects of standardization that occurred towards the end of the 19th century.

Harmonization and European government

For the European Commission, the word "harmonization" has two different meanings. On the one hand harmonization is understood as an ambition. One aim of the European Community, according to the Commission, is to harmonize economic and social life in the Community, to reduce, though not to eradicate, large-scale geographical differences in social and

HARMONIZATION AND EUROPEAN GOVERNMENT

economic power. Article 117 of the Treaty of Rome, for example, states that "Member States agree upon the need to promote improved working conditions and an improved standard of living for workers, so as to make possible their harmonization while the improvement is made".

The second sense of "harmonization", however, is as an instrument of policy. Harmonization is a principle applied to a whole series of policy areas, from telecommunications and the environment to employment and taxation. In some cases, harmonization involves the development of common European standards and regulations that replace existing national procedures. More generally, harmonization involves the "mutual recognition" of national standards (Pelkmans 1987).

In terms of the scale and scope of its ambitions, the current project of harmonization is comparable to the drive towards standardization in the late 19th and early 20th centuries. In the technological field, for example, the aim of harmonization will be to create, in the words of Jacques Delors, a "genuine European technology community" (CEC 1985, 2). Such a community would be formed not through the development of specific high technology artefacts, but through the creation of a space within which technologies and technologists from different European countries can readily move and communicate. In relation to communication technologies, the Commission has argued that harmonization promises to enable the provision of the same technology everywhere, thereby equalizing access to technology for consumers (cf. Berland 1988, 149). In this view, information and communication technologies develop from being controlled by public or private monopolies to being general facilities available for every European citizen. It is hoped that this will create, to adapt a McLuhanite phrase, a "European village – a democratic community of information technology and telecommunication users" (CEC, Ungerer 1988, 194). In this discourse, then, harmonization can help to construct a "European identity", based not so much on large-scale state-supported programmes, but on the diverse and local uses of information and communication technologies (Barry 1990).

The political prominence of standards in the 19th century was, I have argued, closely associated with the consolidation of a form of government based upon the use of knowledge. By contrast, the current European project of harmonization is occurring at a time when the rôle of expert knowledge is already well established, whether in relation to questions of public or private finance (Miller & Rose 1990) or the nation's health or defence. In this context, harmonization acts not so much to foster the development of a relatively new form of power, but to align the capacities of already existing tech-

HARMONIZATION AND THE ART OF EUROPEAN GOVERNMENT

nologies that hitherto had operated within the restricted territorial boundaries of individual nation states.

It is often remarked that the bureaucracy, and indeed the budget, of the European Commission is rather small ("only enough to run the government of a small city", "fewer administrative staff than employed by the translation service"). Yet in the context of the project of harmonization, the small scale of the Commission is not surprising, for, as an agent of government, the EC seeks to operate not by administering anything directly (the Common Agricultural Policy is an exception) but rather by enrolling the diverse powers of existing professional, commercial or state institutions. In this way harmonization appears to provide one solution to the problem of governing such a large economic and social area.

Although a central theme of the EC's programme for government is the principle of harmonization, this does not mean that the principle is employed in the same way across all areas of policy. As is well known, at the Maastricht summit the UK government sought to prevent an extension of the application of the principle to "social" questions. There is, then, a politics to harmonization. Harmonization is far from a neutral programme that will somehow impact upon every country, institution and group with equal force. Questions not only of what practices should be harmonized, but also how and at what rate this process should take place, require political decisions. The idea of "harmonization" re-emerged in the context of the growing importance of neo-liberal economic discourse in western Europe. But, as Grahl and Teague admit, "harmonization" is not, in itself, a neo-liberal project (Grahl & Teague 1989, 50); rather, it is a process with which the widest range of political projects may be articulated (Ross 1992, 56).

If harmonization is a political process it could, nonetheless, be represented as an example of what Habermas called "the scientization of politics": the transformation of an issue requiring open political debate into a technical problem examined by restricted groups of bureaucrats and experts (Habermas 1970). The official institution of democratic accountability within the Community, the European Parliament, has few formal powers and insufficient resources to scrutinize the harmonization process (the so called "democratic deficit"), and the traditional mediators of political debate (parties, mass media, trade unions, etc.) are, as yet, inadequately organized at a European level to provide even a limited critical examination of current developments.

Yet despite these limitations, the current process of harmonization is far from being a movement that is narrowly determined by the concerns of the European bureaucracy or multinationals. Issues that have been problematized through the activities of environmental movements, for example, have become objects of knowledge and regulation. The attempts by the Commission to establish common ways of defining and measuring levels of pollution, environmental damage, industrial safety, or rural poverty suggest a rather more complex and contested project than one that is directed solely by a neoliberal agenda. After the Chernobyl disaster, for example, it was extremely difficult to establish an accurate representation of radiation levels across Europe. Without such a representation it becomes that much more difficult to formulate a "European" response to the problem. Common standards are not only a condition of the formation of a Single Market; they also enable specific dimensions of "Europe" to be known and therefore, in a certain manner, to be governed.

Standardization occurred in the period of what Lash and Urry call "organized capitalism". Standardization was, I have suggested, a central feature of this organization, enabling technologies and expertise to operate across large areas of geographical space. In the late 19th century these large areas of space broadly corresponded to the territories and spheres of influence of the imperial powers.

In the late 20th century the existence of well defined national economic or political spaces has broken down. Individual national governments and nationally based corporations have less capacity to regulate the character of national economic activity (e.g. Lash & Urry 1987, 5). The policy of harmonization was conceived of in the context of a recognition of the weakness of national institutions. Jacques Delors, one of the principal architects of current policies, described the rationale for harmonization to a French audience in the light of the failure of the French Socialist project of 1981–83:

> In 1981, during the first months of the Left government, there was a very strong notion to reverse this tendency [of decreasing national autonomy], so burdensome seemed the interdependences which had proliferated along with the increase in commercial exchanges. Besides the "wall of money", ought one not to challenge the stateless voracity of the multinationals, raging mercantilism, and seek – or rather reconquer – on our national territory the resources needed for technological and industrial recovery on a global scale?
>
> Even if there is such a thing as a creative utopia, this does not deserve such an attractive description. The question is no longer how and to what extent we can break free of external constraint. *What matters from now on is recognizing that the solution to our problems is wholly*

51

HARMONIZATION AND THE ART OF EUROPEAN GOVERNMENT

bound up with the variables of interdependence: exchange rates, interest rates, growth in world trade, but also agreements for harmonizing bank regulations, quality of life and environmental standards, fluctuations in raw material prices and rules governing exports to the Third World – and that's not all.
(Delors & Clisthene 1992, 5–6, my emphasis)

Harmonization is, then, a project that aims to work within the context of global inter-dependences, instabilities and risks. It seeks to provide the conditions within which it is possible to know and to regulate the effects and development of such inter-dependences within a European space.

In this chapter I have not sought to assess the success of the harmonization project in achieving any "real" harmonization within the Community. I have not sought either to evaluate the effects of the project of harmonization in encouraging economic growth within the Community or achieving the desired social and economic harmonization between richer and poorer regions (cf. Cecchini 1988). Rather, what I have tried to do is to illuminate the rather obscure theme of "harmonization" in the history of government. Harmonization makes possible the government of a large economic and social space without the extensive further development of a central state. It is, I suggest, an essential element in the current art of European government.

References

Advisory Council on Applied Research and Development (ACARD) 1980. *Information technology*. London: HMSO.

Barry, A. 1990. Technical harmonisation as a political project. In *The Single Market and the information and communication technologies*, G. Locksley (ed.), 111–20. London: Belhaven Press.

Berland, J. 1988. Placing television. *New Formations* (4), 145–53.

Bright, C. 1914. Inter Imperial telegraphy. *Quarterly Review* **220**, 134-51.

Burchell, G., C. Gordon, P. Miller (eds) 1991. *The Foucault effect: studies in governmentality*. Hemel Hempstead: Harvester Wheatsheaf.

Callon, M. 1987. Society in the making: the study of technology as a tool for sociological analysis. In *The social construction of technological systems*, W. Bijker, T. Hughes, T. Pinch (eds), 83–103. Cambridge, Mass.: MIT Press.

Cecchini, P. 1988. *The European challenge 1992: the benefits of a Single Market*. London: Wildwood House.

Chandler, A. 1977. *The visible hand: the managerial revolution in American business*. Cambridge, Mass.: Harvard University Press.

CEC (Commission of the European Communities) 1985. *Towards a European technology community*. Commission document COM (85) 350 final.

CEC (H. Ungerer) 1988. *Telecommunications in Europe*. Luxembourg: Office for the Official

REFERENCES

Publications of the European Communities.

Conner, R. 1987. *The weights and measures of England*. London: HMSO.

Dandeker, C. 1990. *Surveillance, power and modernity*. Oxford: Polity.

Delors, J. & Clisthene 1992. *Our Europe: the Community and national development*. London: Verso.

Foucault, M. 1979. On Governmentality. *I & C* 6. Reprinted in Burchell, Gordon & Miller (eds) 1991, 5–21.

Foucault, M. 1986. Knowledge, space and power (interview with P. Rabinow). In *The Foucault reader*, 239–46. London: Penguin.

George, S. 1985. *Politics and policy in the European Community*. Oxford: Clarendon Press.

Giddens, A. 1985. *The nation-state and violence*. Oxford: Polity.

Gooday, G. 1990. Precision measurement and the genesis of physics teaching laboratories in Victorian Britain. *British Journal for the History of Science* **23**, 23–52.

Gordon, C. 1991. Governmental rationality: an introduction. In Burchell, Gordon & Miller (eds) 1991, 1–52.

Grahl, J. & P. Teague 1989. The cost of neo-liberal Europe. *New Left Review* **174**, 33–50.

Habermas, J. 1970. The scientisation of politics and public opinion. In *Toward a rational society*, 62–80. London: Heinemann.

Hacking, I. 1990. *The taming of chance*. Cambridge: Cambridge University Press.

Howse, D. 1980. *Greenwich and the discovery of longitude*. New York: Oxford University Press.

Laclau, E. & C. Mouffe 1985. *Hegemony and socialist strategy*. London: Verso.

Lash, S. & J. Urry 1987. *The end of organised capitalism*. Oxford: Polity.

Latour, B. 1987. *Science in action*. Milton Keynes, England: Open University Press.

Latour, B. 1988. *The pasteurization of France*. Cambridge, Mass: Harvard University Press.

Miller, P. & N. Rose 1990. Governing economic life. *Economy and Society* **19**(1), 1–30.

Noble, D. 1977. *America by design: science, technology and the rise of corporate capitalism*. New York: Oxford University Press.

Pavitt, K. 1971/72. Technology in Europe's future. *Research Policy* **1**, 210–73.

Pelkmans, J. 1987. The new approach to technical harmonisation and standardisation. *Journal of Common Market Studies* **25**, 249–69.

Pick, D. 1990. *Faces of degeneration*. Cambridge: Cambridge University Press.

Porter, R. 1986. *The rise of statistical thinking 1820–1900*. Princeton, New Jersey: Princeton University Press.

Ronayne, J. 1984. *Science and government*. London: Edward Arnold.

Rose, N. & P. Miller 1992. Political power beyond the state: problematics of government. *British Journal of Sociology* **43**, 173–205.

Ross, G. 1992. Confronting the New Europe. *New Left Review* **191**, 49–68.

Schaffer, S. 1988. Astronomers mark time: discipline and the personal equation. *Science in Context* **2**, 115–46.

Schaffer, S. 1991. Victorian metrology and its instrumentation. Paper presented at conference on instruments and institutions, Science Museum, London.

Smith, C. & M. N. Wise 1989. *Energy and empire: a biographical study of Lord Kelvin*. Cambridge: Cambridge University Press.

Tagg, J. 1988. *The burden of representation*. London: Macmillan.

Weber, M. 1922. The development of bureaucracy and its relation to law. In *Weber: se-*

HARMONIZATION AND THE ART OF EUROPEAN GOVERNMENT

lections in translation, W. Runciman (ed.), 341–54. Cambridge: Cambridge University Press.

Wise, M. N. & C. Smith 1986. Measurement, work and industry in Lord Kelvin's Britain. *Historical Studies in the Physical Sciences* **17**, 147–73.

Chapter 4

Theses on a post-military Europe
conscription, citizenship and militarism after the Cold War

Martin Shaw

This chapter explores the rôles of war, military institutions and military values in the new Europe of the 1990s and beyond. It is presented, for the sake of brevity and clarity, in the form of a number of theses that attempt to point up the radical changes that are taking place in European society, politics and culture.

The unique rôle of war in European civilization is undergoing historic change

War has almost defined European history up to the very recent past. Indeed war, although known to most societies in most periods in all parts of the world, has played a decisive rôle in the very origins of modern European and Western civilization. A "Western way of war", as trial by battle, evolved in ancient Greece (Hanson 1989). The slave-based social structure of ancient Rome, the first pan-European polity, was dependent on its military operations (Weber 1896). The feudal societies that emerged from the collapse of the Roman Empire were defined by relations of subordination that were primarily military. War remained, through all these social changes, the supreme mode of resolution of conflicts between polities. It played a fundamental rôle in the development of capitalism and industrialism in Europe, as competition between states stimulated trade and innovation (Hall 1987), and war itself was often the leading edge of technological and social change. Military hierarchy and discipline anticipated the social organization of the modern factory (van Doorn 1973a).

Industrial societies, as they emerged in Europe, developed within this framework of competing, war-prone states and highly developed military institutions. The technology and social relations of industrialism were thus adapted to war: improved agriculture fed larger populations and hence larger armies; industrial discipline prepared workers to be members of military machines; industry made weapons more lethal; improved communications, state bureaucracy, and "surveillance" made mass mobilization possible on an unprecedented scale (McNeill 1982; Giddens 1985).

Europe's divided state-system and industrial capitalist society of the first half of the 20th century were thus the context for the most destructive mode of war, total war, that human societies have yet inflicted on themselves. War was total, however, not just in this Clausewitzian sense of "absolute war", but also in the sense of total social mobilization. For Europe especially, this has been a "century of total war" (Marwick 1974).

The end of the Second World War in 1945 marked a historical turning-point for Europe. The great western and central European powers, whose wars had dominated the international system and European societies, were subordinated by defeat (or in the case of Britain, indebtedness) to the new super-powers. They fought no more wars among themselves, but they were centrally implicated in the Cold War, whose central geopolitical fracture ran through the centre of the continent, and the nuclear arms race, which threatened European societies with total destruction even more complete than that of 1939–45. In retrospect, the years up to 1989 can be seen as a period of transition from the total war industrialism of the first half of the century to a new stage of industrial society. The advanced world, including Europe, will be free of major wars between major powers in the 1990s and beyond; but it will be increasingly affected by minor but very destructive wars, especially civil wars, within and between minor nation-states on its margins. The twin collapse of communism and the Cold War has brought instability to the state system in eastern Europe, and has brought war back to the continent for the first time since 1945.

This situation is the result of a double paradox. The Cold War, while it threatened mutual nuclear destruction, also brought about mutual surveillance, with institutionalization of monitoring and routinized contacts, between the rival blocs of states. It created, paradoxically, a framework of co-operation that has led to a Europe in which military antagonism has a marginal rôle between major states. If this fundamentally optimistic conclusion is valid, then a historic transformation of the first order is occurring, with profound implications for every aspect of European society.

On the other hand, however, the very creation of peace between the major powers has allowed socio-political tensions to open up within (espe-

A MORE CRITICAL RESPONSE TO INTERNATIONAL RELATIONS

cially eastern) European societies, and the collapse of the Soviet empire has led to the creation of many new nation-states, the tensions between which are causing the new wars.

European sociology is poorly equipped to confront this new situation, and needs to develop a more critical response to international relations

Sociological theory has had a curious relationship to war and militarism. As Mann has remarked, the dominant version has been – in another central paradox – that of the military victors, the Atlantic powers, whose liberalism denied any "militarist" content. Liberal and Marxist versions of society have triumphed over the "militarist" ideas of writers of writers such as Hintze and Glumpowicz (Mann 1987a). War and militarism have hardly figured in much of the sociological canon, especially in the Anglo-Saxon world.

Nineteenth-century sociology was deeply imbued, moreover, with the aura of automatic industrial progress that dominated western European societies in the century (1815–1914) without major war. At the extreme, founding fathers such as Comte and Spencer speculated on an industrial society in which, in contrast to feudalism, military organization and values played marginal rôles. Even Marx left war and militarism out of his account of the dynamics of industrial capitalism, and saw class violence as dwarfing the inter-state variety in historic significance.

It hardly needs to be said how inappropriate these perspectives seem in the light of 20th-century events. Later Marxists opposed to the "optimistic theory of pacific capitalism" their own "pessimistic theory of militaristic capitalism"; but Mann (whose labels these are) argues, against both these perspectives, that war is the product of older geopolitical relations between states, and that industrialism contributes "only" to the intensity, not to the frequency, of war (Mann 1984). Mann (1987a) argued for growing recognition of the "geopolitical privacy" of states in relation to war, and the separation of war from social systems.

In a contemporary variation on the same theme, Giddens (1985) argued for a partial vindication of the "pacification" thesis. In his view, the consolidation of nation-states meant that societies were internally pacified, through surveillance, although this same development meant that states were able to mobilize greater external violence in their conflicts with other states. Like Mann, he presented a view of international relations, separated from social

57

THESES ON A POST-MILITARY EUROPE

forces, that connected with the dominant "realist" perspectives in international political theory – according to which the international system is an anarchic system of relations between states, regulated by wars.[1]

It has to be said that these works, the most important recent sociological contributions to the analysis of war and international relations – and testimony to the vitality of English macro-sociology – were essential correctives to the neglect of inter-state relations in most sociology, and the economic reductionism with which they were approached in Marxism. They were also, moreover, indirect responses to the renewed military dangers of the second Cold War in the early 1980s.

In retrospect, however, we may argue that the "cold" was more important than the "war" in Cold War. This period in international relations was a transition between the period of total war and a phase of largely warless integration of the major powers, into which we are now entering. The transition was fraught with the danger of nuclear war, and we were right to be overridingly concerned with this at the time, but since these dangers were unrealized, its greater historical importance lay in the system of mutual surveillance, monitoring and even co-operation that emerged, the full significance of which has become evident since 1989. In this respect, the social theorizing of the early 1980s (including this author's own writings) that focused on the historical reality and contemporary danger of large-scale war between anarchic states is now rather anachronistic.

There was another, equally serious, defect of the theoretical framework that is available from this period. In focusing on the autonomous power of states and inter-state relations, writers such as Mann and Giddens understated the continuing impact of social contradictions on international relations. Seeing the Cold War as a system of geopolitical rivalry actually overstated the autonomy of state from society, and limited the relevance of the sociological contribution. In fact "geopolitical privacy" was a feature of the Cold War already challenged by the peace movements of the 1980s; they, and the democratic movements that arose in eastern Europe in 1989, played a critical rôle in breaking down the dominant bipolar structure of international relations (Shaw 1991a).

The post-Cold War situation is one in which social movements and national politics intersect at all levels with international relations. The sociology that is needed is one that challenges, rather than reinforces, the separation of international relations from other social realities. Sociology must criticize the separation of international relations from social theory, its definition of security in terms of state rather than society, and its neglect of the

REVIVAL OF THE NATION-STATE AND NATIONALISM IN EUROPE

rôle of non-state social forces (especially social movements) in international affairs (Shaw 1993).

Of course, the interpenetration of international relations and society is by no means as automatically positive as the balance of the late 1980s might suggest. The instability of state formations and socio-economic systems in east-central Europe, and the social movements to which these have given rise, have played a negative part in the early 1990s revival of nationalism, which in turn has reintroduced war to Europe. A central sociological issue concerns the significance of the new nationalism, which also has powerful echoes in western Europe.

The revival of the nation-state and nationalism in Europe may lead to war and militarism in some cases, but it should not be equated with it

Giddens' account of the nation-state emphasizes the relationship between surveillance and warfare. On the one hand, the state pacifies society through extensive surveillance: firm borders are established, the state's remit runs throughout, and bureaucracy, monitoring, and force ensure that the population is controlled by the state. On the other hand, the violence "extruded" from society is concentrated in the external aspect of state power, in "outward-pointing" warfare directed at other states (Giddens 1985).

The use of this argument is as a general schema: the interesting issues arise where historical developments fail to fit. In general historical terms, two major criticisms can be made. The first is that societies are less than perfectly pacified, with internal violence that can threaten the cohesion of states (and that this violence is partly a product of the contradictions of external war-making in its impact on society, a feature that is explained by "total war" (Shaw 1989)). The second is that surveillance increasingly works at an international as well as a national level – the mutual monitoring of the Cold War, for example – and that this is associated with an increasing pacification of the international system (Rosenberg 1990).

Taking these two points together, we can see a strong relevance to explaining current developments within European society. On the one hand, the process of establishing and consolidating nation-states is hardly complete. The imperfect fit of nations and states, in Europe as in other continents, means that the process of dividing and subdividing states proceeds apace, not just in the former Soviet Union and Yugoslavia, but in western states that

59

THESES ON A POST-MILITARY EUROPE

have for long periods been considered as satisfactory models of nation-states, such as Belgium, Italy and even the United Kingdom. While in western cases (and also, for example, in Czechoslovakia) the pressures for disintegration work in largely non-violent ways, in the ex-USSR and Yugoslavia, violence has often been manifest in societies, between ethnic communities and between newly forming nation-states.

On the other hand, the integrative tendencies of the global economy, culture, and political system are strong. The new nationalism is as much a means of staking out a rôle in a more integrated, multi-national Europe (and world) as it is of achieving the total autonomy of the traditional 19th-century nation-state. From Ukraine, Slovenia and Slovakia to Flanders and Scotland, independence is seen within the context of a more unified, Western-centred economic and political system. Calls for independence are advanced with the framework of the Helsinki process, guaranteed by the USA, and of an extending European Community. The new states premise their very acquisition of sovereignty from old multinational states on a partial surrender to new multi-national structures.

In this context, the classical 19th-century link between political sovereignty and war-making is becoming tenuous and in some cases is, in real terms, lost altogether. All new states seek some national military force as a token of sovereignty, rather like an independent currency or postage stamps. But the real military significance of these developments varies widely. At one extreme, on the eastern and southern margins of Europe, the pull of European integration is so weak, and that of national rivalries so strong, that nasty local wars break out (e.g. Serbia/Croatia, Bosnia, Armenia/Azerbaijan, Moldova/Trans-Dnestra, Georgia). At the other extreme, in the case of forces within smaller Western nations seeking to break up existing EC states and achieve "independence within Europe" (as the Scottish Nationalists have it), it is virtually inconceivable that any new nation-states would have much more than symbolic military autonomy. The militaries of the smaller NATO states, after all, have hardly had an autonomous rôle for more than four decades; with the end of the Cold War, the real rôle of military power in even the largest European states becomes more and more attenuated.

The revival of nationalism and the creation of many new nation-states means more armies, some local wars on the margins of Europe, and a period of instability in the military make-up of the continent after the dangerous certainties of the Cold War. It does not, however, threaten a new militarization of European society as a whole; on the contrary, once the new system of states is consolidated, a patchwork of minor armed stalemates in

MILITARY SERVICE AS A DEFINING ELEMENT OF CITIZENSHIP

the East is likely to be more than matched by the supra-national integration of the European Community, and of the Western-dominated international system in general. In this context, the pacification of Europe is likely to gain new strength, and the rôles of military institutions and values will be brought into question as never before.

Military service will decline in significance as a defining element of citizenship in the new Europe

There is a striking contrast between the rôle of compulsory military service in continental Europe and elsewhere in the Western world (Shaw 1991b). All continental states, including NATO members, former Warsaw Pact members and neutrals, with insignificant exceptions such as Monaco and Liechtenstein, maintain conscription. All "offshore" Western states, from the UK, Ireland, and Iceland, to the USA, Canada, Japan, Australia, and New Zealand, lack the institution, most of them having dispensed with it during the Cold War period. The split is quite exact, and it can be explained in terms of both basic geo-strategic facts – a continental location implies the possibility of invasion across land borders – and long historical traditions – in most continental states, it is central to concepts of citizenship and can be traced back a century or more, whereas in most offshore states it has a much more limited rôle and history.

The rôle of conscription as a social institution is far more than that of a purveyor of cheap manpower to the military. Conscript armies play a central part in the political culture of many states. They have been important as a context of political socialization, an institution within which ethnically, linguistically and socially disparate components of the nation are welded into a unified force. Historically, conscription has been central to the emergence of an all-inclusive citizenship in many European states, with electoral and civic rights conceived as trade-offs for military duty.

Trends in military technology and organization have rendered conscription increasingly problematic, even during the Cold War period. The supremacy of nuclear weapons and the general trend towards high technology have sent the mass army of the age of total war into irreversible decline (van Doorn 1973b). In the offshore states, this has meant the abandonment of conscription; on the Continent, it has meant the attenuation of the system. Western European states have reduced terms of service and introduced greater safeguards of individual rights to conscientious objection. In the

THESES ON A POST-MILITARY EUROPE

German case, by the late 1980s over one third of young men eligible for call-up were opting for civilian service, despite the penalty of a longer term (Kuhlmann 1990). In southern Europe, terms have been longer and conditions poorer, Greece and Turkey having, for obvious reasons, the longest as well as the most illiberal regimes in the West. In the USSR and eastern Europe, terms averaged two years, nearly double the Western average, in the 1980s, and rights of conscientious objection were weak.

The collapse of communism and the end of the Cold War have widened and accelerated these trends. The military system was a central target of the Gorbachev reform movement from its early days, and the failure of the Afghan war also played a major part in its delegitimation. The Soviet withdrawal from eastern Europe removed one major rôle; the *détente* with the West undermined the core function of military institutions. *Glasnost* opened up a host of further fractures. Nationalist motives led to widespread resistance to military call-up in many smaller Soviet and Yugoslav republics in the late 1980s. In Russia itself there was opposition to young men being sent to police distant ethnic conflicts, as well as criticism of the bullying and authoritarianism of the Red Army. The 1991 coup finally undermined its remaining credibility.

The residual militaries are slimmed down, divided in uncertain ways between the newly independent states and – while discontent still simmers – a shadow of the powerful system that existed in the late 1980s. Terms of conscription are being radically reduced, and rights of conscientious objection and alternative service are being institutionalized in many states. The goal of a professional army has been embraced by politicians such as Russia's Yeltsin and Czechoslovakia's Havel, as well as by some military leaders and junior officers, even if its achievement is probably some way off.

The repercussions of these changes in the West have been slower to develop, but they are real enough. Everywhere armies and arsenals are being reduced in size, and in continental states, terms of military service are being radically cut back. The big question that remains to be answered is whether – or when – the very institution of conscription will be abolished, rather than merely reformed, in continental western Europe. Even in France, where the institution can be traced back two centuries to the revolutionary *levée en masse*, and continuously for over a century to the early Third Republic, powerful voices have been raised for an all-professional military. In Germany, where the origins of the modern system of conscription lie in mid-19th-century Prussian militarism, it is now seen as a bulwark of the democratic order in the Bundeswehr. However, so many young men are taking advantage of the

MILITARY SERVICE AS A DEFINING ELEMENT OF CITIZENSHIP

democratic right to *Zivildienst*, that, whatever the benefits to social work in the Federal Republic, there must be a serious long-term question mark over the survival of the system. New cuts envisaged in 1993 also raise the prospect of an all-professional force. Even in Spain, where military service is seen, rather as in Russia, as a matter of residual military pride by most leaders of the post-authoritarian army, there are widespread challenges to its continuance.

The pressures from above and below seem likely to combine to make the longer-term survival of universal military service untenable. Politicians and military leaders are likely to see it as a costly and, in the age of technological militaries, increasingly inefficient form of armed force. Young men are likely to see it – however much it is cut back – as an increasingly unjustifiable slice out of their lives and careers, now that the prospect of large-scale warfare between East and West has been removed. Military sociologists have long seen armies as facing a "legitimation crisis" (van Doorn 1976), and it seems that with the end of the Cold War this is gathering new force. The movement for gender equality places a large new question-mark against conscription: why should men carry out national service if women do not? The wholesale incorporation of young women into the system would, however, make no military or social sense, so that in the longer term this seems a powerful additional factor likely to undermine the institution.

The historic European link between conscription and citizenship seems set, therefore, to be cut. A formidable array of factors is overdetermining its demise: the undermining of the nation-state by European and global integration, the ending of the Cold War, the shift from manpower to technology in armed forces, the cultural changes in the situation of young men. In EC states the nature of citizenship will, in any case, be open for fundamental redefinition as we move into the 21st century. The emergence of an increasingly federal Europe, in reality if not yet in name, will pose the European as well as the national dimension of citizenship as a basic issue.

It is very difficult to conceive of this new Euro-citizenship as a mere continuation of national citizenship, with its essential component of military duty. Apart from the fact that the UK and Ireland do not have conscription, and that in other states it is becoming problematic, the EC is not defined on a military basis. The Community's development of a security dimension should not be seen, primarily, as the development of a military policy or institutions, although it will involve these as a subordinate part. Security is likely to be formulated, for the most part, in political, economic, and social terms, and military activity will mostly be restricted to peace-keeping, most probably under wider international (chiefly UN) rather than EC auspices.

63

(Indeed the striking lesson of the Yugoslav crises of 1991–93 has been the abject failure of specifically European institutions, including the Conference on Security and Co-operation (CSCE) as well as the EC.) The development of a European army, from its beginnings in the Franco-German brigade, is likely to be mainly if not exclusively in professional form. The Europeanization of military power will be a symbol of the marginal rôle of military force in both the international relations and the socio-political relations of the new Europe.

Culture is the last refuge of European militarism, but here too it will be increasingly contested

If the institutional side of militarism is further weakened, its cultural manifestations are likely to remain its most potent feature. Indeed the literature on militarism in the nuclear age, based mainly on the dominant American model, has increasingly highlighted the critical importance of cultural forms. Mann (1987b) argued that we could distinguish Eastern and Western varieties, with a bifurcation into elite "deterrence science" and different popular militarisms, "spectator sport" in the West and "socialist militarism" in the East. Luckham (1984) argued that institutionally based militarism is giving way to "armament culture", centred on the fetishism of the weapon; similar insights seem to inform much of Thompson's (1982) more polemical argument.

Mann's model needs to be modified because "socialist militarism" has self-destructed: the communist military ideology and its permeation of work, education, and family life in the eastern countries have been rejected even more thoroughly than the military institutions themselves. The distinction of elite and popular forms, while analytically useful, can also be questioned if, as Luckham suggests, similar principles underlie each. The shift from traditional institutionally based military culture and values to a weapon-based insertion in both elite and popular cultures is indeed a crucial manifestation of the nuclear age.

The idea of such a transition is useful as a statement about the direction of change, but we need to be careful about ascribing to it an absolute and evenly distributed character. There are elements of universality in the diffusion of American-derived weapons systems and strategic doctrines, on the one hand, and cultural forms such as war films on the other (Luckham in fact provides a far more complex, multi-faceted characterization of armament

CULTURE AS THE LAST REFUGE OF EUROPEAN MILITARISM

culture). At the same time, these are embedded in cultural forms that relate both to the ongoing development of military institutions and to the residues of past wars. Since militarism is, of its nature, highly nationally specific as both a social institution and a cultural phenomenon, we need to understand the significance of armament culture in the context of national differences.

The wars of the Cold War and even more the post-Cold War era are major social events, but they have nothing like the impact that total war had on society. Much of contemporary military activity, indeed, takes place out of sight of society. Although nuclear weapons and high tech armaments are crucial cultural symbols, it is arguable that their significance for most members of societies is still less fundamental than that of the world war that was actually experienced by older generations still alive today, and that remains a matter of folk memory for all. Indeed we can argue that nuclear weapons and other contemporary military issues are largely interpreted, in European cultures, within a frame derived from the last world war.

We all live in "post-war" societies, and 1945 is our benchmark. Although on the face of it this is the assertion of a modernity that has advanced beyond war, beneath lies an implicit recognition that the war is the most fundamental of historical experiences that still shapes our worlds. Some evidence for this is stark and recent, notably from regions such as the Baltic and Yugoslavia where new conflicts have activated issues dormant since the 1940s. The same pattern can be observed, however, throughout Europe, where memories are benign as much as where they are bitter. Britain's war was best of all, without the occupation, defeat and massive loss of life that marked most continental societies; a collective triumph over all these dangers. As a result, British culture is suffused with a "nostalgia militarism" that contributes to national myths of war that have been highly potent in the 1980s and early 1990s (Shaw 1991b, Ch.4).

The specific character of wartime experience, and its subsequent articulation in national cultures and ideologies, determines much of the pattern of contemporary European militarism. The sharp contrasts between Britain, with its nostalgic indulgence of "democratic" militarism, France with its even stronger consensus on a national nuclear force, and Germany where demilitarization is not only culturally strong but institutionalized in the constitution, the structure of the armed forces and the arrangements for national service, are obvious reflections of different Second World War outcomes. The national military cultures thus established are major determinants of the incorporation of "armament culture", in the sense of universal commodities such as Second World War and Vietnam war films.

65

THESES ON A POST-MILITARY EUROPE

In the discussion just referred to, I have taken Britain as an extreme case of a society that is institutionally highly demilitarized, but culturally and ideologically still strongly dominated by militarism. The key issue is whether this case can be seen as a model for other European societies, as they undergo a parallel decline of mass military participation. At the most general level it is probably true that an abstract militarism, divorced from real military practice but linked to the historic myths of reviving nationalisms, will have an appeal to major sectors of many European societies. More specifically, however, the British case is unlikely to provide a model. British militarism has flourished under two conditions that are unlikely to apply to most European societies in the future: a context of general Cold War, in which communism has provided a ubiquitous "threat"; and a situation of declining imperialism which has furnished pretexts for military action, such as the Falklands War, which are inconceivable for most other European states.

Except on the eastern and southern margins where local wars occur, European cultures seem likely to be characterized in the coming years by tensions between historic nationalist military myths, the realities of a declining and increasingly internationalized rôle for military institutions, and strong anti-militarist strands. Anti-militarism, especially among the educated young, showed its strength in western Europe in the early 1980s, and has emerged more recently in the former communist states as a reaction to the militarism of the old system. The declining institutional space of the military is likely to create new social space for non- and anti-militarist culture; the adjustment of terms of conscription is likely to provide a constant agenda for anti-militarism among the young.

The rôle of European states in global policing will provide the critical test of the future of militarism in European societies

On a global scale, the end of the Cold War has largely completed the process of removing the dangers of war among the major industrial states. The military rôles of Western states are likely to be confined to activities on a range best described as "peace-keeping" and "policing", increasingly under the auspices of the United Nations. In the years since the fall of the Berlin wall, we already have had good indications of the nature and scope of the military activities which are likely. At one extreme there will be an increasing number of peace-keeping operations under UN auspices, interposing

THE RÔLE OF EUROPEAN STATES IN GLOBAL POLICING

neutral troops between combatants under terms of strict impartiality and non-aggression. At the other, there will be more active, punitive and even warlike interventions, such as those against Iraq, the maximum form of which is probably represented by the Gulf War. At the time of writing, the failure of purely "humanitarian" UN interventions in Croatia and Bosnia is raising the prospect of a larger-scale "peace-making" intervention on the continent of Europe.

Many western and possibly some ex-communist European states are likely to be involved in all these operations. They will all be different from the historic wars of European states, possessing minimal national dimensions (although of course the conflict with Iraq involved national issues such as the fate of specific groups of Western hostages). They will generally take place either under multinational UN control, or under the leadership of the USA. There will be some similarities with classic colonial wars and the neo-colonial conflicts of the more recent past, in the policing of "unruly" and distant regions, the superiority of Western technology and the small numbers of Western casualties, leading to criticisms of interventions as new forms of "imperialism".

The Gulf War and the crises in Yugoslavia have provided the strongest and in some ways contrasting test cases of the rôle of war in post-Cold War European societies. There are good reasons to believe that the Gulf represents something like a maximum case: a strongly armed, aggressive regional power testing Western-imposed international order. There has been a good deal of general discussion of the general features of the war: the rôles of Western weapons superiority and the control and reception of media coverage; the combination of minimal direct attacks on civilian populations with devastating strikes on the physical infrastructure of civil society; the effect of Iraq's defeat on the Kurdish and Shi'ite minorities. Most of the emerging literature deals with the military, political, economic, and environmental consequences, little with the sociology of the war in Western (let alone Arab) societies. Such sociological works as exist are generally US-centred and focus closely on the media in the war.

There is little literature that deals specifically with European societies, and yet Europe presents, both in general and in its national peculiarities, a different picture from that of the USA. Because the rôle of European states was subordinate to that of the USA, European populations were at a further remove than Americans from the real political debate about the recourse to war. There were, however, major differences between the responses in European societies that can be explained in terms of the institutional and cul-

67

THESES ON A POST-MILITARY EUROPE

tural/ideological features of contemporary militarism that we have discussed (see Shaw 1991b, Ch.6).

In general, it can be said that all-professional militaries were easier to mobilize for war than conscript armies. The USA and UK were the earliest and most committed participants in the anti-Iraq coalition, and their governments had least difficulty in securing popular support once war broke out.[2] Continental European states that participated sent professionals rather than conscript forces; in Germany, the presence of German conscripts at Turkish airbases became an issue, while in general the possibility (however remote given the constitutional position) of German conscripts being sent to fight was a powerful anti-war mobilizer. Even in Britain, where no one had been conscripted for over 30 years, it was interesting to note a moral panic among young people, especially students, at the (wholly unreal) prospect of being conscripted to fight in the Gulf.

More specifically, the rôle of national cultures in general, and of military values in particular, can be seen to have influenced the level of support for the war. Britain, where the myths of war (based on the comparable Falklands experience as well as the Second World War) were uniquely strong and positive, saw less opposition than the USA (where Vietnam was a potent symbol of the dangers). In France, the position of the Arab minority reinforced national pride in leading the government to pursue an independent policy in the build-up to war; but powerful national military traditions saw strong support once war broke out. In Germany, on the contrary, post-war antimilitarism was reflected in widespread anti-war protests in the build-up to the coalition attacks. In Italy, a unique combination of papal and communist opposition led to the largest national protests. In Belgium, the government refused military participation, and was widely supported. In Czechoslovakia, on the other hand, the post-communist regime was supported by most political forces as it demonstrated its pro-Western credentials by giving support (albeit token) to the war. In all European states, poll minorities against war shrank rapidly once the fighting started.

The American-inspired literature on the media in the Gulf War needs to be reinterpreted in the light of these national differences in Europe. Although global media influences – and not just CNN – were strong, many European media had their own coverage that reflected, and influenced, national perceptions.

The experience of the Gulf War thus provides varied and contradictory evidence on contemporary European militarism. The war, unlike those of the recent past but like virtually all wars in the foreseeable future, was expe-

68

THE RÔLE OF EUROPEAN STATES IN GLOBAL POLICING

rienced in a highly mediated form. This mediation was defined, however, by the cultural context as well as by the specific activities and products of "media"; indeed the latter can only be understood in terms of the former. The cultural context in which moves towards war were undertaken was complex, and provided many sources of resistance to war. Certainly it was the case that once powerful international military, political, economic, and media forces were decisively mobilized, this resistance was largely overwhelmed.

The wars in various parts of the former Yugoslavia and Soviet Union, however, have produced different responses. In the regions of crisis themselves, the demilitarization caused by the collapse of communist state militarism has been quickly superseded by regression to modes of war that, until recently, appeared historically outmoded in Europe. Within the newly mobilized nation-states of Serbia and Croatia, Armenia and Azerbaijan, not to mention the internationally unrecognized enclave mini-states of the Bosnian Serbs and Croats and others in the Caucasus, grisly caricatural forms of militarism, replete with both the symbols and realities of the Second World War, have had an influence unimaginable in the past four decades of European history, apparently sweeping aside advances in the development of a peaceful, pluralist, and democratic civil society.

These dark developments, even more than those in the Gulf, which were more consonant with recent historical experience, have created a crisis in both the states and civil societies of the rest of Europe. We have already commented on the weaknesses of European Community interventions in Yugoslavia; we can go farther and argue that this ineffectiveness has contributed a fatal element to the gathering crisis of EC institutions and political leadership. The inability of a united Europe to respond even as well as the UN or the USA (neither of which, at the time of writing, has covered itself in glory) has shown up the deep moral and political weakness of European integration.

The incapacity of western European states has reflected itself in European civil societies and especially in the northwest of Europe, comfortably removed from the new wars. Political parties, churches and even (or particularly) peace movements have been caught off guard, without clear perspectives or responses. Even the mass media have been found pursuing contradictory policies: the occasional sensational exposé of atrocities has been surrounded by seas of silence. In comparison to the Gulf, western European society's response has, for the most part, been even less evident. There are, of course, marked national differences: in Germany, and in countries such as Austria (and Hungary) that border the conflict zones, there has been a much higher

THESES ON A POST-MILITARY EUROPE

profile of the issues, with particular partisanships to the fore. In Greece, which is politically part of western Europe but geographically in the Balkans, there has been a rapid and repressive surge of nationalism.

These weak cultural, social, and political responses to the new wars are in part a product of the demilitarization that we have discussed. They show, however, the inadequacies of this passive reflection of a declining militarism, and the need of the demilitarized civil societies of western Europe to respond to the crisis of civil societies in the Balkans and elsewhere, engulfed by violence. There is a danger that, in the post-Cold War world, the violence of Europe's margins will have a highly negative effect on the integrity of its peaceful core.

Notes

1. This convergence with realism has been noted by a number of writers, most recently Scholte (1993, 4n) who points out in addition that "Theda Skocpol and John Hall explicitly acknowledge their realist orientation".
2. The British case is examined more fully in ongoing work. For a preliminary report based on survey work, see Shaw & Carr-Hill (1991). A wider study is in preparation: Shaw (forthcoming).

References

Giddens, A. 1985. *The nation-state and violence.* Oxford: Polity.

Hall, J. A. 1987. War and the rise of the West. In *The Sociology of War and Peace,* C. Creighton & M. Shaw (eds), 37–53. London: Macmillan.

Hanson, V. D. 1989. *The Western way of war.* New York: Knopf.

Kuhlmann, J. 1990. National service policy and programs: the case of West Germany. München: Sozialwissenschaftliches Institut der Bundeswehr.

Luckham, R. 1984. Of arms and culture. *Current Research on Peace and Violence* **VII**(1), 1–64.

Mann, M. 1984. Capitalism and militarism. In *War, state and society,* M. Shaw (ed.), 25–46. London: Macmillan.

Mann, M. 1987a. War and social theory. In *The sociology of war and peace,* C. Creighton & M. Shaw (eds), 54–72. London: Macmillan.

Mann, M. 1987b. The roots and contradictions of modern militarism. *New Left Review* **162**.

Marwick, A. 1974. *War and social change in the twentieth century.* London: Macmillan.

McNeill, W. H. 1982. *The pursuit of power.* Oxford: Basil Blackwell.

Rosenberg, J. 1990. A non-realist theory of sovereignty: Giddens' *The nation-state and violence. Millenium* **19**, 249–60.

Scholte, J. A. 1993. From power politics to social change: an alternative focus for international studies. *Review of International Studies* **19**, 3–21.

REFERENCES

Shaw, M. 1989. War and the nation-state in social theory. In *Social theory of modern societies: Anthony Giddens and his critics*, D. Held & J. B. Thompson (eds), 129–46. Cambridge: Cambridge University Press.

Shaw, M. 1991a. State theory and the post-Cold War world. In *State and society in international relations*, M. Banks & M. Shaw (eds), 1–24. Hemel Hempstead: Harvester Wheatsheaf.

Shaw, M. 1991b. *Post-military society: militarism, demilitarisation and war at the end of the twentieth century.* Oxford: Polity.

Shaw, M. 1993. "There is no such thing as society": beyond statism and individualism in international security studies. *Review of International Studies* **19**(3).

Shaw, M. & R. Carr-Hill 1991. *Public opinion, media and violence.* Working paper. Department of Sociology, University of Hull.

Shaw, M. (forthcoming). *Distant violence: civil society in the new crises of global order.* London: Routledge.

Thompson, E. P. 1982. Notes on exterminism, the last stage of civilization. In *Exterminism and Cold War*, E. P. Thompson et al., 1–34. London: Verso.

van Doorn, J. 1973a. The genesis of military and industrial organisation. In *The soldier and social change*, 51–61. London: Sage.

van Doorn, J. 1973b. The decline of the mass army. In *The soldier and social change.* London: Sage.

van Doorn, J. 1976. The military and the crisis of legitimacy. In *The military and the problem of legitimacy*, G. Harries-Jenkins & J. van Doorn (eds). London: Sage.

Weber, M. 1896. The social causes of the decay of ancient civilisation. In *Max Weber*, J. E. T. Eldridge (ed.), 254–75. London: Nelson.

Chapter 5

Changing attitudes in the European Community

Sheena Ashford and Loek Halman

Introduction

The main aim of this chapter is to consider the extent to which the values and outlook of the peoples of the various member countries of the European Community agree or differ. We are particularly interested in three things: first, are EC member countries quite distinct in terms of the values and attitudes their peoples hold, or can they be said to take a common approach to the issues that confront them; secondly, are countries more in agreement upon some issues than others; and thirdly, are the countries of western Europe in the process of growing closer in terms of their values and opinions, or are they moving farther apart? These questions have both theoretical and practical importance. Durkheim (1893) and Talcott Parsons (1935), among others, have proposed that value consensus is a basic requirement for social stability. If the values and beliefs of EC member countries are broadly in agreement, the cohesion that this confers will pave the way for greater mutual co-operation and communication among countries in the future. On the other hand, areas marked by value dissensus have the potential to become foci for future social and political conflict. In what follows, we shall show that Europe is in fact best thought of as a loose collection of countries with disparate rather than similar values. We shall also show that over the past ten years European values have tended to become less cohesive in some respects.

The European Values Systems Study Group (EVSSG), whose surveys produced the data on which our analysis is based, was initially mooted just prior to the first elections to the European Parliament. Given the processes of economic, political and cultural transnationalization that might result, it was thought important to discover whether the emerging concept of a European cultural identity had an empirical base.

VALUES AND SOCIAL CHANGE

In 1981 the first Values Study was carried out in all the then EC member countries and in Spain. A second wave of surveys was carried out in 1990, again in all the EC member countries (except Greece). (For a full report of the European findings, see Ashford & Timms 1992.) This chapter draws on data from both EVSSG surveys to examine value changes that took place between 1981 and 1990 in the nine EC member countries that participated in both surveys (Great Britain, Northern Ireland, the Republic of Ireland, France, West Germany, Italy, Spain, Belgium, and the Netherlands).

Values and social change

A central theme in sociology has been the evolution from agrarian society to modern industrial and now post-industrial society, and the dramatic although gradual change in traditional and civic values that has accompanied societal development. Commentators are generally agreed about the direction of these changes. Most modernization theories point to the increased differentiation within societies, the diminished authority of traditional sources of values such as the Church, and with this an increase in individualism (Klages 1985). By individualism we mean that the individual has become the point of reference in the shaping of values and attitudes: more importance has come to be attached to self-development and personal fulfilment, while the importance of values which derive their authority from external sources such as family, society, and Church have declined. What we are seeing is a cultural change in which values are no longer fixed or given but have become options that individuals may choose or reject.

Some writers (e.g. Sennett 1977; Lasch 1979; Zijderveld 1979; Bloom 1987; Finkielkraut 1989) see greater individualism as resulting in narcissism and hedonism; preoccupation with self means selfishness, a decrease in concern for others. But not all commentators share this view. For example, Yankelovich (1981) argues instead that greater individualism brings with it an increased sense of personal responsibility, an "ethic of commitment", rather than personal opportunism. Common to these various theories of value change, however, is the ultimate direction of change. All theories point towards increased individualism and self-expansion. We therefore consider the extent to which changes in values are consistent with the hypothesis that there is a gradual movement towards greater individualization and a growing tendency to reject externally imposed moralities (cf. Inglehart 1990).

With the 1981 and 1990 data now available, we are in a position to as-

73

CHANGING ATTITUDES IN THE EUROPEAN COMMUNITY

sess the nature of any changes that took place in European values during the 1980s. We shall focus on the following areas: family life, religion, and the socio-political domain.

Family life

We would argue that individualism is not very conducive to conventional forms of family life, since these require responsiveness to the needs of partners and offspring and so interfere with the pursuit of self-interest. Yet our figures show that very few people believe marriage to be an outdated institution and that a very large majority of Europeans would like to see more emphasis on family life. In 1981, 75% of Europeans disagreed that marriage is an outdated institution; ten years later, the proportion had actually risen slightly, to 78%. Young people are still less committed to the institution of marriage than are older people, but the evidence suggests that even among young people, support for marriage has been growing. There is also growing support for the view that more emphasis on family life would be a good thing. In 1981, 83% of Europeans were in favour of more emphasis on family life; by 1990, 87% were in favour.

Having children is not easy to reconcile with the pursuit of purely individual pleasures, and so a growth in individualistic values might be expected to entail a decrease in the importance placed upon children and their position in family life. Yet our figures indicate that, rather than rejecting children, Europeans may even be coming increasingly to see them as necessary to personal fulfilment; in 1981, 36% thought that a woman needs children if she is to be fulfilled, while by 1990 this had gone up to 40%.

Nor is there any indication that the values that govern the parent–child relationship are becoming more individualistic. Most Europeans believe that it is the duty of the young to love and respect their parents regardless of the qualities and failings they might have, and again support for this "conventional" view is growing, from 65% in 1981 to 69% in 1990. Likewise, most Europeans believe that parents have a duty to do their best for their children even if it is at the expense of their own well-being; fewer than one in five take the view that parents have a life of their own and should not be expected to sacrifice their own interests for the sake of their children. Again, the conventional view has been spreading, with 65% of our 1981 respondents extolling parental self-sacrifice, compared with 69% in 1990.

There are, however, some areas of personal relationships where individu-

74

alistic values are more in evidence. There is evidence of individualistic, anti-conventional values in the increase in support for women who want to have a child outside a stable relationship, from 33% in 1981 to 37% in 1990. Yet even here there is a suggestion that this "support" for single parenthood is more a question of toleration than endorsement, since an already vast but still growing majority of Europeans believe that a child needs a home with both a father and a mother to grow up happily (80% in 1981 compared with 87% in 1990).

Other areas where public opinion has become more individualistic include attitudes towards complete sexual freedom, towards relatively unconventional forms of sexual behaviour such as homosexuality and prostitution, and towards abortion. The proportion of people who agree that individuals should have the chance to enjoy complete sexual freedoms without being restricted went up from one in five (22%) Europeans in 1981 to more than a third (34%) in 1990. Similarly, the proportion of people who believe unconventional forms of sexual behaviour can never be justified has fallen; Europeans generally are more prepared than before to consider the case for homosexuality, prostitution, and under-age sex; fewer people are now prepared to condemn these behaviours outright. Tolerance of abortion and divorce has also increased since 1981, suggesting again a greater willingness than previously to allow individuals to make an independent choice in their personal lives. The findings of the Values Study suggest that this tolerance extends to a fairly wide variety of groups and so might be taken to indicate that attitudes in this area have generally become more liberal.

The nature of value change in the domain of family life and personal relationships is therefore somewhat ambiguous. One the one hand we have evidence of individualism where sexual behaviours are concerned, but on the other we have a picture of personal relationships, such as those between parents and offspring, that involve just as many mutual obligations and responsibilities as in the past.

Religion

In the religious domain there has been considerable debate about the importance of what observers describe as the growing secularization of Europe. Seen as another example of the process of individualization of values, it is manifest in the recent decline in church attendance almost everywhere, and in a reluctance to accept the Church as a voice of authority in moral and

CHANGING ATTITUDES IN THE EUROPEAN COMMUNITY

personal matters. The Values Study provides further evidence of these changes. Even over a period as short as ten years, church attendance fell dramatically. In 1981 nearly half (49%) of our respondents claimed to attend church at least once a week; by 1990, the proportion had fallen to less than one in three (29%). The drop in attendance was particularly acute among the young, but even older people, generally more conscientious in their religious observance, have become less likely to attend church at least once a week.

Our findings also show that the Church has lost some of its historical authority, especially in the area of personal and moral problems. Confidence in the Church as an institution has fallen somewhat, from 52% in 1981 to 48% in 1990. Fewer people now than in 1981 believe that the Church has credible answers to family (39% compared with 44%) or moral (44% compared with 48%) problems. Perhaps for this reason Europeans have also become less likely to find comfort in religion – only 54% claimed to do so in 1990, compared with 59% in 1981. Only in the domain of spiritual matters has the Church maintained its position as a respected source of answers; indeed here at least it has increased its authority, with the proportion of Europeans who see the Church as answering spiritual needs rising from 59% to 64% by 1990.

Independently of conventional worship, the European public have become somewhat less prepared to recognize the authority of God in their lives. For 55% of Europeans in 1990, God was considered to occupy a relatively important place in their lives, a drop of five percentage points since 1981. Orthodox religious beliefs, e.g. in sin, the devil, and heaven, have declined, but personal spirituality does not appear to have declined to the same extent as has conventional observance. Belief in a soul was unchanged (71%), and the average European in 1990 was only marginally less likely to see him/ herself as a religious person and to believe in God, a spirit, or life force than ten years previously. By 1990, Europeans had become no less likely than before to take moments of prayer, and the proportion of people who claimed to think about death and about the meaning of life had actually increased. Most striking of all, given the decline in formal religious authority, was the increase, albeit small (from 30% to 33%), in the proportion of Europeans who took the rather authoritarian view that there are absolutely clear guidelines about what is good and evil that always apply to everyone, whatever the circumstances. External forms of authority may be losing their legitimacy for many people, but personal, individualistic spirituality does not appear to be declining. Conventional religion may have lost some of its popularity as

SOCIO-POLITICAL OUTLOOK

a source of guidance, but the need for some source of moral certainties does not appear to have abated.

Socio-political outlook

What sort of political and social future is in the making for Europe? Are values in EC member countries becoming more individualistic, giving less ground for common purpose, or are countries moving towards consensus in their socio-political aims?

In this area, comparisons are unfortunately restricted to a small number of items that were present in both the 1981 and 1990 surveys (Table 5.1). These show changes that are small but consistent with the view that in the socio-political domain, as in others, individualistic values are becoming more widespread. In Europe as a whole, feelings of national pride appear to be declining, albeit only slightly: while 39% of Europeans claimed to be "very proud" to belong to their country in 1981, the proportion had fallen to 37% by 1990. Unlike most other socio-political attitudes, national pride showed considerable inter-country variation. Two countries in particular stand apart

Table 5.1 Socio-political outlook by country, 1981 and 1990.

	Total (%)	GB (%)	NI (%)	RI (%)	WG (%)	N (%)	B (%)	F (%)	I (%)	S (%)
Those who are "very proud"										
1981	39	55	46	66	21	19	26	33	41	49
1990	37	52	52	76	17	22	26	32	41	45
Those wanting social change										
1981	70	70	69	71	52	62	61	76	77	82
1990	74	80	74	78	60	71	68	74	86	78
Those preferring freedom over equality										
1981	49	69	58	46	37	56	46	54	43	36
1990	51	63	61	45	59	54	48	48	42	43
Those with a great deal/quite a lot of confidence in Parliament										
1981	44	40	47	51	53	44	34	48	30	48
1990	44	46	46	50	50	53	42	43	32	41
Those agreeing that government should be made much more open to the public										
1990	81	82	81	88	86	75	81	82	84	76

Note: GB – Great Britain; NI – Northern Ireland; RI – Republic of Ireland; WG – West Germany; N – Netherlands; B – Belgium; F – France; I – Italy; S – Spain.

CHANGING ATTITUDES IN THE EUROPEAN COMMUNITY

from the rest. In the Republic of Ireland, levels of national pride were particularly high, with something over three-quarters (76%) claiming to be "very proud" of their nationality. In contrast, residents of West Germany had the lowest levels of national pride in Europe: just one in six (17%) were "very proud" to be German. What is more, national pride diminished in West Germany between 1981 and 1990, while pride in being Irish rose over the same period.

Another potential indicator of growing individualism is the increase in the number of Europeans who appear to feel some dissatisfaction with the way society is run, in that they favour social change and are prepared to take positive action to achieve their ends. In 1990, Italy was the country most in favour of change (86% support) while, at the other extreme, West Germany was the country most strongly committed to maintaining the existing order, although the majority (60%) still wanted change. Furthermore, with the sole exception of Spain, desire for change grew over the decade; this was particularly noticeable in Italy and Great Britain.

Information on the sorts of changes that Europeans want was available from the 1990 survey but not from the 1981 survey, so we do not know whether these represent new issues or long-standing concerns. Nevertheless, it is interesting to consider the issues that are currently of concern to Europe (Table 5.2).

Concern about the environment and about human rights is almost universal; around nine out of ten Europeans (93% and 91% respectively), regardless of nationality, were in favour of the ecology and human rights movements. Other movements that received widespread support include anti-apartheid and disarmament (80% and 78% respectively); somewhat

Table 5.2 Support for political movements, 1990.

	Total (%)	GB (%)	NI (%)	RI (%)	WG (%)	N (%)	B (%)	F (%)	I (%)	S (%)
Those who support the movement for:										
ecology	93	92	89	94	97	95	93	91	92	90
human rights	91	89	78	95	87	94	92	92	96	90
anti-apartheid	80	73	64	90	74	82	79	76	86	82
disarmament	78	51	52	86	83	71	83	72	84	79
anti-nuclear energy	71	56	57	85	72	68	74	64	67	76
women's rights	62	73	74	85	62	64	66	62	44	58

Note: GB – Great Britain; NI – Northern Ireland; RI – Republic of Ireland; WG – West Germany; N – Netherlands; B – Belgium; F – France; I – Italy; S – Spain.

SOCIO-POLITICAL OUTLOOK

fewer but still a large majority (71%) came out against nuclear energy. Least widely supported was the women's movement, which was approved of by just over six out of ten Europeans (62%). For the most part, similar levels of support for each movement were observed in the different countries. However, human rights and the anti-apartheid movement received markedly less support in Northern Ireland than elsewhere in Europe, while Great Britain and Northern Ireland together were significantly less likely than the rest of Europe to support disarmament and oppose nuclear energy. With regard to the women's movement, the two endmarkers were both Catholic countries: strongest support came from the Republic of Ireland, where 85% approved, while support was weakest in Italy, where only 44% approved.

Another indication that individualistic values may be on the increase is suggested by the slight rise, from 49% to 51%, in the proportion of Europeans who prefer freedom to equality. There was a clear public preference for freedom in Great Britain and Northern Ireland, closely followed by West Germany, where the largest majorities preferring freedom were to be found, while the Spanish and Italians tended to feel that equality was the more important goal. In relative terms, national positions had changed little since 1981, except in West Germany, where the figures suggest a substantial shift away from equality and in favour of freedom.

More significant, perhaps, is the increase in the proportion of people ready to take action to achieve political ends (Table 5.3). Compared to 1981, Europeans in 1990 were more likely to have participated, or were prepared to participate, in a range of political actions such as signing petitions, boycotts, lawful demonstrations, unofficial strikes, and the occupation of buildings and factories. Milder actions such as signing petitions are still by far the most common form of political protest, and unlawful behaviour remains relatively rare, but the likelihood of all forms of protest has increased. The potential for unconventional political actions of a more extreme sort appears to be greater among the residents of continental Europe than among residents of Great Britain, Northern Ireland and the Irish Republic. Indeed, signing a petition can almost be said to be a uniquely British form of protest, with three-quarters (75%) of British respondents claiming to have signed a petition, compared with 45% for Europe as a whole. Despite this, petitions remain the most widespread form of unconventional protest in all countries, followed in decreasing order of frequency by attending demonstrations, joining in boycotts, taking part in unofficial strikes, and occupying buildings or factories. Among Europeans, the French are the most likely to become involved in actions of a more extreme sort, and France has the highest propor-

CHANGING ATTITUDES IN THE EUROPEAN COMMUNITY

Table 5.3 Political protest potential by country, 1981 and 1990.

	Total (%)	GB (%)	NI (%)	RI (%)	WG (%)	N (%)	B (%)	F (%)	I (%)	S (%)
Those who have or might										
sign a petition										
1981	69	89	74	73	79	71	56	73	64	58
1990	74	92	84	80	85	80	73	79	73	50
join in boycott										
1981	36	37	40	37	33	34	24	46	33	33
1990	39	48	37	39	42	40	34	47	51	24
attend lawful demonstration										
1981	46	41	45	50	44	42	42	52	42	53
1990	55	47	47	57	58	63	51	62	67	54
join unofficial strike										
1981	20	22	26	26	13	14	15	32	11	24
1990	22	26	27	27	14	23	23	32	21	20
occupy building or factory										
1981	16	12	9	16	11	20	17	28	14	16
1990	18	12	9	20	10	24	23	30	24	16

Note: GB – Great Britain; NI – Northern Ireland; RI – Republic of Ireland; WG – West Germany; N – Netherlands; B – Belgium; F – France; I – Italy; S – Spain.

tion of respondents who have actually taken part in demonstrations and have occupied buildings or factories.

Finally, there is evidence to suggest that Europeans are less than happy with a political system that allows them little voice, and want more participation in the process of government. Fewer than half (44%) place a great deal or quite a lot of confidence in their parliament, a proportion that has not changed since 1981. The Italians stand out as being particularly disillusioned. Confidence in parliament has increased in some countries, notably the Netherlands, Belgium, and Great Britain, but this is countered by a decrease in confidence among the French and Spanish. Further evidence from the 1990 survey suggests that the problem derives in part from a widespread sense of alienation from the processes of government, for more than eight out of ten (81%) Europeans would like to see government made more open to public scrutiny.

Convergence or divergence?

Is Europe coming closer together? We have noted that European countries vary widely in the position taken by public opinion on many issues. For example, in the countries of northern Europe, there is extensive support for modern, individualistic values, while in southern Europe, Northern Ireland, and the Republic of Ireland, religiosity is much more pronounced and conventional views have a stronger hold. But is there any evidence to suggest that the countries of Europe moved closer together during the 1980s, or do they remain a collection of countries with disparate outlooks, linked together politically but not in spirit? If we compare the spread of opinion among EC member countries in 1981 with the spread of opinion in 1990 and find it to have decreased, then we have a rough indication that countries have become less diverse in their outlook. If, on the other hand, the spread of opinion in 1990 is greater than in 1981, then we would suggest that countries have become more diverse. For items measured using individual scales – an example would be a ten point scale of "acceptability" where 0 indicates "totally unacceptable" and 10 "totally acceptable" – this is done by comparing the standard deviations obtained in 1981 and 1990. For items measured using an ordinal scale, such as "agree a lot, agree a little, don't agree at all", this is done by computing an index of dissimilarity based on the sum of the differences between the distribution of responses given by the two most extreme countries, divided by two. The index of dissimilarity is therefore an indication of the extent to which the two most dissimilar distributions differ.

In the domain of family life and personal relationships, public opinion had, in some areas, become more diverse by 1990 than it was in 1981 (Table 5.4). National views on whether marriage is outdated have become more varied, as have views on whether children are necessary to a woman's fulfilment. In particular, views on rights to sexual freedom have become much more diverse. In other areas, though, there has been little change, while views about parents' responsibilities towards their children have moved towards consensus.

The extent to which nations agree in their religious beliefs has not changed very much. National differences in views about whether the Church gives adequate answers to moral problems have decreased, but countries differ much more now than before over the comfort and strength that their publics derive from religion. There has been a move towards dissensus in the frequency with which publics reflect upon the meaning of life, and in their belief in the devil, although the extent of inter-country agreement with re-

Table 5.4 Index of country dissimilarity, 1981 and 1990.

	1981 (%)	1990 (%)
Marriage is not an outdated institution	18	23
More emphasis on family life is a good thing	21	27
Women need children for fulfilment	57	62
Parents' duty is to do their best for children	36	29
One must always love and respect parents	41	40
Approve of a woman having a child as a single parent	39	37
A child needs a home with a father and a mother	23	23
Individuals should enjoy complete sexual freedom	21	45
Under-age sex is justifiable	3	3*
Prostitution is justifiable	3	3*
Homosexuality is justifiable	4	5*
Abortion is justifiable	3	3*
Divorce is justifiable	2	2*
Attend church weekly or more often	69	65
Church answers family problems	24	27
Church answers moral problems	35	22
Church answers spiritual needs	31	35
Confidence in church (great deal + quite a lot)	15	24
Get comfort and strength from religion	35	54
God is relatively important	37	49
Am a religious person	32	34
Believe in God/spirit or life force	46	47
Believe in a soul	36	36
Take moments in prayer	37	39
Often think about death	18	17
Often think about the meaning of life	13	18
Believe there is absolute good and evil	24	27
Very proud to be (e.g. British)	59	47
Confident in parliament	18	18
Want social change	23	26
Have or might − sign petitions	26	36
− join boycott	10	12
− attend lawful demonstration	10	10
− join unofficial strikes	11	6
− occupy buildings, factories	9	11
Prefer freedom over equality	33	20
Post-materialism	34	23

Note: Countries included West Germany, Great Britain, Northern Ireland, the Republic of Ireland, Belgium, Netherlands, Spain, Italy, France.

* Difference between mean scores of highest and lowest scoring countries.

CONVERGENCE OR DIVERGENCE?

gard to other beliefs is much as before. In the socio-political domain the biggest changes have been in the direction of greater consensus. International agreement about the merits of freedom over equality has increased, as has agreement about the merits of post-materialism. In other areas, agreement has remained at the same level as previously, or has decreased by only a small amount.

Perhaps the last word about the benefits and possible costs of European unity should be given to the participants in the Values Study. In 1990, a question was included for the first time that asked whether national identities would disappear or be enhanced in a united Europe. Overall, 50% of those who answered felt that on the whole there was more chance of a united Europe protecting national identities than undermining them. A further one in five (22%) felt that a truly united Europe would probably mean the end of member states' national, historical and cultural identities, while the remainder had middling views or no view on the matter at all (see Table 5.5). Countries varied in their outlook: Britain and Northern Ireland were particularly sceptical, whereas France and Italy were the most enthusiastic. Across Europe the dominant view is that national and cultural identities will

Table 5.5 Attitudes towards the EC by country, 1990.

There is much talk about what the individual member states of the European Community have in common and what makes each one distinct. Which opinion is closest to your own opinion, the first or the second?

a) Some people say: If the European member states were truly to be united, this would mean the end of their national, historical and cultural identities. Their national economic interests would also be sacrificed.

b) Others say: Only a truly united Europe can protect its states' national, historical and cultural identities and their national economic interests from the challenges of the superpowers.

	Total (%)	GB (%)	NI (%)	RI (%)	WG (%)	N (%)	B (%)	F (%)	I (%)	S (%)
those who agree that EC means the end of identities										
	22	33	31	28	25	22	17	19	12	17
those who agree that EC protects identities										
	50	35	38	49	44	45	48	59	65	47
those who are unsure/ don't know										
	28	32	31	23	31	33	35	22	23	36

Note: GB – Great Britain; NI – Northern Ireland; RI – Republic of Ireland; WG – West Germany; N – Netherlands; B – Belgium; F – France; I – Italy; S – Spain.

CHANGING ATTITUDES IN THE EUROPEAN COMMUNITY

be maintained, even enhanced, by membership of a united Europe, but there is still a significant contingent in most member states who feel that membership poses a threat to historical identity.

Conclusion

Certainly the 1980s saw changes in the attitudes and outlooks of the various member countries of the European Community. In very general terms we can conclude that there is some evidence of individualization in values in all the domains we considered. It is also clear that this process of individualization is far from universal. Individualization is evident in the way in which people think about certain issues in certain areas, but thinking on other issues in the same area may be unchanged or may even have become more conventional as, for example, in the ways in which people think about family and personal relationships. European values cannot be simply described as "modern" or "individualistic". The transformation is incomplete, and our data point in several different directions at once. More freedom is advocated in relation to sexual interests and political participation, yet concern with spirituality may be growing. Conventional sources of authority, such as the Church, are increasingly rejected, yet morality is no less well grounded than before, although it is now more likely to be based in individual discernment than in external dictate. The extensive support for a range of movements concerned with social change suggests a possible widening of interpersonal interests in the environment and in issues concerning the human condition; if individualism is on the increase, it would seem to take the form of a greater sense of individual responsibility and concern for others rather than an inward-looking preoccupation with self at the expense of the community.

Equally, there is little evidence to support the view that the countries of Europe are moving towards greater consensus in their outlook. Commitment to a united Europe varies substantially from country to country, and variations in national opinion are as marked now as in 1981. In terms of identity, differences within countries such as those due to age, gender, or political or religious affiliation are almost without exception smaller, sometimes considerably smaller, than differences between countries. The picture of western Europe that emerges from these findings is rather complicated. Some indicators point towards value convergence, while others suggest value divergence. Clearly it is not possible to conclude unequivocally that values in Europe are moving in the direction of either consensus or dissensus.

REFERENCES

References

Ashford, M. S. & N. Timms 1992. *What Europe thinks: a values handbook*. Aldershot: Dartmouth.

Bloom, A. 1987. *The closing of the American mind*. New York: Simon & Schuster.

Durkheim, E. 1893. *De la division du travail social: Etude sur l'organisation des sociétés supérieures*. Paris: Alcan.

Finkielkraut, A. 1989. *De ondergang van het denken*. Amsterdam: Contact.

Inglehart, R. 1990. *Culture shift in advanced industrial society*. Princeton, New Jersey: Princeton University Press.

Klages, H. 1985. *Wertorientierungen im Wandel*. Frankfurt: Campus.

Lasch, C. 1979. *Haven in a heartless world*. New York: Basic Books.

Parsons, T. 1935. The place of ultimate values in sociological theory. *International Journal of Ethics* **45**, 282–316.

Sennett, R. 1977. *The fall of public man*. New York: Knopf.

Yankelovich, D. 1981. *New rules*. New York: Random House.

Zijderveld, A. C. 1979. Het ethos van de verzorgingsstaat. *Sociale Wetenschappen* **22**, 179–203.

Chapter 6

Support for new social movements in five western European countries[1]

Dieter Fuchs and Dieter Rucht

Introduction

In Western democracies, in the wake of the student revolts of the late 1960s, several waves of collective protest have been superimposed and have coalesced to form a relatively stable, new type of movement. Along with these "new social movements", there have come into being in the system of political interest mediation collective actors that are distinctly different from established collective actors, political parties, and interest groups. These differences relate to some of the movements' goals, but most of all to their forms of action, their organization, and their resource base (Rucht 1991). In particular, social movements depend to a greater degree on the willingness of citizens to become involved than do established collective actors, which rely on professional apparatuses and direct access to the political system. Therefore, whether these movements can have an impact on distinct policies, change the structure of the system of political interest mediation (Offe 1985; Roth 1989), or whether they may even challenge the entire political order (Dalton & Kuechler 1990), depends essentially on the extent to which they are supported by mass publics. It is the degree of mass support that finally limits the movements' ability to mobilize for collective action, and that is their key means to reach their goals.

Conceptions of the amount and stability of support for new social movements diverge greatly. Whereas some consider these movements to be a peripheral and cyclical phenomenon, other observers see them as long-term and politically relevant. Such positions are often based on selective observation or data that refer only to a single movement, a single country, or a single point in time. Assumptions are often derived from mobilization campaigns of movements that vary greatly in scope, and as a result the mobi-

CONCEPTS AND OPERATIONALIZATION

lization potential is typically overestimated or underestimated. More realistic and generalizable statements can be made only if they are based on measurements of the mobilization potential of several movements in several countries at several different points in time.

So far, such data are available only from the four Eurobarometer surveys conducted during the 1980s, which included questions on the kind and degree of support for various new social movements in France, the Netherlands, West Germany, Italy and Great Britain. Until now, these data have not been used for an analysis of several movements in several countries for four points in time. In aiming to fill this gap, we shall mainly be concerned to ask: what trends and levels of support can be determined for the new social movements in the five countries during the 1980s, and how are variations to be interpreted? In answering this question, we shall examine not only the supporters and specifically the mobilization potential of new social movements, but also their opponents, a group that has been neglected in previous studies.

Given the lack of empirical knowledge and of strictly theoretically guided hypotheses regarding the trends and levels of support for new social movements in cross-national comparison, our analysis is mainly descriptive. Instead of studying support for social movements among the broader public, most researchers in this field have offered explanations for the emergence of movements, their level of mobilization, strategies and outcomes. Despite the neglect of theories dealing explicitly with support for social movements, we think that modernization theory offers ideas that could serve to interpret some of our findings. All five countries investigated here have reached a relatively high level of modernization. If the formation of new social movements can be understood to be one expression of this transformational process (Raschke 1985; Inglehart 1990a, 1990b), then similar and stable patterns in the support for these movements in the five countries should also result. Though all countries are likely to fit this overall pattern, their relative differences could be attributed to the fact that they are at different stages in the transformational process (Fuchs & Klingemann 1993). These assumptions will serve at least as a rough heuristic guide for explaining cross-national variation.

Concepts and operationalization

Difficulties with the concept "social movements" are already apparent in the very different attempts at definition. For the most part these difficulties have

NEW SOCIAL MOVEMENTS IN FIVE COUNTRIES

to do with general characteristics of social movements, for example their often rapid changes in scope and form over time, and their ambiguous boundaries. We assume that social movements are constituted for citizens primarily by perceptions – usually mediated by mass media – of these movements' collective actions. In these collective actions, the fundamental dimensions of social movements appear in a specific way. Certain goals are formulated and are articulated within the framework of certain forms of action and organized by certain groups.[2] Citizens' attitudes to a social movement are presumably formed by generalization from perceptions of the movement's individual collective actions.

In the first instance, "new social movements" as a specific object of support is simply a sociological construct. Difficulties in clarifying this concept result especially from the fact that it serves as an umbrella concept for quite heterogeneous individual movements – among others, the anti-nuclear power movement, the ecology movement, and the second waves of feminism and the peace movement (Roth 1985; Brand, Büsser & Rucht 1986). The rather ambiguous adjective "new" implicitly refers to differences from the socialist movement as the "classic" movement since the mid-19th century. Although the new social movements share with it a radical democratic orientation, they share neither its belief in the worker as the revolutionary subject nor its trust in the rôle of central, bureaucratic, avant-garde organizations. A further difference can be found in the fact that the workers appear neither ideologically nor socio-structurally as important carriers of new social movements, whose activist core is formed much more by the "new middle class", especially those employed in human services (Raschke 1985, 415).

Since the justification of the umbrella concept "new social movements" is not uncontested within the social sciences (even its promoters emphasize the heterogeneity of the various individual movements) and the concept cannot necessarily be presumed to be familiar to many western Europeans, it makes most sense to collect data for several of the above-mentioned individual movements. Drawing on these results, the possibilities and limitations of more generalizing statements can then be discussed. The most important of these individual movements are at the very least familiar to most western Europeans from the news reporting of the mass media. These movements can therefore be assumed to be objects to which citizens have developed certain attitudes and behavioural dispositions. These can be determined by means of direct questions in representative opinion polls (Pappi 1991). In a causal analysis of the support for new social movements in West Germany, it was shown that in addition to the attitude to the goals of movements, the

88

CONCEPTS AND OPERATIONALIZATION

attitude to their modes of action was one of the strongest predictors (Fuchs & Kühnel 1990). This can be seen as an empirical indication that those questioned reacted not only to the inherent goal dimension of a certain movement (e.g. peace), but that in fact they also had the actual movement in mind.

By "support" we mean a fundamental disposition of a person to an object: "Support refers to the way in which a person evaluatively orients himself to some object, either in his attitudes or his behaviour" (Easton 1975, 436). This concept defines a quality of relationship between a subject and an object. Whereas the subject of support – a person or an aggregate of people – can be clearly determined, categories of support and of the object of reference, "new social movements", are in need of further clarification. This general concept of support borrowed from Easton is without directed content, can be based on either a positive or a negative attitude to an object, and leaves open the question whether support is simply a matter of an attitudinal dimension or a matter of a behavioural dimension. A more exact definition of the different types of support can be undertaken only in regard to the specific character of the object in question.

Established politics is essentially channelled into the form of parties, which interpret the passivity of citizens as agreement, and may operate routinely on the basis of the strength of their institutional resources. Social movements, by contrast, are in need not just of toleration but of active support that manifests itself in concrete mobilizations. Without the commitment and participation of many people in a movement's actions and campaigns, the movement would sink into insignificance. Thus it makes sense to make the behavioural dimension a necessary condition of "support", at least in regard to the mobilization potential of social movements.

"Mobilization potential" is one of the most important questions in studies of the support for (new) social movements (Klandermans & Oegema 1987; Schmitt 1990; Kriesi 1992). It is insufficient to regard everybody who has a positive attitude to a goal that a movement is trying to achieve as comprising the mobilization potential of this movement. In the case of the ecology movement in West Germany in 1989, for example, more than three-quarters of the population asserted the importance of environmental protection (Hofrichter & Reif 1990, 130). But such a definition of potential carries little weight when one considers the small scale of participation even in large campaigns. If the concept of mobilization potential is to have better predictive value, it must be defined in closer accordance with behaviour so that only those people who evince a fundamental willingness to participate in a move-

89

NEW SOCIAL MOVEMENTS IN FIVE COUNTRIES

ment are defined as part of its mobilization potential. Thus Klandermans and Oegema (1987) and Kriesi (1992) relate the mobilization potential of a movement to "the people in a society who could be mobilized by a social movement. It consists of those who take a positive stand toward a particular movement. Attitudes toward a movement involve the means and/or goals of a movement." (1987, 519) However, in contrast to Klandermans and Oegema, it is our view that, in order to establish the mobilization potential of a movement – the reservoir from which it can draw for its collective actions – a positive evaluation of the goals and the means of the movement is necessary (Fuchs & Kühnel 1990).

For mobilization actually to occur, other conditions must be met in addition to a positive stance towards the goals and means of a movement. The mobilization potential must thus be directly or indirectly realized on the micro- and meso-levels by the mobilizing actors (Gerhards & Rucht 1992); motivation and expectations of success must be present for participation, and certain barriers against participation must be overcome (Klandermans & Oegema 1987; Klandermans 1989).

In the sense of the general concept we use here, social movement support can then be positive or negative. By contrast, the mobilization potential of a movement refers solely to those people who evidence a positive, behaviourally relevant disposition towards the goals and means of a movement.

Opposition to a movement can only be investigated symmetrically to the mobilization potential in exceptional cases. Whereas, in the case of an actually existing movement, one can make enquiries about a positive attitude as well as about a behaviourally relevant disposition (actual participation or intent to participate), an analogous negative spectrum could be construed only if there existed a clearly identifiable antipode to that movement, especially an oppositional movement. In so far as this condition is not met, we consider it sufficient to determine opposition solely on the basis of a negative attitude to the movement; answers to questions that asked about potential support for a purely hypothetical oppositional movement would be of doubtful value.

One condition of the empirical determination of a movement's support is that this object must also be known to the citizens in a way in which reference to supporting it makes sense. Fundamental difficulties arise here and parallel those connected with the problems discussed earlier of defining "new social movements".

In Eurobarometer surveys (numbers 17, 21, 25, and 31a) conducted in 1982, 1984, 1986, and 1989 in France, the Netherlands, West Germany,

CONCEPTS AND OPERATIONALIZATION

Italy, and Great Britain, the following two questions were posed:

> "There are a number of groups and movements seeking the support of the public. For each of the following movements can you tell me . . .
>
> A. Whether you approve (strongly or somewhat) or you disapprove (somewhat or strongly)?
> B. Whether you are a member or might probably join or would certainly not join?"

Four movements were named that those questioned were asked to evaluate using the choices of answers in A and B:
- The nature protection associations
- The ecology movement
- Movement concerned with stopping the construction or use of nuclear power plants
- Anti-war and anti-nuclear weapons movements.

From responses to these two questions, both the attitudinal and the behavioural dimensions of the "support" concept can be defined at least approximately, but the questions, drafted by other authors, are for a number of reasons[3] less than ideal. First, it must be questioned whether the membership question is a valid indicator of the behavioural dimension. Strictly speaking, membership can exist only in formal organizations that have clear boundaries with their environment. By contrast, the organizational forms of new social movements are marked on the whole by a rather small degree of formalization (Gundelach 1984) and lack clear boundaries, although these movements also include regular membership organizations. The question of membership is a valid indicator of the behavioural dimension only if those questioned understand "membership" not in this strict sense, but rather as a designation of forms of participation that are possible within the context of new social movements: participation in collective actions of these movements, or more or less binding membership in groups that organize such collective organizations.

From the linkage of the attitudinal and the behavioural dimensions, we constructed a measuring instrument to determine the support for the movements addressed in the surveys. The environmental protection groups are, however, excluded because they are neither new nor left-libertarian and so do not qualify as "new social movements".

All those questioned who declare that they are members of a certain or-

NEW SOCIAL MOVEMENTS IN FIVE COUNTRIES

Table 6.1 Typology of support for new social movements – construction of variables.

Attitudinal dimension	Is a member	Might join	Would not join	Missing data
Approve strongly	1	2	3	3
Approve somewhat	1	2	3	3
Disapprove somewhat	MD	MD	4	4
Disapprove strongly	MD	MD	5	5
Missing data	1	2	3	MD

The categories of the resulting typology are:

1 – activists
2 – potential activists   } mobilization potential }
3 – sympathizers   } proponents
4 – weak opponents
5 – strong openents   } opponents
MD – missing data

ganization and who simultaneously evaluate the movement positively are labelled "activists". Those who "somewhat" or "strongly approve" of the movement but do not consider themselves to be members, but instead only "might join", are considered "potential activists". Those who evaluate the movement positively but would not join it are called "sympathizers". "Weak opponents" are people who "somewhat disapprove" of the movement, and "strong opponents" are those who "disapprove strongly". In this way a typology of the support for a social movement is created with five categories that form an ordinal hierarchy ranging from activists of the movement to its strong opponents (see Table 6.1).

Only the "activists" and "potential activists" from our typology meet our criteria for inclusion in a movement's "mobilization potential". If one adds "sympathizers", the group of "proponents" results; these are those citizens who, in one way or another, take a positive stance towards the movement. Against the proponents stands the group of "opponents" formed by aggregating the "weak" and "strong opponents".

Trends and levels of support

Preliminary inspection of the data for each of the five types of support just described for each of the five countries revealed that the numbers of activists and strong opponents were so small that differences between countries and between different points in time could not sensibly be interpreted. For

TRENDS AND LEVELS OF SUPPORT

this reason and for clarity and simplicity of representation, the data are graphically presented in a somewhat condensed form (see Figures 6.1–6.3; for tabular presentation of the data, see Appendix, pp. 109–111). These figures represent only the trends for the mobilization potential and for strong and weak opponents; trends for the mobilization potential have been placed above, and those of the opponents below, the central horizontal axis.

There is no homogeneous pattern of development in the trends of support for the three movements either within one country or between countries. In none of the five countries was there a monotonic increase or decrease in support for the three movements; nor was there a monotonic increase or decrease in support for any of the three movements in all five countries. Clearly the development of the support of new social movements is determined by country-specific and movement-specific factors.

If the attempt is made to distil from the trend data at least some common, overarching characteristics for the movements and the countries, then this is most easily done by a comparison between 1986 and 1989. The general pattern can be seen in Figures 6.1–6.3: the mobilization potential of the three movements increased in 1989 in all five countries compared to 1986; at the same time the number of opponents decreased. But there are also two exceptions to this general pattern: in Italy, the mobilization potential of the peace movement actually decreased, and in Great Britain the number of opponents to the anti-nuclear power movement increased.

In a comparison of the first (1982) and the last point in time (1989), there are different results for the individual countries: in Italy and France, the mobilization potential for all three movements decreased, whereas in the Netherlands and West Germany it increased; in Great Britain, it increased for the ecology movement and decreased for the other two movements. The mobilization potential of new social movements in Italy and France was at its greatest in 1982, then dropped off, and even with the general upswing between 1986 and 1989, it did not regain its former level.

If we compare the data presented here with the survey data on the importance of environmental protection and the risks of atomic energy (Hofrichter & Reif 1990), there are indications that the development of support for new social movements does not depend solely on the extent to which those questioned accept the movements' goals. A further important factor encouraging support is presumably the perceived overall performance of the movements (among other things, the way in which they pursue their goals). In all five countries, the number of those questioned who agreed with the development of atomic energy declined between 1982 and 1989; conversely,

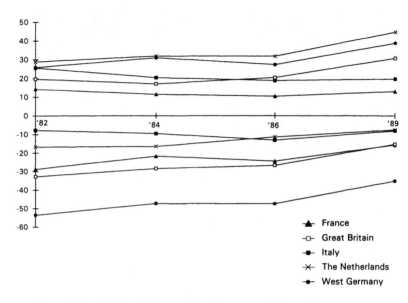

Figure 6.1 Mobilization potential and opponents in the ecology movement.

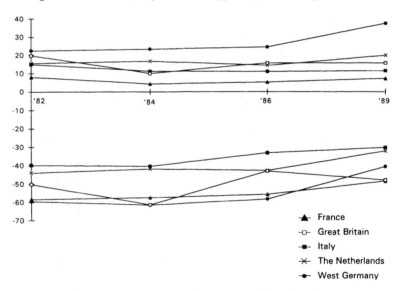

Figure 6.2 Mobilization potential and opponents of the anti-nuclear power movement.

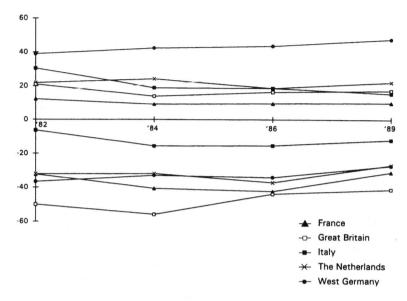

Figure 6.3 Mobilization potential and opponents of the peace movement.

the number of people who perceived the risks to be unacceptable rose (Hofrichter & Reif 1990, 137). (The Chernobyl catastrophe in 1986 strengthened but did not create the trend.) Even more clearly, recognition of the environmental problem increased steadily in all five countries during the period 1983 to 1989 (ibid., 129).

These positive trends at the level of goals or issues are also evident in France and Italy, yet the mobilization potential for the corresponding movements declined in both countries. This finding should serve as a warning against directly inferring the size of the mobilization potential or even manifest participation in social movements from the level of agreement with movement goals. Such a reservation is all the more valid in the case of the converse inference from actual mobilization to the size of the mobilization potential and the attitudes of mass publics to movement goals.

By contrast with the trends described above, some rather clear patterns emerge within as well as among individual countries (see Figures 6.1–6.3) in the levels of support for new social movements. The ecology movement has the highest mobilization potential of the three movements, the anti-nuclear power movement the lowest. The peace movement lies between them. The converse is true for opponents: the ecology movement has fewest opponents, followed by the peace movement. The anti-nuclear power movement chalks up most opponents. This picture holds true for almost all countries and almost all points in time. West Germany is the primary exception: in all four years the mobilization potential of the peace movement is larger than that of the ecology movement; conversely, there are more opponents of the ecology movement than the peace movement. The low mobilization potential of the ecology movement can, however, be attributed to a methodological artefact,[1] and may well be markedly higher in reality. In Italy and Great Britain, the mobilization potential of the peace movement in 1982 was also somewhat larger than that of the ecology movement, but this changed at other points in time.

Thus it can be assumed that, during the 1980s in the five countries analyzed, the ecology movement had the largest and the anti-nuclear power movement the smallest mobilization potential, with the peace movement in between. However, this order of the three movements in the individual countries occurs at very different levels. If one orders the countries according to the size of the mobilization potential and the number of opponents of the individual movements, striking differences become apparent. The mobilization potential of all three movements in the country that is ranked first is more than three times as large as that in the country that is ranked last. The same holds true, with the exception of the anti-nuclear power movement, for the opponents.

The ranking of the countries in regard to mobilization potential is almost identical for all three movements. The highest mobilization potential is present in West Germany, followed by the Netherlands, Great Britain, and Italy; the lowest mobilization potential with respect to all three movements is found in France. The ecology movement in West Germany, which is ranked slightly behind that of the Netherlands, is an exception to the general pattern in the ranking of countries, probably for the methodological reasons already mentioned (see note 4).

In addition to the determination of the mobilization potential of individual movements, an appropriate description of the resonance of new social movements for mass publics also requires a systematic treatment of the opponents of these movements. If the numbers for 1989 are considered, the ecology movement in all five countries has markedly fewer opponents than the peace movement and, in particular, the anti-nuclear power movement. Italy and the Netherlands tend to have fewer opponents, France and West Germany considerably more. (The average number of opponents of all three movements in West Germany is more than twice that of Italy.) The relatively high number of opponents to the peace movement in Great Britain and their middling number in Germany are the only exceptions to this pattern.[5]

The basic patterns that result from the relations of different orders of magnitude of mobilization potential and opponents can be illustrated in a simple four-fold table. If one proceeds from the simple dichotomy "strong/weak", four different categories of movements can be distinguished. Borrowing from the concept of valence issue used in election research (Butler & Stokes 1969, 390–94), Kaase (1990, 93) has suggested the concept "valence movement" to characterize the case of a movement that attracts a large measure of approval and a low number of opponents. Analogously, one could characterize a movement that strongly divides mass publics, one for which there is high mobilization potential and a high number of opponents but little indifference, as a polarizing movement. For movements with little mobilization potential and a small number of opponents, we speak of a marginal movement. We call the case in which low mobilization potential coincides with a large number of opponents a provocative movement.

The relations between the strength of the mobilization potential and the proportion of opponents, and thus the categorization of empirically existing movements in terms of the four constructed types, can be illustrated in a two-dimensional space (see Figure 6.4).

This space is structured by two axes, of which the horizontal axis shows the extent of mobilization potential and the vertical axis the number of opponents. The matrix created in this way is subdivided into four quadrants, each characterizing one type of movement. The closer a movement lies to the outside corner of a quadrant, the more closely it corresponds to the type of movement characterized by the quadrant. Thus we get a clear picture of the overall constellation of all movements within a two-dimensional field.

The anti-nuclear power movement in France and the ecology movement in the Netherlands each come closest to one of the constructed ideal types, the former a provocative movement, and the latter a valence movement. On the level of movements as well as on the level of countries, some patterns emerge. All three movements in West Germany are in the polarizing movement quadrant; in France, Great Britain and the Netherlands, two movements each are in the provocative movement quadrant, and in Italy two movements are in the marginal movement quadrant. Thus in all five countries, a certain type of movement is dominant.

With regard to individual movements, the anti-nuclear power movement can be most clearly classified: in four countries it can be characterized as a provocative movement and in one country as a polarizing movement. The

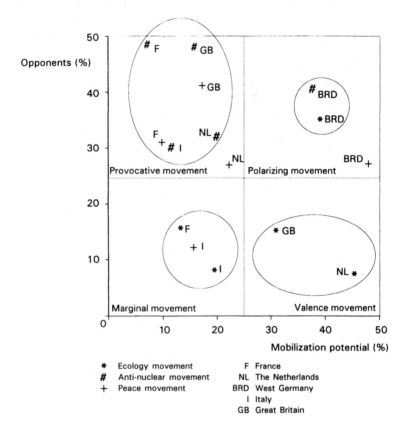

Figure 6.4 Types of new social movements (1989).

peace movement can be characterized least clearly: in one country it is a marginal movement, in another country a polarizing movement, in two a provocative movement, whereas in the Netherlands it lies on the border between quadrants. The ecology movement is a valence movement in two countries, a marginal movement in one, and a polarizing movement in one. In contrast to other quadrants, the one for valence movements contains only ecology movements: those of Great Britain and the Netherlands.

This structure of support makes it clear that the question of levels of mobilization potential and of numbers of opponents must be addressed quite

TRENDS AND LEVELS OF SUPPORT

differently for the five countries. Even within the individual countries – with the exception of West Germany – no uniform ordering of the individual movements can be performed.

Thus far we have carried out a separate analysis of the support for new social movements for each of the three individual movements. A question often discussed in the more recent literature on movements is whether the individual movements are just different forms of expression of a single more general type of movement, or whether they must be considered to be independent of one another. In characterizing the ecology movement, the anti-nuclear power movement and the peace movement as "new social movements", commonality is conceptually implied. In what follows, we address this implication only in so far as we attempt empirically to determine how thoroughgoing the relationship between the three movements is. As an indicator of this, we draw on the average size of mobilization potentials on the one hand, and of opponents to the three movements on the other.

The basis of the percentages presented in Table 6.2 is the total mobilization potential of new social movements or, in other words, all of those questioned who could be counted as part of the mobilization potential of at least one of the three movements. The percentages show how this total mobilization potential of three movements is distributed. In Table 6.3, the same procedure is used for the opponents. In this distribution, seven classes are created: the average potential of all three movements (one case), the average potential for two movements each (three cases), and the exclusive mobilization potential that can be assigned in each case only to one movement (three cases). Table 6.3 operates in the same way in regard to the opponents. In

Table 6.2 Overlap of the mobilization potential of new social movements (percentages).

Movements	France		Netherlands		Germany		Italy		Great Britain	
	1982	1989	1982	1989	1982	1989	1982	1989	1982	1989
ecology + nuclear										
+ peace	28.0	25.0	23.9	24.2	31.4	52.6	30.6	36.0	19.8	27.2
nuclear + peace	6.3	8.4	7.9	2.0	11.8	11.0	5.4	7.0	26.2	6.4
ecology + peace	17.0	11.7	12.1	10.3	12.0	8.7	23.9	12.7	5.1	8.4
ecology + nuclear	6.7	5.8	3.7	9.0	5.9	1.5	1.2	0.9	3.8	8.0
peace	14.9	12.6	12.0	8.0	27.7	13.6	21.0	7.9	10.8	5.5
nuclear	2.3	4.2	5.0	3.5	2.5	4.3	3.0	2.6	7.3	1.7
ecology	24.7	32.2	35.5	43.0	8.7	8.4	14.9	32.9	26.9	42.9
N	190	166	393	474	400	562	372	288	347	*

NEW SOCIAL MOVEMENTS IN FIVE COUNTRIES

Table 6.3 Overlap of the opponents of new social movements (percentages).

Movements	France		Netherlands		Germany		Italy		Great Britain	
	1982	1989	1982	1989	1982	1989	1982	1989	1982	1989
ecology + nuclear										
+ peace	18.8	13.9	16.6	8.5	42.8	36.8	5.6	8.0	26.8	14.3
nuclear + peace	26.9	25.6	25.1	30.9	5.9	10.2	9.5	22.2	30.2	42.0
ecology + peace	4.3	3.8	3.1	3.0	2.3	4.2	0.0	0.9	5.8	1.0
ecology + nuclear	10.8	6.5	3.5	5.1	20.1	14.8	10.2	9.3	4.3	4.2
peace	8.7	10.4	12.6	20.8	4.4	4.4	1.2	4.3	9.4	11.3
nuclear	24.4	36.4	33.0	30.5	15.1	15.7	69.3	49.1	11.0	20.3
ecology	6.1	3.4	6.1	1.2	9.3	13.9	4.1	6.2	12.6	6.9
N	741	581	572	387	639	498	414	324	696	485

order to be able to illustrate the changes in the subtotals, the percentages for 1982 and 1989 are shown.

First we will concentrate on the results from 1989. With the exception of West Germany, a pattern among the countries is identifiable: a relatively large proportion of the total mobilization potential for the three movements individually consists of those people who could be mobilized by all three movements. In this case we speak of the consistent mobilization potential of new social movements. It is apparent that the mobilization potential exclusively ascribed to the ecology movement also comprises a large part of the total mobilization potential.

In West Germany in 1989, the consistent mobilization potential of all three movements is, at 52.6%, markedly higher than that in the other four countries. The proportion of those in the total mobilization potential who exclusively form the mobilization of the ecology movement (8.4%) is, by contrast, markedly lower than in other countries. Thus in Germany, unlike the other countries, the ecology movement has no special attraction by comparison with the peace and anti-nuclear power movements.

For the opponents, the movement-specific overlapping is less clearly marked. Comparatively, the largest overlapping of opponents to movements is found for the anti-nuclear power and the peace movements, yet because of the extent to which they are thematically related, a larger overlapping between the anti-nuclear power and the ecology movements would be expected. Except in Italy, the consistent opponents of all three movements also form a significant group; they are especially strongly represented in West Germany. Comparable to the ecology movement with regard to mobilization potential, the anti-nuclear power movement takes on a special position

SUMMARY AND DISCUSSION

for the opponents. Of the seven different categories, in almost all countries the proportion of the group that is composed solely of opponents of this movement is either the largest or second largest, in Italy reaching almost 50%. Once again, West Germany is the exception: the group of consistent opponents is clearly strongest (although it drops from 42.8% in 1982 to 36.8% in 1989), whereas the proportion of exclusive opponents to the anti-nuclear power movement is clearly the smallest.

The pattern described for 1989 also applies for 1982, albeit somewhat less clearly. The largest difference between 1989 and 1982 is in the mobilization potential in West Germany, where the consistent mobilization potential for all three groups increased from over 31% (1982) to over 50% (1989). On this evidence, in contrast to the other countries, there was a clear broadening of consistent mobilization potential for the new social movements in West Germany. By contrast, in France the consistent mobilization potential, clearly small at the outset, decreased slightly between 1982 and 1989.

Thus, on the whole, it can be concluded that in all five countries a considerable proportion of those who belong to the mobilization potential of one movement can also be included in the mobilization potential of all three movements. The differences that can be determined for 1989, at 25% in Italy and over 50% in West Germany, are, however, considerable. In any case, the consistent mobilization potential in 1989 is considerably higher than the number of consistent opponents. Thus a significant and (except in France) growing consistent mobilization potential is evident. This is presumably an indication that citizens see the individual movements, which clearly differentiate themselves in terms of concrete themes, as part of a larger whole. The consistent mobilization potential or, in other words, that which exceeds the mobilization potential of individual movements, indicates that people believe the individual movements to share common, ideological background characteristics, and supports the thesis that there is a single type of new social movement.

Summary and discussion

Firstly, there is evidence of a considerable or even high mobilization potential for all five countries and all three movements. Secondly, this pattern remains relatively stable between 1982 and 1989; there are no dramatic changes in the mobilization potential or number of opponents. In general, the mobilization potential increases rather than decreases. Thus the proposition that the new social movements are a politically marginal and transitory phenomenon is not supported by the evidence. We did not examine the reasons for the surprising size and stability of the mobilization potential, but our results lend support to those arguments that tie the unfolding of new social movements to structural rather than cyclical factors. If one considers the broad and stable mobilization potential of new social movements, it can be assumed that a new line of political conflict is indicated that is also expressed by changes in the party system (Inglehart 1984; Müller-Rommel 1990). Although the mobilization potential is broad and stable, only a small part of this potential is actually mobilized into concrete actions.[6] The mobilization cycle of new social movements determined by Koopmans and Duyvendak (1991, 243) on the basis of protest event data, which culminates in West Germany and in the Netherlands between about 1981 and 1986, is thus not accompanied by an analogous development in mobilization potential. In the second half of the 1980s, a decrease in actual mobilization accompanies an expansion of mobilization potential.

In cross-national comparison, clear differences in the levels of support can be seen. West Germany and the Netherlands tend to have the highest and France the lowest levels of mobilization, with Great Britain and Italy in between. The country-specific findings regarding the level of mobilization potential correspond to our expectations. In the light of modernization theory, it is not surprising to find most support for new social movements in West Germany and the Netherlands. Were one to place the countries on a modernization scale, we would situate Germany and the Netherlands at the top and the remaining three countries below. Obviously, such a ranking depends on the definition of modernization and the indicators chosen. In our view, one has to distinguish at least between the economic and the cultural dimensions of modernization. Unlike many other authors, we would not measure economic modernization only in terms of the relative size of the service sector; in considering the highly advanced economies of, say, Switzerland or West Germany, this indicator can be misleading (Esping-Andersen 1991). A more adequate measurement would refer to productivity rates, economic competitiveness on the world market, and only the technologically most advanced segments within the service sector. On these criteria, West Germany and the Netherlands are in front of the other three countries. On the cultural dimension, one could choose the level of postmaterialism as a key indicator of modernization. According to Eurobarometer data (1982 to 1989), the average proportions of postmaterialists in the population were: West Germany 22.5%, Netherlands 22.2%, Great

SUMMARY AND DISCUSSION

Britain 15.5%, France 14.3%, and Italy 9.3%. Moreover, the traditional left–right cleavage is also less viable in West Germany and the Netherlands. Though we do not dare to place the five countries on an ordinal scale according to their overall degree of modernization, we do find a consistent pattern for the two sets of countries. Hence, in West Germany and the Netherlands especially favourable conditions for the development of new social movements seem to exist. The mobilization potential determined here suggests this, as does the actual mobilization achieved by the movements,[7] as well as their more condensed and developed infrastructural basis compared with those of Great Britain, Italy, and France.[8]

Modernization theory may, then, help to explain why movements in West Germany and the Netherlands have higher mobilization potential than those in the other three countries. Nevertheless, such a framework is too general consistently to explain the order of all five countries investigated here. For example, the French movements have lower mobilization potential than those in Italy and Great Britain, despite the fact that France, according to most indicators of modernization, ranks higher than Italy and Great Britain. We therefore conclude that other explanatory factors, such as political opportunity structures (Tarrow 1989; Kriesi 1991; Kriesi et al. 1992), must be considered.

Clear differences also arise in a comparison of individual movements. The higher mobilization potential of the ecology movement by comparison with the peace movement and especially the anti-nuclear power movement could be related to the fact that, first of all, there are now hardly any significant political forces that speak out against ecological concerns, and ecological issues are also considered important by mass publics (Hofrichter & Reif 1990). Secondly, the ecology movement seems to have a more diffuse appearance than the other two movements; it is more fragmented and disintegrates into a multitude of individual subtopics, partial movements and campaigns. This facilitates wider public acceptance, because the ecology movement is associated to a lesser degree with strongly polarizing issues such as the NATO double track resolution (in the case of the peace movement) and the construction of nuclear power plants.

On the basis of the relations of the mobilization potential for individual movements (low/high) and the number of opponents (few/many), we have constructed four movement types and related empirical movements in the five countries to them. We found the following patterns. In cross-national comparison (data from 1989), there is evidence of a tendency towards polarizing movements (high mobilization potential and many opponents) in

West Germany and a contrary tendency towards marginal movements (low mobilization and few opponents) in Italy. Comparing movements, the number of opponents to the anti-nuclear power movements is relatively high. The most marked provocative movements (low mobilization potential, many opponents) are the anti-nuclear power movements in Great Britain and, above all, France. The most marked case of a valence movement (high mobilization potential, few opponents) is that of the Dutch ecology movement.

The example of West Germany shows that movements that are quite active and strong by comparison with those of other countries not only draw on or actively create a high mobilization potential, but can also simultaneously assemble a relatively large number of opponents. This is especially true of the anti-nuclear power movement in West Germany. The strong mobilization of this movement, which did not shy away from sometimes militant forms of action, has apparently also created a definite and broad opposition, so that the group of those who are indifferent is very small. The opponents of the West German anti-nuclear power movement in the 1980s did not, however, express themselves in large-scale counter-mobilizations.

The relatively insignificant anti-nuclear power movements in France and Great Britain, which have only a low mobilization potential, have an even larger number of opponents than in West Germany. We suspect that in the former two countries, the dominant party political consensus on the question of nuclear power influenced public opinion and branded anti-nuclear power movements as outsiders. That they did not degenerate into marginal movements with little mobilization potential and few opponents despite their relative weakness could be related to the fact that Great Britain and France quite early and strongly backed the civil uses of nuclear power and tied it closely to their military nuclear power as well as to an industrially rooted concept of progress. Under these conditions, the issue of nuclear energy gains great material and symbolic significance (Rucht 1993). It is consistent with this that peace movements find most opponents in France and in Great Britain; in both countries, criticism of nuclear armaments is for the most part interpreted as an attack on national independence and strength rooted in their identities as nuclear powers.

As for the overlapping of mobilization potentials, it was seen that significant proportions of the mobilization potential of individual movements comprise the people who could be mobilized by all three movements. With the exception of Italy, this consistent mobilization potential, as we have called it, increased between 1982 and 1989, most especially in West Germany. This supports the hypotheses that there is a generalized mobilization potential of

NOTES

new social movements that exceeds individual issues, and that this type of movement is consolidating its position. These findings, together with the high and remarkably stable level of total mobilization potential, support our belief that the new social movements will remain a significant political factor well into the 1990s.

Notes

1. An earlier version of this chapter was presented at the ESF/ESRC conference on Political Participation in Europe, Manchester, 5–8 January 1990. We are grateful to Robert Rohrschneider, Edeltraud Roller and colleagues in our research unit for their comments and to Sherri Sokerland for translating the manuscript.

2. Tilly (1978, 8ff.) distinguishes between three fundamental dimensions that constitute a social movement: a group of people, beliefs or goals, and events or collective actions. We see the formal characteristic of the majority of social movements in that they exist as a relatively loose association of subgroups and organizations – as "mobilized networks of networks" (Neidhardt 1985, 197). In regard to their beliefs, social movements typically stand in contradiction to some central elements of an established order (Melucci 1989, 29). Since in our societies this order is politically legitimated and, as a rule, guaranteed by the state, social movements are always also political challengers. Finally, it is characteristic that, due to a lack of other resources and channels of influence, they rely primarily on the means of collective protest actions (Neidhardt & Rucht 1991, 452).

3. First, the positive and negative possibilities for answers are not always symmetrically constructed. Although the English version meets this criterion with the paired concepts approve/disapprove, the German version, with *Unterstützung/Mißbilligung* (support/disapprove) (instead of *Billigung/Mißbilligung* (approve/disapprove)), does not. Secondly, some of the translations are at best inexact. This occurred in part because translations were not always done from the English original; apparently the French translation served as a model for the Italian translation, and further ambiguities were thus created. Additionally, detailed descriptions were chosen ("anti-war and anti-nuclear weapons movement" instead of "peace movement") in some languages, but were translated by simple categories (German: *Friedensbewegung* ("peace movement")) in others. In part, inappropriate stimuli were also presented out of ignorance of linguistic and empirical nuances. Thus instead of the French concept *mouvement de la paix*, the concept *mouvement pacifiste*, which has historically negative connotations and is for the most part associated with the communist party, was used. On the basis of this stimulus, it is likely that the potential of the French peace movement was underestimated. Thirdly, important attributes are missing in some questions. For example, the French version of Eurobarometer 31a did not ask about nuclear power plants (*centrales nucléaires*), but instead only about power plants (*centrales*). Fourthly, even within individual languages the formulation of questions was not kept completely consistent at different points in time. Fifthly, the completely

105

NEW SOCIAL MOVEMENTS IN FIVE COUNTRIES

appropriate English concept "activist" was replaced in some languages with the category of "member", which in reference to movements is both theoretically and empirically problematic. For an additional flaw, see note 4.

4. In West Germany only, the question gave the "Greens" as a supplemental example for the ecology movement. This addition surely caused some of those questioned who have a positive stance towards the ecology movement to give a negative answer, in so far as they adopt a critical or disapproving stance towards the Greens. Data from a 1989 survey that contains questions regarding attitudes towards new social movements supports this assumption; in that survey, evaluations of the ecology movement were clearly more favourable than those of the peace movement (Fuchs 1991).

5. The relation between mobilization potential and opponents is not necessarily transparent in the sense that a high mobilization potential corresponds to a low number of opponents (and vice versa) because the two categories are not symmetrical and a relatively high number of sympathizers were not included in the mobilization potential.

6. The percentages of actual activists vary according to country, point in time, and movement, between 0.1% (anti-nuclear power movement in France in 1986) and 4.4% (ecology movement in the Netherlands in 1989). These percentages are too small to be interpreted.

7. The results of Koopmans and Duyvendak's (1991, 236) study of the quantitative mobilization of different new social movements in the Netherlands, West Germany, and France show this quite clearly. For the period 1975 to 1989, with the exception of the solidarity movement (primarily with third world countries), the mobilization per million residents in France, at 86,000, is much weaker than in the Netherlands (154,000) and West Germany (188,000).

8. For a comparison of the movements in Italy and West Germany, see della Porta & Rucht (1991); for a comparison of France and Germany, see Rucht (1993).

References

Brand, K.-W., D. Büsser, D. Rucht 1986. *Aufbruch in eine andere Gesellschaft. Neue soziale Bewegungen in der Bundesrepublik.* Frankfurt/M.: Campus.

Butler, D. & D. Stokes 1969. *Political change in Britain.* New York: St. Martin's Press.

Dalton, R. & M. Kuechler (eds) 1990. *Challenging the political order: new social and political movements in Western democracies.* Oxford: Polity.

della Porta, D. & D. Rucht 1991. *Left-libertarian movements in context: a comparison of Italy and West Germany, 1965–1990.* (Discussion Paper FS III 91–102.) Berlin: Wissenschaftszentrum Berlin.

Easton, D. 1975. A re-assessment of the concept of political support. *British Journal of Political Science* **4**, 435–475.

Esping-Andersen, G. 1991. Three postindustrial employment regimes. *International Journal of Sociology* **21**(4), 149–88.

Fuchs, D. 1991. *The normalization of the unconventional: forms of political action and new social*

REFERENCES

movements. (Discussion Paper FS III 90–203.) Berlin: Wissenschaftszentrum Berlin.

Fuchs, D. & S. Kühnel 1990. *Determinants of the mobilization potential of new social movements.* Paper presented at the ISA World Congress, Madrid, July 9–13.

Fuchs, D. & H.-D. Klingemann 1993. Economic and cultural modernity: an attempt to analyse macro-relations. Unpublished manuscript.

Gerhards, J. & D. Rucht 1992. Mesomobilization: organizing and framing in two protest campaigns in West Germany. *American Journal of Sociology* **98**, 555–9.

Gundelach, P. 1984. Social transformation and new forms of voluntary associations. *Social Science Information* **23**, 1049–81.

Hofrichter, J. & K. Reif 1990. Evolution of environmental attitudes in the European Community. *Scandinavian Political Studies* **13**, 119–46.

Inglehart, R. 1984. The changing structure of political cleavages in Western society. In *Electoral chances in advanced industrial democracies: realignment or dealignment?*, R. J. Dalton, S. C. Flanagan & P. A. Beck (eds), 25–69. Princeton, New Jersey: Princeton University Press.

Inglehart, R. 1990a. *Cultural shift in advanced industrial society.* Princeton, New Jersey: Princeton University Press.

Inglehart, R. 1990b. Values, ideology and cognitive mobilization in new social movements. In *Challenging the political order: new social and political movements in Western democracies*, R. J. Dalton & M. Kuechler (eds), 43–66. Oxford: Polity.

Kaase, M. 1990. Social movements and political innovation. In *Challenging the political order: new social and political movements in Western democracies*, R. J. Dalton & M. Kuechler (eds), 84–101. Oxford: Polity.

Klandermans, B. 1989. Grievance interpretation and success expectations: the social construction of protest. *Social Behaviour* **4**, 113–25.

Klandermans, B. & D. Oegema 1987. Potentials, networks, motivations, and barriers: steps towards participation in social movements. *American Sociological Review* **52**, 519–31.

Koopmans, R. & J. W. Duyvendak 1991. Protest in een pacificatie-democratie: De Nederlandse nieuwe sociale bewegingen in internationaal vergelijkend perspectief. *Mens en Maatschappij* **66**, 233–56.

Kriesi, H. 1991. *The political opportunity structure of new social movement: its impact on their mobilization.* (Discussion Paper FS III 91–103.) Berlin: Wissenschaftszentrum Berlin.

Kriesi, H. 1992. Support and mobilization potentials for new social movements: concepts, operationalizations, and illustrations from the Netherlands. In *Studying collective action*, M. Diani & R. Eyerman (eds), 219–44. London: Sage.

Kriesi, H., R. Koopmans, J. Duyvendak, M. Giugni 1992. New social movements and political opportunities in western Europe. *European Journal of Political Research* **22**, 219–44.

Melucci, A. 1989. *Nomads of the present: social movements and individual needs in contemporary society.* London: Hutchinson.

Müller-Rommel, F. 1990. New political movements and "new politics" parties in western Europe. In *Challenging the political order: new social and political movements in Western democracies*, R. J. Dalton & M. Kuechler (eds), 179–208. Oxford: Polity.

Neidhardt, F. 1985. Einige Ideen zu einer allgemeinen Theorie sozialer Bewegungen. In *Sozialstruktur in Umbruch*, Stefan Hradil (ed.), 193–204. Opladen: Leske.

Neidhardt, F. & D. Rucht 1991. The analysis of social movements: the state of the art and

NEW SOCIAL MOVEMENTS IN FIVE COUNTRIES

some perspectives for further research. In *Research on social movements: the state of the art in western Europe and the USA*, D. Rucht (ed.), 421–64. Frankfurt: Campus; Boulder: Westview Press.

Offe, C. 1985. Challenging the boundaries of institutional politics. *Social Research* **52**, 817–68.

Pappi, F. U. 1991. Die Anhänger der neuen sozialen Bewegungen im Parteiensystem der Bundesrepublik Deutschland. In *Neue soziale Bewegungen in der Bundesrepublik Deutschland*, 2nd edn, R. Roth & D. Rucht (eds), 458–86. Bonn: Bundeszentrale für Politische Bildung.

Raschke, J. 1985. *Soziale Bewegungen. Ein historisch-systematischer Grundriß*. Frankfurt/M.: Campus.

Roth, R. 1985. Neue soziale Bewegungen in der politischen Kultur der Bundesrepublik – eine vorläufige Skizze. In *Neue soziale Bewegungen in Westeuropa und den USA. Ein internationaler Vergleich*, K.-W. Brand (ed.), 20–82. Frankfurt & New York: Campus.

Roth, R. 1989. Neue soziale Bewegungen als politische Institution – Anregungen für einen theoretischen Perspektivenwechsel. *Forschungsjournal Neue Soziale Bewegungen*. Special Issue 1989, 33–51.

Rucht, D. 1991. Parteien, Verbände und Bewegungen als Systeme politischer Interessenvermittlung. (Discussion Paper FS III 91–107.) Berlin: Wissenschaftszentrum Berlin.

Rucht, D. 1994. New social movements in France and West Germany: explaining differences in their overall strength and dynamics. In *New social movements: European and American interpretations*, M. Mayer (ed.). London: Routledge.

Schmitt, R. 1990. *Die Friedensbewegung in der Bundesrepublik Deutschland. Ursachen und Bedingungen der Mobilisierung einer neuen sozialen Bewegung*. Studien zur Sozialwissenschaft, Vol. 90. Wiesbaden: Westdeutscher Verlag.

Tarrow, S. 1989. *Struggle, politics, and reform: collective action, social movements, and cycles of protest*. Western Societies Program Occasional Paper No. 21. Cornell University.

Tilly, C. 1978. *From mobilization to revolution*. Englewood Cliffs, New Jersey: Prentice Hall.

Appendix

Table 6.4 Support for the ecology movement (%).

	France				The Netherlands				West Germany				Italy				Great Britain			
	'82	'84	'86	'89	'82	'84	'86	'89	'82	'84	'86	'89	'82	'84	'86	'89	'82	'84	'86	'89
Activists	0.6	0.3	0.4	1.0	3.2	2.4	2.8	4.4	1.9	0.8	0.7	1.1	0.5	0.9	0.9	0.8	0.4	0.8	1.1	2.7
Potential activists	13.6	11.2	10.1	12.1	25.6	29.5	29.0	40.6	23.9	30.2	26.7	37.9	27.1	19.5	18.0	19.0	19.3	16.3	19.4	28.2
Sympathizers	56.9	66.6	64.9	71.1	54.3	51.5	56.8	47.6	20.6	21.7	25.1	25.7	64.6	69.9	71.9	72.0	47.6	54.5	52.7	53.8
Weak opponents	22.8	18.0	19.5	12.6	11.0	11.8	8.2	6.0	34.9	25.5	29.7	19.7	6.7	7.7	6.6	6.4	24.6	23.6	23.5	12.8
Strong opponents	6.1	3.8	5.0	3.2	5.8	4.7	3.3	1.5	18.7	21.8	17.8	15.6	1.1	1.9	6.6	1.7	8.2	4.9	3.3	2.5
No. of cases	1069	1009	1003	1040	1088	1015	1001	971	1197	992	987	1202	1174	1060	1102	1011	1256	1042	1055	957
Missing cases	24	26	39	12	25	37	24	28	207	149	117	123	91	57	60	28	167	56	116	107

Source: *Eurobarometer* 17, 21, 25, 31a.

Table 6.5 Support for the anti-nuclear power movement (%).

	France				The Netherlands				West Germany				Italy				Great Britain			
	'82	'84	'86	'89	'82	'84	'86	'89	'82	'84	'86	'89	'82	'84	'86	'89	'82	'84	'86	'89
Activists	0.2	0.3	0.1	0.6	0.8	0.4	0.6	1.6	1.8	0.6	0.6	1.1	0.2	0.9	0.7	0.6	0.4	0.4	1.1	1.8
Potential activists	7.8	4.0	5.1	6.6	14.7	16.2	13.7	18.3	20.7	22.7	23.8	36.3	14.7	10.2	10.2	10.8	19.3	9.5	14.5	13.9
Sympathizers	33.5	38.3	39.1	44.4	40.6	41.5	42.9	47.8	17.9	15.2	17.2	22.0	45.4	48.6	56.0	58.3	30.1	28.8	41.3	36.3
Weak opponents	39.8	42.0	34.8	34.7	19.9	19.2	19.7	20.3	33.5	34.7	32.4	23.5	23.6	28.4	19.0	20.8	26.7	39.4	28.2	31.5
Strong opponents	18.7	15.5	20.9	13.7	24.1	22.7	23.1	11.9	26.1	26.9	25.9	17.1	16.2	12.0	14.2	9.5	23.5	22.0	14.9	16.5
No.of cases	1069	1009	1003	1040	1088	1015	1001	971	1197	992	987	1202	1174	1060	1102	1011	1256	1042	1055	957
Missing cases	34	39	56	34	35	21	14	30	190	165	129	121	154	76	89	45	84	50	56	69

Source: *Eurobarometer* 17, 21, 25, 31a.

Table 6.6 Support for the peace movement (%).

	France				The Netherlands				West Germany				Italy				Great Britain			
	'82	'84	'86	'89	'82	'84	'86	'89	'82	'84	'86	'89	'82	'84	'86	'89	'82	'84	'86	'89
Activists	0.6	0.3	0.1	0.6	1.5	2.2	1.0	1.6	2.4	1.8	1.5	2.7	1.4	1.3	1.2	0.7	1.4	2.1	2.6	2.5
Potential activists	11.7	8.8	9.4	9.4	20.3	21.9	17.7	20.7	36.6	40.5	42.1	45.0	29.0	17.6	17.5	14.8	19.5	11.8	13.8	14.8
Sympathizers	45.4	50.1	48.1	58.8	46.3	43.9	43.9	50.7	24.3	24.6	22.1	24.9	63.1	65.4	66.0	72.5	28.9	30.2	39.5	41.5
Weak opponents	27.4	27.0	25.4	18.0	16.0	14.6	16.9	14.8	21.1	19.8	19.9	15.3	3.8	10.4	9.7	7.7	24.3	32.0	25.4	24.9
Strong opponents	15.0	13.8	17.1	13.2	16.1	17.5	20.4	12.2	15.6	13.4	14.4	12.1	2.6	5.3	5.7	4.3	25.8	24.0	18.7	16.4
No. of cases	1069	1009	1003	1040	1088	1015	1001	971	1197	992	987	1202	1174	1060	1102	1011	1256	1042	1055	957
Missing cases	31	35	42	27	20	16	15	19	169	122	106	117	65	57	60	32	76	39	51	58

Source: *Eurobarometer* 17, 21, 25, 31a.

Chapter 7

Environmentalism in Europe: an east–west comparison

Petr Jehlicka

Introduction

The east European upheavals have profoundly changed a situation that had been stable for 40 years. Each country recently liberated from the Soviet sphere of influence has already requested entry to the European Community (EC), but western countries are lukewarm in their response. Whereas in economic or military affairs this cautious approach is understandable, hesitation about close east–west co-operation in the area of environmental protection is less justified; environmental problems are, after all, essentially transnational, long-term and threaten the entire continent, and confronting environmental problems might establish a precedent for pan-European co-operation in other areas.

Free elections and the installation of new parliaments in the former eastern bloc countries meant, in theory at least, that serious environmental problems could be tackled. The old regimes entered into few agreements, and when they did they were unable in practice to meet their requirements. Only shortly before the regimes' collapse, when the depth of environmental problems started profoundly to affect the population and could no longer be disguised, did they admit the seriousness of environmental issues. Until then, communist governments had not manifested enthusiasm for the solution of environmental problems, partly because of lack of finance, but mainly for ideological reasons. No obstacles, including environmental considerations, should impede socialist society on its way towards the communist paradise. The dense smoke of factory chimneys was presented as evidence of socialist well-being, and when a certain level of environmental degradation was admitted, it was presented as the inevitable but temporary cost of progress.

However, as Trudgill (1990, 102) argued, any form of government can be

INTRODUCTION

involved in creating and perpetuating environmental problems: the ecological crisis in western Europe differs from the eastern one only in its depth and the approach of society to it; otherwise, its essence and the reasons for it are identical. Kara (1992) precisely describes the present situation when he argues that Europe is probably the most polluted and, at the same time, the most polluting part of the globe: "Fragmented into a number of small and medium size national states with different economic power and different environmental legislation, into a variety of regions, both affluent and declining, well preserved and fatally damaged, it is a very difficult object to 'deal with' and coordinate."

In this respect, the EC countries are a special group. Although they contain regions that differ in economic development, history, traditions, and culture, they have tried to approach problems, including environmental ones, as a unit. Despite common legislation, less developed EC countries such as Spain, Ireland, Portugal, and Greece are not always so keen on their duties because they sometimes see them as jeopardizing their economies. As Ripa di Meana, then EC environment commissioner, commented: "It is quite misleading to see the problem of the environment as a purely legislative problem and to expect legislation alone to reduce pollution levels. It is essentially a problem of awareness of environmental damage, and of inspirers of decisions which the various governments adopt world-wide" (in Alberti and Parker 1991).

As Trudgill (1990, 102) remarked, politicians are motivated by perceived practical or ideological advantage, whether in terms of votes or of demonstrating or reinforcing the value system or ideology. Thus, the environmental consciousness of society and the pressure of environmental groups is the essential motivator in the "greening" of governments and their policies. How this comes about is the focus of this chapter.

Environmentalism – the movement in favour of a cleaner world, with less pollution, less depletion of natural resources, conservation of wilderness areas and recycling of resources (Vedung 1991) – can be understood as an evolving set of political ideas. Paehlke (1989) even believes it has the potential to become the first original ideological perspective to develop since the middle of the 19th century. By focusing on its impact in Europe, I shall deal with environmentalism as a social phenomenon aimed at achieving desirable changes in the state of the environment.

A major shortcoming of literature on environmentalism is the lack of international comparisons that deal with more than two or three countries. Among the rare exceptions are the analyses of Kitschelt (1990), Hofrichter and Reif (1990), and Dijkink and van der Wusten (1992). Thus the main problem of grappling with environmentalism from an international perspective is the lack of reliable and comparable data; the only usable information is the electoral results of Green parties and the results of enquiries into the level of environmental awareness or "consciousness". Since environmentalism takes many forms, this limitation means tremendous simplification.

If government policies favouring the environment are the consequence of pressure from the population, movements, and parties, the origins of public environmental awareness are less clear. On the one hand, it is obvious that general awareness has been increased by the activity of environmental groups as well as through the media. On the other hand, EC opinion polls show a high level of environmental concern in Italy and Spain but without any political or organizational counterpart. Dijkink and van der Wusten (1992) accounted for this by suggesting that awareness of problems is only the beginning. Frequently mentioned as a reason for the development of environmentalism is the "greening" of other parties and consequently the whole political spectrum. The same explanation may be applied to the ecological policies of governments.

Development of environmentalism in West and East

Western environmentalism was, from the beginning of the 1960s, closely related to scientific findings of the negative impact on the environment of a highly developed civilization, mainly focused on pollution, and apolitical (Paehlke 1989, 1). This new interest in pollution was quickly joined by concern with other more global issues – population growth, depletion of resources, and nuclear energy.

Later, in the 1970s and 1980s, environmentalists concentrated largely on single-issue problems. Environmentalism took the form of pressure groups, followed by the founding of environmental political parties. As the ecological crisis in Europe deepened, the strength of environmental movements grew. Two main peaks can be identified: one at the beginning of the 1970s and another at the end of the 1980s. Although environmentalism has passed through various stages and taken on various forms, the social profile of its bearers has not significantly changed (Rüdig et al. 1991; Rootes 1992a).

Under communist regimes, despite severe environmental problems comparable to or worse than those in the West, environmental issues never achieved the recognition from state authorities that they did in the West, and

DEVELOPMENT OF ENVIRONMENTALISM IN WEST AND EAST

the exclusion of public participation precluded any possibility of politicizing them. In response to continued environmental degradation, ruling communist parties allowed the founding of nature protection organizations but, as such organizations were under the strong control of communists, they could hardly have had any serious impact. However, in the last years of the old regimes, such organizations changed their orientation towards a more global approach to environmental problems, and some independent currents emerged within them.

At the same time, in the 1980s, some completely illegal activities started to appear but were not prosecuted, partly due to *glasnost* (as in the case of the Bulgarian Ecoglasnost), and partly due to the weakening of communist regimes themselves. This unofficial environmental movement took several forms: in Czechoslovakia samizdat reports were published, while in East Germany the Green Network developed under the influence of the Protestant Church and consequently forged ties with the underground East German peace movement (Fura 1991). Elsewhere, environmental groups grew up primarily on single-issue matters, such as the Hungarian Danube Circle, which opposed the construction of giant dams on the river.

Jancar (1992, 164) identified two goals of east European environmental groups under communist regimes: first and foremost, the aim was to save the environment; second, and linked to it, was the promotion of democracy. Jancar emphasized the qualitatively different connection between ecology and democracy in state-socialist systems from that in pluralist systems. In Western democracies, the rights to speak and organize are constitutionally guaranteed, preconditions of the political system, while under socialism, the single party's exclusive right to govern was premised upon its ability to promote economic and social well-being. Silence on the extent of environmental damage, rampant environmental pollution, and events such as Chernobyl challenged the party's exclusive right at its base.

Political mobilization in reaction to environmental devastation became one of the most significant factors within the movement towards democracy in the East, especially in the central European countries and Baltic republics of the former Soviet Union.

Firstly, many people joined and worked in environmental groups because it was the only more or less legal way actively to oppose the regime. When the regimes fell, these environmental activists entered the political scene as relatively well-known figures, no longer as "green" politicians, but as regular politicians.

Secondly, it is a frequent allegation that the rise and development of eastern environmentalism, mainly in the republics of the former Soviet Union, were closely connected to the wave of nationalism. The present model of west European ethnonationalism cannot be applied to the situation in the former Soviet Union. There "nationalism" was very often mainly the reaction of indigenous inhabitants to the influx of Russians followed by the spread of the Russian language in their native territory, as in the case of the Baltic republics, which, having the highest living standards in the USSR, were highly attractive to newcomers. Native populations opposed not only such migration, but the Soviet system in general. As Connor (1984) wrote: "Baltic peoples have resisted new investment capital from the Soviet government because of the conviction that greater industrialization brings with it more Russians into the Estonian, Latvian or Lithuanian homeland, a price deemed too high to pay for increased living standards." The Baltic peoples found it effective to oppose industrial growth on environmental grounds in order to keep down the number of Russians coming into their country. Thus the environment was used as a shield to hide xenophobia and the loss of national identity.

Some "pure" environmentalism did exist in the USSR. Yanitsky (1991) emphasized its difference from the Western model in terms of the conditions under which Soviet environmental movements emerged and the context in which they operated. The environmental movement was relatively young, but often a haven for the old who wanted to find a new application for their experience and wisdom. Most were male and professionals, usually scientists and scholars, writers and journalists.

Environmentalism: facilitating and inhibiting factors

Of the overwhelming majority who feel that the environment is an important problem, few are environmentalists and fewer are Greens. In western Europe those who vote for the Greens are usually young, highly educated, urban, leftist, postmaterialist, middle class, and working in the public sector. Franklin and Rüdig (1991), investigating the profile of the Green electorate within the European Community, found Green voters to be more leftist than the general electorate in each country, and especially so in Germany and the Netherlands. Similarly, the relationship between Green voting and postmaterialism exists in each country, but is rather weak except in Germany and the Netherlands. The correlation between Green voting and the significance of the environment as a political issue was strong in all countries.

ENVIRONMENTALISM: FACILITATING AND INHIBITING FACTORS

Franklin and Rüdig's analysis provides strong evidence that the theories that have dominated the academic literature on Green politics – Inglehart's theory of postmaterialist value change and Kitschelt's left-libertarian theory – are applicable mainly to the German Greens. Their results also show the diversity and variable significance of factors stimulating green politics across Europe and, at the same time, that the only common concern peculiar to Green voters is the environment itself. This supports Rüdig's basic presumption that Green parties are not a political manifestation of new postmaterialist values or left-libertarianism, but instead express a new ecological cleavage based on a structural conflict about the environment; people did not become involved in environmental politics because their values changed, but because the negative impact of man on the environment overcame the thresholds of attention and acceptability.

According to Rohrschneider (1988), in order to be able to understand the political implications of the environmental movement, it is necessary to know the origin of citizens' attitudes towards the environment. Rohrschneider's starting point was recognition that the psychological model of postindustrial value change neglects to link environmental concern to the true state of ecological affairs. He concluded that the "sociotropic dimension" displayed the strongest direct effect. Experience of ecological problems in one's immediate environment does not lead directly to favouring environmental regulation. This conclusion seems surprising, but it corresponds with the findings of Rüdig et al. (1991): "learning about particular events highlighting national or global environmental problems" was endorsed twice as often as "being confronted with a specific environmental problem locally" as a reason for joining the British Green Party. Generalized values appear more strongly predictive of favourable attitudes to environmentalism than personal experience, and because the perception of environmentalism as a global issue requires people to utilize information that goes beyond their immediate circumstances, in the most developed countries it was mainly educated people who were concerned with the complex problem of the environment. Consistent with this, Hofrichter and Reif (1990) pointed to the gap between "personal (environmental) complaint" and "general (environmental) concern": "general concern" is predominantly influenced by the value orientation and political ideology of the respondent and is higher among those with postmaterialist and politically leftist orientations.

ENVIRONMENTALISM IN EUROPE: AN EAST–WEST COMPARISON

"Personal complaint" versus "general concern"

Hofrichter and Reif (1990), on the basis of Eurobarometer data, found that, since it was first measured in 1976, environmental concern in EC countries decreased during 1976–78, increased in the early 1980s, and in 1989 was at an unprecedentedly high level. They noted stable groupings among EC countries according to the saliency of environmental issues: Luxembourg, Denmark, West Germany, and the Netherlands were above the EC average; Italy and Belgium were average; and the UK, France, Spain, Greece, Portugal, and Ireland were below average, albeit that in 1989, the last year of their investigation, the saliency of environmental issues increased in several countries (France, the UK, and Greece) that previously ranked below average.

While such an identification of the "core" and "periphery" of environmentalism in a spatial or geographical sense might seem quite predictable, the geographical distribution of "personal complaint" and "general concern" with the state of environment in the EC is more intriguing. Hofrichter and Reif discovered that only 18–20 per cent of the EC population register complaints about their local environment, whereas 80–86 per cent are worried about the national and global situation. Countries with saliency of environmental issues as a global problem (Denmark, Luxembourg, and the Netherlands) have very low levels of "personal complaint", while southern countries (Spain, Portugal, and Italy) manifest a high level of "personal complaint" and a lower saliency of environment as a global issue. The UK, France and Ireland show low levels both in personal and general concern with the environment.

The core and periphery of west European environmentalism

Kitschelt's (1990) study of left-libertarian parties concluded that countries with low per capita income, low growth rate, underdeveloped welfare state provision, low degree of labour corporatism, high strike rate and lack of major socialist/communist party participation in government are unlikely to develop significant left-libertarian parties. Conversely, the Western countries that provide favourable conditions for the development of left-libertarian parties are Austria, Belgium, Denmark, Luxembourg, the Netherlands, Norway, Sweden, Switzerland, and West Germany. Not all the left-libertarian parties he considers are Green parties, and in Denmark, Iceland, and Norway the Greens are weak or non-existent.

THE CORE AND PERIPHERY OF EUROPEAN ENVIRONMENTALISM

Unlike Kitschelt, Dijkink and van der Wusten (1992) looked at Green parties as a clear political manifestation of environmentalism. The aim of their analysis was the identification of factors that account for the development of green politics in the EC and the demarcation of their west European stronghold. Four explanatory variables favouring the spread of green ideas were examined: the occurrence of environmental problems; differences in economic prosperity; differences between electoral systems; and the diffusion principle. The countries in which the Greens thrive best (Belgium and West Germany) belong to the elite club of highly developed states, are centrally located within the EC, are culturally "open", and possess political structures marked by a high degree of governmental decentralization and strong regional tradition.

This argument is supported by evidence from the subnational level. It is southern German states (Hesse, Baden-Württemberg, and Bavaria) that form the Greens' stronghold; only the city states (Hamburg, Bremen, and Berlin) show higher Green gains. Not only do both linguistic regions of Belgium, and Luxembourg, belong to the area of highest Green support, but in countries that border Germany, the regions directly adjoining Germany are those of strongest Green support. Alsace, culturally and historically closely related to Germany, has been a good area for the French Greens (Prendiville 1989, 90); the northern German-speaking Swiss cantons (from Neuchâtel to Thürgau), as well as French-speaking cantons Genève and Vaud, together form the area of highest Green support in Switzerland (Church 1991); in Austria, the Greens are electorally most successful in the western part of the country (Salzburg, Tirol, and Vorarlberg) adjoining Germany (Haerpfer 1989; Sully 1991); South Tyrol, the only Italian territory settled by German speakers (65 per cent in 1981 according to Markusse 1991, 138) was one of the first places in Italy where the Greens made significant gains (in 1983, Alternative Lists polled 4.5 per cent in the province of Bolzano (South Tyrol) with a peak of eight per cent in the main town (Diani 1989)); northern Italy, and specifically the province of South Tyrol, has since been a stronghold of the Italian Greens.

These facts support Dijkink's and van der Wusten's assumptions of the influence of kindred political culture as well as the favourable rôle of decentralization (or regionalism) for the spread of green ideas. The process of spatial diffusion of political innovation from the centre to the surroundings with similar circumstances is encouraged by such linkages.

The situation beyond the "core" is more complicated. Without doubt, the populations of Scandinavian countries are also very concerned with the en-

ENVIRONMENTALISM IN EUROPE: AN EAST WEST COMPARISON

vironment, but this is not so clearly mirrored in the political sphere: in the only Nordic EC member country, Denmark, the Green party's performance is weak but the level of environmental awareness is above average (Hofrichter & Reif 1990). This paradox is probably explained by special conditions of social arrangements and political culture in these countries and by the capacity of the "old" parties successfully to absorb the demands of the public into their agenda.

Greece, Italy, Spain, and Portugal also have weak Green parties and other environmentalist organizations, but a relatively high level of general environmental concern; but in contrast to the Danish pattern, the high level of environmental "personal complaint" in southern Europe is accompanied by low levels of perception of the environment as a global problem.

The UK, France, and Ireland represent a special group, with low perceptions of environmental issues both on the personal and global levels. Britain, however, presents a paradox: its Green party, although the first in Europe, is extremely weak, whereas its many traditionally non-political environmental groups number over three million members (McCormick 1989, viii). The low electoral impact of the British Green Party is usually explained by the electoral system and by institutional arrangements that constrain the environmental movement towards integration rather than opposition (Rootes 1992a).

Environment, religion and relative economic deprivation

The contribution of environmental degradation to environmental consciousness is often underestimated or even rejected (Dijkink & van der Wusten 1992), but some authors do take it into account. Rootes (1991), for instance, suggested that the lower British concern about global environmental problems simply reflects the fact that such problems as acid rain and river pollution are less noticeable in Britain than in countries such as West Germany, Denmark, and the Netherlands, whose geographic position means that they import more of other countries' pollution and have fewer opportunities for discreetly disposing of their own.

The construction of any complex map of environmental pollution and devastation on the European scale is complicated, but the most affected area coincides more or less with the already identified "core" or "cradle" of European environmentalism. Air pollution, acidification, forest death, soil degradation, and river pollution are, in western Europe, most severe in Germany,

ENVIRONMENT, RELIGION AND ECONOMIC DEPRIVATION

Belgium, Luxembourg, and the Netherlands. Yet these are countries where environmental concern is "global" rather than "personal". The historical evolution of environmentalism provides the explanation. At the beginning of its development in the 1960s, pollution and personal perceptions of it were the initial stimuli for environmentalism. Since then, environmentalism has been transformed into a more global issue, partly due to the extension of environmental problems to the worldwide scale, partly due to a shift in people's value systems and the ability to perceive pollution as a global problem. In this light, the countries of the EC periphery (Greece, Italy, Spain, and Portugal) seem to be at an earlier stage of development of environmentalism, similar to that which more developed countries experienced in the past.

Besides the level of environmental degradation, the "core" region of the EC and its southern "periphery" differ also in the level of their economic development. High levels of economic development and affluence correspond to levels of high environmental concern, especially in terms of "global concern". If the laggardly development of environmentalism in countries such as Greece, Spain, Ireland, and Portugal is explained by the lag in economic and social development, how can this delay be explained in the Italian case? The common denominator is non-Protestant religion and, with the exception of Greece, Catholicism. Conversely, all other west European states are predominantly Protestant, except Belgium, France, and Austria, where the impact of the Church, as measured by the rate of regular church attendance, is significantly lower than in Ireland, Portugal, or Italy (Lane & Ersson 1991, 71–2).

The debate on the relationship between Christianity and environmentalism started with White's (1967) argument that Christianity would either have to be altered significantly or abandoned entirely if we were to solve our environmental problems (Hargrove 1986, xiii). More subtly, Munz (1991) argued that the present ecological crisis is the result of "paths which were taken primarily by science and technology"; the Catholic Church resisted scientific development and new currents of thought, and industry, together with liberalism and capitalism, took root only slowly in Catholic countries, which even today are poorer than Protestant ones; the Protestant religions were modern, more flexible than Catholicism and, originating during the early capitalist era and to some extent a consequence of capitalism, they also in their turn stimulated its development; Protestant countries, capitalist and industrialized, are as a consequence very much implicated in the contemporary ecological crisis, but it is to their credit that action has caused reaction, and they are today the centres of ecological action.

121

ENVIRONMENTALISM IN EUROPE: AN EAST WEST COMPARISON

This religious influence on the spread of environmentalism is reflected at the subnational level: the Swiss Greens gained most votes in Protestant cantons (Church 1991), while the party was weakest in Catholic cantons; of the three strongholds of the French Greens, two (Alsace and Ile-de-France) concentrate most of the Protestant minority (Lane & Ersson 1991, 67).

The same religious factor is identifiable at the personal level too. In West Germany, among both Catholics and non-Catholics, the weaker the Church attachment, the stronger the support for the Greens, and in 1987 there was a negative correlation of −0.2 between the Catholic percentage of a district's population and the Greens' share of the vote (Frankland 1989, 72). Even in predominantly Catholic Belgium, Green voters see themselves either as "Christians outside the Church" or simply as non-believers (Deschouwer 1989, 47).

In general, although most Greens and environmentalists are non-believers, countries with substantially Protestant histories or populations provide much more favourable conditions for the evolution of environmentalism than do purely Catholic countries.

The German case demonstrates the difficulty of distinguishing the rôle of religious cleavage from that of relative economic deprivation. The almost purely Protestant north German states, Niedersachsen, and Schleswig-Holstein, display the lowest support for the Greens, but these are also the states with the lowest per capita GDP. The three southern states (Hesse, Baden-Württemberg, and Bayern) that constitute the Green stronghold belong to a religiously "mixed zone".

Countries other than Germany also display significant correlations between levels of regional economic development and Green voting or environmental concern. Thus voters from the more affluent north and centre of Italy were much more sympathetic to the Greens than voters from the south, who in 1985 elected only ten Green representatives (out of a total of 141) to local councils (Diani 1989). In 1987 the Greens won no parliamentary seats in the south, while their best results came from smaller, more affluent northern towns with developed economic structures (e.g. Trento 7.3 per cent, Vicenza 5.7 per cent, Mantova 5.8 per cent). Alsace and Ile-de-France, regions with the highest Green votes in France, are also among the most developed parts of the country. The same pattern is evident in Austria, where Greens attracted most support in the richest western lands of Salzburg, Tirol, and Vorarlberg. In Britain an electoral system unfavourable to smaller parties makes Green votes a generally unreliable indicator of environmental concern, but on the one occasion that the Greens did well – the European

122

elections of 1989 – their vote was highest in the affluent south and lowest in the economically depressed north-east (Rootes 1991). Similarly, recent research[1] shows that members of four national environmental groups are concentrated in southern England.

The fact that the German city states display the highest stable support for the Greens is not surprising. That it is mainly city dwellers who back environmentalism is as true of Greece, where almost 50 per cent of Green voters are concentrated in the Athens area (Demertzis 1991), as it is of Germany. Yet in Britain Green party members as well as voters in the 1989 European elections lived mainly in the south of England and in "rural and suburban areas" (Rüdig et al. 1991). This apparent contradiction is resolved when we consider the high level of urbanization in England; England's southern rural areas bear scant resemblance to those in Scandinavia or Spain. Moreover, the Green vote shifted towards urban Labour-held seats in the 1992 British general elections (Rootes 1992b). The urban character of environmentalism is entirely in accord with the "novelty" of this social and political phenomenon; rural areas, with their tougher social structure and relations anchored in traditions, are always relatively resistant to innovation.

Environmentalism and nationalism

The recent tide of ethnonationalism throughout Europe has had a significant impact in many fields, including the environmental one. At first glance, one can find nationalist parties and movements highlighting environmental issues or entirely ignoring them. The Slovak National Party, which supports independence for Slovakia, was the only parliamentary party in Czechoslovakia in 1990 that made no reference to the environment in its programme. Furthermore, in the southern Slovak districts, where the political party of the Hungarian minority, "Coexistence", received more than 50 per cent of votes in both 1990 and 1992 elections, the Green party recorded its lowest support in Czechoslovakia, despite the proximity of the Gabcikovo dam project. On the other hand, the Scottish and Welsh nationalist parties have the reputation of being environmentally conscious.

Kellas (1991, 165) pointed to the links between nationalism in advanced industrial societies and the spread of postmaterialist values; nationalist and Green parties in western Europe and popular fronts in the former Soviet Union are supported by citizens whose political concerns are with the environment and with constitutional freedoms, and they express these concerns

ENVIRONMENTALISM IN EUROPE: AN EAST WEST COMPARISON

through nationalism rather than through class politics. Kellas may be right to suggest that present western green and nationalist movements are linked to postmaterialism, but it is doubtful whether the same is true of eastern Europe, where postmaterialism is hardly widespread. As far as the former Soviet Union is concerned, Ziegler (1992, 35) identified two important factors shared by nationalism and environmentalism that significantly affected political participation: first, both nationalism and environmentalism have generated highly emotional forms of mass political participation directed against the political establishment; secondly, both nationalism and environmentalism are closely associated with physical territory. Environmental problems perceived as imposed from outside by political forces of questionable legitimacy threaten the well-being of the territorial homeland and therefore strike at an essential aspect of sovereignty.

These "emotionally" motivated movements seem to be led by people of very similar social profile. The "humanist" intelligentsia play the key part in the resurgence of nationalism and environmentalism alike, but nationalism always gains stronger support, its appeal to material well-being in the wake of national independence apparently being stronger than the Greens' demands for sustainable development and, unlike environmentalism, nationalism often appeals to the less well-educated.

Fundamental differences between nationalism and environmentalism are theoretically clear cut. If the Greens' "anti-statism" and their bias towards decentralization stem from their rejection of present centralized forms of the state, nationalists want to break the state in order to create other, usually smaller, but otherwise unreformed states. Another difference between environmentalism and nationalism consists in the former's relative "openness" and the strong bias of the latter towards isolationism and "closedness". Among Paehlke's (1989, 144) 13 central value assertions of environmentalism, "a global rather than a nationalist view" occupies fourth place.

Eastern Europe

Environmental concern undoubtedly played a prominent rôle in the period of transition from communism to post-communist democracy in eastern Europe. However, as several authors have recently remarked (Georgieva 1992; Jehlicka & Kostelecky 1992; Waller & Millard 1992), the initially strong appeal of environmental issues withered surprisingly quickly. Waller and Millard explained the lower than expected votes for east European

Green parties in the early free elections by the character of these elections as plebiscites on the communist regimes, the inclusion of the environment in the programmes of most political parties, the fact that many leading champions of the environmental cause joined other political parties, the internal divisions of Green parties, the limited social base of the green movement, and the economic crisis. In subsequent elections in Bulgaria (1991), Czechoslovakia (1992) and Romania (1992), the Green decline continued. This suggests that green was a protective colour during the last years of communist rule but that it has withered under the impact of the unpopular performance of Green politicians and the economic crisis.

Under present east European conditions, the relaunch of environmental politics is not likely, especially in countries that are undergoing the most difficult period of their post-war history (Albania, Bulgaria, Romania, and republics of former Yugoslavia and the former Soviet Union). The very existence of some of these countries may be in question, and problems of food and energy supply have priority. The only parts of the former eastern bloc where environmentalism has much chance to develop are Poland, Hungary, and Czechoslovakia. However, only Czechoslovakia continues to display some environmental concern; recent electoral results indicate that in Hungary and Poland environmental awareness is less developed. In the 1990 Hungarian general election, in "the worst Green party performance in East Central Europe" (Waller & Millard 1992), the Green party won no seats; an opinion poll in August 1992 showed that only one per cent of Hungarians intended to vote Green. Even in Poland, whose electoral system is much more favourable to smaller parties, none of the three green coalitions gained a seat in parliament, even though the Polish Beer Lovers' party has 16 deputies and Tyminski's mysterious Party "X" has three.

One of several questions posed in April 1992 by the Hungarian agency Szonda IPSOS to people in five central and east European countries asked respondents to select three items out of ten that they thought would cause the greatest difficulties in the next one to two years. Only 12 per cent of Hungarian and 33 per cent of Polish respondents included environmental problems among the three items selected, compared with 44 per cent of Czechs and Slovaks. The Czechoslovak case is worthy of closer analysis.

The position and public perception of Green parties in eastern countries shortly after the fall of the communist regimes were significantly different from those of western Greens. The general public saw them only as saviours from ecological disaster rather than as bearers and representatives of a new political model and values. Thus, in Czechoslovakia, the Greens found their electoral base in the north Bohemian brown coal basin, the region most severely damaged by the negative impact of obsolete heavy industry (coal mines, power plants, metallurgy, and heavy chemical industry), where air pollution has a direct impact on morbidity and mortality of the population (Jehlicka & Kostelecky 1991).

According to a 1991 opinion poll, the typical Czech Green voter was relatively young and had a middle level of education. More striking was the finding that in the most environmentally damaged districts (mainly in northern Bohemia), voting for the Greens did not follow the overall Czech trend of the bigger the municipality, the higher share of votes; there the percentage of votes was identical in the smallest villages and in cities (Jehlicka & Kostelecky 1991). The Green Party attracted no support in the Catholic regions of southern Moravia and northern Slovakia, despite the existence of serious environmental problems. By contrast, its stronghold, north-western Bohemia, is traditionally the most atheistic region in the Czech Republic and Slovakia.

Green voting in the 1990 general elections was not negligible (in the Czech Republic 3.7 per cent, in Slovakia 3.2 per cent) by comparison with Poland (1991) and Hungary (1990). The Green party was generally accepted as legitimate, with only one per cent of respondents stating that they would never vote for it (Jehlicka & Kostelecky 1992). It is highly likely that almost none of the potential or actual Green voters knew much about the programme and policies of the Green party; many would be shocked if they found out that in none of the Greens' conferences did ecological issues come onto the agenda[2].

Despite this, the Green party had several times more members (several thousand) than most other environmental groups, the only exception being the Czech Union of Nature Protectionists, with approximately 15,000 members. This ratio between the membership of the Greens and non-political environmental groups was the opposite of the situation in the UK, where the membership of Greenpeace or Friends of the Earth overwhelmingly exceeds the numbers of the Greens. The spatial distribution of conservationists or protectionists and Greens was also different. In Britain, the Green party's members and voters are concentrated in the affluent areas of southern England where amenity and environmental groups are most active, while neither has strong support in the Midlands. By contrast, in Czechoslovakia, the spatial distribution of Green voters and the members of the Czech Union of Nature Protectionists did not coincide; in heavily environmentally affected regions, where the Green party had many of its local groups, almost no protectionist branches exist.

EASTERN EUROPE

Thus, a very strange situation within the environmental movement had evolved in the Czech Republic. Non-political environmental pressure groups were much less numerous than the Green party, and these did not support the Greens in the elections. Furthermore, the Greens had no credible environmentalists among their members, although they sought unsuccessfully to contact and draw upon them. For many of those active in environmental groups under the old regime, the environment was the only platform for resistance to the communists; the Green party had been established "artificially", without connection to previous environmental movements or any experience in either environmental issues or politics. Very few of the Greens' members had participated in environmental groups in the past.

At the time when most western environmental groups were shifting from direct action to campaigning, the increasing number of occupations and demonstrations in Czechoslovakia gave evidence of delay in the development of environmentalism. Strong international environmental organizations, such as Greenpeace, were only starting to develop their operations in Czechoslovakia. The very weak organizational basis of environmentalism in Czechoslovakia sharply contrasted with the high level of environmental awareness of the general public. According to an opinion poll in March 1991, 83 per cent of respondents considered the environmental issue to be most important, the highest score among the 13 issues offered.

Taking all the above into account, there is a certain resemblance between the Czechoslovak case in 1990 and 1991 and countries outside the core of Western environmentalism (Greece, Portugal, and Spain). Poorer southern European countries and Czechoslovakia both gave high priority to advancing to the level of economically more developed countries. This inevitably led to neglect of severe environmental problems. A relatively high level of general environmental awareness, combined with underdeveloped organizations, is another common feature. The perception of environmental problems as "personal complaint" in these southern countries parallels the location of the Greens' stronghold in the environmentally devastated area of Czechoslovakia.

Since the middle of 1991 the situation has been changing. The level of environmental concern has been steadily declining. Environmental issues now figure between fifth and eighth in position of importance, according to various polls. There is other evidence of this decline: the drop in circulation of the ecological journal *Nika* (from 10,000 in 1989 to 3500 in summer 1992); the shrinkage of membership of the Green party (from approximately 15,000 in 1990 to 3000 in 1992); its entering the coalition with socialists and

ENVIRONMENTALISM IN EUROPE: AN EAST WEST COMPARISON

agrarians in the Czech Republic; and the poor electoral results of this coalition as well as the electoral failure of the Slovak Greens in the June 1992 parliamentary elections. Because since 1991 it has campaigned as part of the Liberal Social Union, the electoral performance of the Czech Green party cannot be subjected to analysis, but indirect evidence indicates that it gained fewer votes than in the 1990 parliamentary elections and that it has lost support in northern Bohemia; the coalition did worse in 1992 than the Greens alone in 1990.

It is not easy to explain the speed and deep decline of environmental concern. Although the Czech Republic is undergoing a period of economic reform, unemployment is, at two per cent, one of the lowest in Europe. With respect to the state of the heavily devastated environment, nothing has changed; people in the most environmentally devastated regions are disenchanted because they continue to suffer from air pollution and illness as they did under the communists. The lack of environmental concern is more understandable in Slovakia which has five times the unemployment as well as emerging national tensions between Slovaks and the Hungarian minority; the principal Slovak environmental problem, the Gabcikovo dam, has become an object of nationalist attention in the conflict with Hungary. Undoubtedly, the break-up of Czechoslovakia also diverted people's attention from the environment. Not surprisingly, in a time of profound, painful economic transition in a disintegrating country where crime rates are increasing, people are engaged with less abstract, more manageable problems than the environment.

Conclusions

In Europe, environmentalism is most developed in the "core" area of central western Europe (Belgium, southern Germany, northern France, Switzerland, and the Netherlands). Both organizational forms of environmentalism – parties and movements – are well developed in this area. The features of this region are: the most severe environmental damage in western Europe, developed economies providing material well-being to populations, the highest degree of urbanization, central location at the European "crossroads", openness to international influences, and relative political decentralization.

The western areas (e.g. Saarland and Rhineland in Germany, the Midlands in England) most devastated by "old" industrialization (mines, metallurgy, heavy chemical industry, etc.) manifest relatively low environmental

NOTES

concern. Until recently the opposite pattern prevailed in eastern Europe, where the most severe ecological damage stimulated the highest environmental concern. Since the regions of old heavy industry are especially vulnerable during the current recession and the process of economic restructuring, environmentalism is losing its strong regional basis. People facing the threat of unemployment and crime have replaced environmental devastation as a top concern with social and personal security. The lower level of environmental concern in old western industrial areas can be explained in several ways: either people living in these areas have become accustomed to environmental degradation as they have become dependent on polluting industry for employment or, as a result of a decade of deindustrialization, local environmental problems are not as severe as they used to be.

The second area, which includes Scandinavia and southern Britain, can be called the "outer core". It is marked by a lesser extent of environmental deterioration and by affluent societies with high global environmental concern politically expressed mainly by "old" parties able to absorb this issue into their agenda and encouraging a "moderate" form of environmentalism. The Protestant background of these countries facilitates the development of environmental concern.

In the peripheral EC countries (Ireland, Portugal, Spain, and Italy), together with Hungary, the Czech Republic and Slovakia, Croatia, and Poland, development of environmentalism is impeded by the influence of Catholicism, lower levels of economic development, the peripheral location of these countries in relation to the "core", the lower degree of urbanization, and their less "open" character as evidenced by the emergence of ethnonationalism in many regions. Environmentalism here is a late developer, and takes mainly the lower level of concern connected with weak organizations and electoral performance.

Finally, we come to eastern Europe (Bulgaria, Serbia, Romania, Ukraine, and Russia), the part of the continent that has been experiencing unprecedented economic crisis accompanied by a wave of "aggressive" nationalism. So extreme are its other problems and so peripheral is it with regard to the "core" that any political expression of environmental issues here seems improbable.

Notes

1. Research conducted by R. Cowell and P. Jehlicka focused on three organizations with divergent aims: Friends of the Earth, County Wildlife Trusts and Civic Trust. The result of this research was a set of maps depicting the support for these organi-

ENVIRONMENTALISM IN EUROPE: AN EAST WEST COMPARISON

zations according to counties; members of all three are concentrated in southern England, and all have least support in the English industrial heartland (the Birmingham–Liverpool–Hull triangle).

2. Author's interview with the chairman and chief of the political committee of the Czech land organization of the Green party in January 1992.

References

Alberti, M. & J. D. E. Parker 1991. The impact of EC environmental legislation on environmental policy in Italy. *European Trends* **2**, 84–90.

Church, C. 1991. The consolidation of green politics in Switzerland. Paper presented at ECPR Joint Sessions, University of Essex. Revised version forthcoming (1994)iin *The Green challenge*, D. Richardson & C. Rootes (eds). London: Routledge.

Connor, W. 1984. Eco-or ethno-nationalism? *Ethnic and Racial Studies* **3**, 342–59.

Demertzis, N. 1991. The green movement and Green party in Greece. Paper presented at ECPR Joint Sessions, University of Essex. Revised version forthcoming (1994)iin *The Green challenge*, D. Richardson & C. Rootes (eds). London: Routledge.

Deschouwer, K. 1989. Belgium: The Ecologists and AGALEV. In *New politics in western Europe*, F. Müller-Rommel (ed.), 39–54. Boulder, San Francisco & London: Westview Press.

Diani, M. 1989. Italy: The "liste verdi". In *New politics in western Europe*, F. Müller-Rommel (ed.), 113–22. Boulder, San Francisco & London: Westview Press.

Dijkink, G. & H. van der Wusten 1992. Green politics in Europe: the issue and the voters. *Political Geography* **1**, 7–11.

Frankland, E. G. 1989. Federal Republic of Germany: "Die Grünen". In *New politics in western Europe*, F. Müller-Rommel (ed.), 61–80. Boulder, San Francisco & London: Westview Press.

Franklin, M. & W. Rüdig 1991. *The greening of Europe: ecological voting in the 1989 European elections*. Strathclyde Papers in Government and Politics 82. Department of Government, University of Strathclyde.

Fura, Z. 1991. Pollution in eastern Europe: catalyst for democracy. Paper presented at ECPR Joint Sessions, University of Essex.

Georgieva, K. 1992. Environmentalism in Bulgaria: what colour are the Greens? *European Environment* **5**, 14–17.

Haerpfer, C. 1989. Austria: The "United Greens" and the "Alternative List/Green Alternative". In *New politics in western Europe*, F. Müller-Rommel (ed.), 28–38. Boulder, San Francisco & London: Westview Press.

Hargrove, E. C. 1986. *Religion and environmental crisis*. Athens, Georgia: University of Georgia Press.

Hofrichter, J. & K. Reif 1990. Evolution of environmental attitudes in the European Community. *Scandinavian Political Studies* **13**, 119–46.

Jancar, B. 1992. Chaos as an explanation of the rôle of environmental groups in east European politics. In *Green politics two*, W. Rüdig (ed.), 156–84. Edinburgh: Edinburgh University Press.

Jehlicka, P. & T. Kostelecky 1991. The greens in Czechoslovakia. Paper presented at ECPR Joint Sessions, University of Essex. Revised version forthcoming (1993) in *The Green*

REFERENCES

challenge, D. Richardson & C. Rootes (eds). London: Routledge.

Jehlicka, P. & T. Kostelecky 1992. The development of the Czechoslovak Green party since the elections of 1990. *Environmental Politics* 1, 72–94.

Kara, J. 1992. Geopolitics and the environment: the case of central Europe. *Environmental Politics* 1, 186–95.

Kellas, J. G. 1991. *The politics of nationalism and ethnicity*. London: Macmillan.

Kitschelt, H. 1990. New social movements and the decline of party organization. In *Challenging the political order: new social and political movements in Western democracies*, R. J. Dalton & M. Kuechler (eds), 179–208. Oxford: Polity.

Lane, J. E. & S. O. Ersson 1991. *Politics and society in western Europe*, 2nd edn. London: Sage.

Markusse, J. 1991. Autonomy in a multiethnic region: the case of South Tyrol. In *States and nation:. the rebirth of the "nationalities question" in Europe*, H. van Amersfoort & H. Knippenberg (eds.), 130–52. Amsterdam: Koninklijk Nederlands Aardrijkskundig Genootschap, Instituut voor Sociale Geografie, Universiteit van Amsterdam.

McCormick, J. 1989. *The global environmental movements: reclaiming paradise*. London: Belhaven.

Munz, T. 1991. Reflections on Christianity and ecological crisis. Paper presented at Environment for Europe Conference, Dobris.

Paehlke, R. 1989. *Environmentalism and the future of progressive politics*. New Haven, Connecticut: Yale University Press.

Prendiville, B. 1989. France: "Les verts". In *New politics in western Europe*, F. Müller-Rommel (ed.), 87–100. Boulder, San Francisco & London: Westview Press.

Rohrschneider, R. 1988. Citizens attitudes towards environmental issues: selfish or selfless? *Comparative Political Studies* 21, 347–367.

Rootes, C. A. 1991. The greening of British politics? *International Journal of Urban and Regional Research* 15, 287–97.

Rootes, C. A. 1992a. The new politics and the new social movements: accounting for British exceptionalism. *European Journal of Political Research* 22, 171–91.

Rootes, C. A. 1992b. The Green vote in the British general elections of 1992. Mimeo, University of Kent at Canterbury. Revised version forthcoming (1994) in *The Green challenge*, D. Richardson & C. Rootes (eds). London: Routledge.

Rüdig, W., L. Bennie, M. Franklin 1991. *Green party members: a profile*. Glasgow: Delta.

Sully, M. A. 1991. The Austrian election of 1990. *Electoral Studies* 1, 77–80.

Trudgill, S. T. 1990. *Barriers to a better environment: what stops us solving environmental problems?* London: Belhaven.

Vedung, E. 1991. Ecologism, the state, and the formation of Green parties. Paper presented at ECPR Joint Sessions, University of Essex.

Waller, M. & F. Millard 1992. Environmental politics in eastern Europe. *Environmental Politics* 1, 159–85.

White, L., Jr 1967. The historic roots of our ecological crisis. *Science* 155, 1203–7.

Yanitsky, O. 1991. Environmental movements: some conceptual issues in East–West comparisons. *International Journal of Urban and Regional Research* 4, 524–41.

Ziegler, C. E. 1992. Political participation, nationalism and environmental politics in the USSR. In *The Soviet environment: problems, policies and politics*, J. S. Massey (ed.), 24–39. Cambridge: Cambridge University Press.

Chapter 8

Order, crisis and social movements in the transition from state socialism

Nick Manning

Introduction

This chapter is concerned with several basic questions about the transition from state socialism.[1] It begins with a review of models of social and political order that focus on the nature of elite groups under state socialism. A longer discussion follows about the nature of the crisis, and some models that might be used to explain it and the rôle of social movements in it. The main part of the chapter is then taken up with an examination of the place of social movements in the transition from state socialism, and presents some evidence from Estonia, Russia, and Hungary. The chapter concludes with comments on social movements and the future of post-transition societies.

Models of social order in state socialism: from totalitarianism to elite factions

The nature of the traditional social and political order and its transformation in eastern Europe has been a matter of particular dispute. The available models can be ranged between the strictly totalitarian, and the "suppressed" pluralist (Brown 1984). The latter in particular have attempted to apply Western theory in the search for the "real" nature of the system. Each stresses certain features of the political and social system, and hence the nature and direction of recent changes.

The first, traditional, model is that these societies were totalitarian. They were characterized by a single-party state, widespread police or military control, centrally organized economy, all-embracing ideology, and a fettered media. Social movements had no place in the model; the monolithic hierarchi-

MODELS OF SOCIAL ORDER IN STATE SOCIALISM

cal structure was controlled by just one elite – a fusion of state and party – and citizens had little autonomy. The main weakness of this model is highlighted by recent events, in that it had no mechanism for explaining change.

At the opposite extreme is the notion that beneath an apparently monolithic exterior, eastern European societies consisted of a wide array of pluralist interest groups, vying for political influence and material advantage. While this view has never made the naïve assumption that all groups had the chance to advance their interests, a long list of groups can be assembled from the literature asserting the existence of common interests generated by occupational, geographical, managerial, military, technical, ethnic, and other structures (Skilling & Griffiths 1971). In this model there is an intimate relationship between interest groups and the elite. Indeed the interest groups are really elite factions, themselves created by the growing complexity of the post-Stalin era, which differentiated their material interests in the system and its development, and gave rise to consciously expressed differences.

Clearly this approach would have a major advantage for examining change. Indeed it has been developed enthusiastically by Zaslavskaya (1989, 1990) in recent years to explain the course and fate of *perestroika* in the former Soviet Union in the 1980s. Her argument is simply that different groups have different interests in recent changes, and will either support or resist change accordingly. Survey research makes this pattern clear: on the whole, managers were in favour of *perestroika* in the late 1980s, while shop floor workers were not (Mason & Sydorenko 1990). However, the open acknowledgement of wide differences of interest has tended to overshadow the analysis of how those interests are actually organized and have effects. Both the interests and the effects of these groups are assumed, or "read off" from changes that have occurred, with little opportunity for any independent corroboration. The articulation of interests by elite factions, and the avenues for political expression (including social movement activities) have been poorly researched. This creates difficulties in the explanation of the relative balance between stability and change in different parts of eastern Europe.

Between these polar types come a variety of models that combine varying degrees of totalizing control and interest pluralism. We cannot review them all here, and will confine ourselves to two examples relevant to our subsequent discussion.

In the first model, Konrad and Szelenyi (1979) suggested that since the demise of Stalinism, there had grown up in eastern European countries a new dominant class composed of an uneasy alliance of the old bureaucratic elite and the new intellectuals – scholars, artists, teachers, engineers, and

133

THE TRANSITION FROM STATE SOCIALISM

physicians. Their knowledge and ideas reflected their interests, such that while they pursued the particular interests of their group, they were also increasingly aware of their common (class) interests *vis à vis* the rest of society in terms of both material privilege and ideas. In this model it is suggested that there were differences of interest between these intellectual elite groups, but that there was a slow consolidation in opposition to a working class whose interests continued to be suppressed. Change in Hungary, for example, was thus seen to arise out of debates within the elite, rather than reflecting any widespread grievances within the population as a whole. Indeed the stress is mainly on the consolidation and stability that has arisen with the incorporation of intellectuals into the material privileges of elite life. The recent crises were therefore not anticipated in this model.

A second model (Bahro 1978) does, however, develop a mechanism to explain change. It, too, located the key groups in society in the intellectual elite. But rather than seeing this development as resulting in the stable consolidation of a new ruling stratum, Bahro attempted to identify contradictions within the elite that would in the end lead to system transformation. Indeed he was at pains to suggest that the apparent stability of eastern Europe in the 1970s was misleading. The main contradiction for him was that the intellectual elite, through education and experience, was coming to realize ("surplus consciousness") that life did not always have to be as it was; in other words, alternatives should be possible. In particular, he argued that there was an alternative to the widespread dependence of individuals on an oppressive social totality (termed "subalternity"). Thus it would not be working-class demands that would lead to the end of the system, but rather demands arising within the very group charged with developing and managing the system itself. In the absence of political parties with which to express these interests, Bahro discussed a hoped-for renewal of communism through emancipatory consciousness. He was thus not too far from the mark in anticipating recent changes. Indeed there are influential members of the Soviet elite who have recently argued for a return to the original emancipatory hopes of socialism (e.g. Zaslavskaya 1990).

Our conclusion at this point is that with the progressive relaxation of total control, differentiation and contradiction were detected. Elite factions with separate interests appeared in a variety of theoretical models from the early 1970s. However, social movements were not included in discussions of eastern Europe until the emergence of Solidarity in Poland in the early 1980s, and the early stirrings of environmental movements discussed in more detail later in this chapter.

134

Crisis theory and the crisis in state socialism

Just as models of eastern European social order have inevitably drawn on Western ideas, recent changes have stimulated the use of Western crisis theory. We can summarize this in terms of political, economic, and mixed or system crisis models.

First there are political models that suggest that modern Western states have suffered a revolution of rising expectations about the outputs that governments can secure for key groups in society. This has resulted in an overload of demands that the state cannot meet, with the consequence that society has become ungovernable – indeed popular belief in the efficacy of politicians has declined along with voting turnout. This has clear applicability to eastern European governments, which in the 1980s always claimed that related to their monopoly of power they had a duty to supply welfare, consumer goods, employment, housing, and so on to citizens as a "gift of the state". Since the definition of adequate quantities of these goods and services is subject to debate, particularly among elite sections of society, control over both this definition as well as the physical supply of "state gifts" was politically crucial. This control began to fail in the 1970s, not least because the state became the victim of its own ideology of steadily expanding provision. It was fuelling expectations through slow political liberalization at the same time as its capacity to deliver was shrinking.

Economic models start with the simple observation that growth rates in the whole of Europe have been declining since the 1950s, but that in the East the rate of decline has been accelerating to a point of economic collapse. Some observers find the reason for this in the expansion of employment in "non-productive" jobs in, for example, the health, education, military, and bureaucratic sectors, where levels have grown in all industrialized countries, but are notably high and rising in eastern Europe. A related observation is that as a country's economy matures, a limit is reached for extensive growth achievable by simple additions of labour and capital. Further growth can be created only through intensive methods such as increasing productivity as a result of technological investment and greater efficiency. However, as this takes place, growing interdependence and complexity in the economy leads to particular problems in eastern Europe in terms of the effective processing of the exponential growth of information required for central planning (Ellman 1989). This information is located at both the periphery of the economy and in the hands of technical experts, from where it is difficult to retrieve quickly and accurately, not least because it can form the basis of

THE TRANSITION FROM STATE SOCIALISM

bargaining between the centre and the periphery. In the West, the encouragement of quasi markets is seen as the only mechanism for improving these necessary information transactions.

A more general model that includes some of these points is the notion that economic growth is inherently self-limiting. A major reason for this is that many desirable goods and services are closely interwoven in such a way that they cannot be endlessly expanded. Power, social status, clear roads, convenient urban locations, and so on cannot be enjoyed by everyone; they are dependent on unequal distribution ("positional goods"). The politics of distribution is thus closely connected to the problems of economic growth, and it this kind of connection that has given rise to mixed or system or political economy models of crisis.

Lane (1987, 221–31) has proposed that one kind of model that is designed to handle these total system problems is classical functionalist theory, in which a society is conceptualized as consisting of a number of interdependent subsystems, each of which is both internally specialized and externally dependent upon and functional for the other systems. As we know, this approach has been heavily criticized for over-emphasizing stability and value consensus, and for circularity of argument. Nevertheless, shorn of some of its assumptions of stability and consensus, it can be useful for handling complex system crises. For example, Habermas's designation of a crisis in legitimation in Western societies in the 1970s has much to offer here.

Habermas (1976, 4–5) explicitly follows Parsons in dividing society into subsystems of economic and political activity, while collapsing the cultural and social into a common sociocultural system. However the whole direction of his analysis is to examine and explain system and subsystem crisis rather than stability. In his model, the political subsystem is the key "steering" mechanism, guiding economic activity from which it in turn derives "fiscal skim off". Similarly it provides social welfare support for the sociocultural system in return for mass loyalty. However, he is concerned to point out that this model lacks an "action" dimension, which he provides by positing for each subsystem a continuing tension between normative claims to validity and real material limits of each subsystem. It is in the management or eruption of these tensions that the source of crises in the system lie.

Habermas suggests that there are six potential crises in the system. For each subsystem, crisis in the form of tension between normative expectations and material conditions can occur at both the input and the output stage: for example, if economic production falls too far below expectations (economic output crisis), or the motivation to work or to vote fails to induce mass

CRISIS THEORY AND THE CRISIS IN STATE SOCIALISM

production or mass support (sociocultural output crisis). However, he suggests that the most important site for crises is the political system. Here output tensions are termed a "rationality" crisis in the sense that the political system can no longer generate sufficient administrative means to steer the economy or to motivate and support social and community life. This is intimately connected to input tensions, whereby the necessary (normatively required) inputs to the political system such as mass loyalty and fiscal resources fail, with a resultant "legitimation" crisis.

This latter crisis is, he argues, the key to system failure. Poor economic performance, and a reluctance to work, can continue within many social systems for long periods of time. But once there is mass disaffection from the political subsystem, even the use of terror will only delay the point at which the system breaks down or is radically transformed. In view of the birth of Solidarity in Poland in the early 1980s, the revolutions of 1989 in central Europe, and the collapse of the Soviet Union in 1991, Habermas's model seems to make a great deal of sense.

However, there is one important problem with it which needs further discussion here. This is a lack of specification, perhaps inevitable in such a general model, as to which are the individuals or groups that become aware of subsystem tensions between normative expectations and material limits. Is it every citizen who loses faith in the government, or evades working? Is it all workers who feel that economic policy is failing, or object to paying their taxes? The originator of this debate, Max Weber himself said:

> Naturally, the legitimacy of a system of domination may be treated sociologically only as the probability that to a relevant degree the appropriate attitudes will exist, and the corresponding conduct ensue. It is by no means true that every case of submissiveness to persons in positions of power is primarily (or even at all) oriented to this belief. Loyalty may be hypocritically simulated by individuals or by whole groups on purely opportunistic grounds, or carried out in practice for reasons of material self interest. Or people may submit from individual weakness and helplessness because there is no acceptable alternative. (Weber 1968, 214)

In this tradition, Mann (1970) and Abercrombie et al. (1980) have argued from evidence drawn respectively from survey research and historical research, that most people do not in fact hold consistent views in line with the prevailing normative requirements of the political subsystem (conventional values or the "dominant ideology"). This kind of consistent belief is peculiarly the property of key influential or ruling groups. It is only they who are required to hold values consistent enough to manage the various subsystems. And it is they who initially detect the rise of tensions between their beliefs and subsystem material conditions, signalling an impending crisis.

The implication of this amendment is that a model along these lines is in fact addressing the concerns of local and national elite groups, in the sense that crisis is reached at the point when these groups begin to register their concerns about subsystem failure. Indeed, Mann's argument that elite or dominant groups are the key level at which value consensus must be maintained indicates that internal disagreements within elite groups are the sure sign of crisis. In the absence of alternative parties, or significant social movement activity, a crisis point means these significant groups will be subject to particularly intense pressure and change will be rapid when it comes. This analysis incidentally provides justification for the traditional political science approach to "Kremlin watching". Rigby (1991) shows clearly the rapid change in elite constitution at points of crisis in the Soviet Union, culminating with the unprecedented thoroughness with which Gorbachev replaced almost all senior national and regional leadership incumbents in the five years following 1985.

These remarks suggest that eastern European legitimation crises differ from those in the West that Habermas had in mind, since it can be argued that elites occupy a more significant, and hence vulnerable, position. Lewis (1984) suggests that the singular position of the dominant elite based round the party is inevitably vulnerable to two kinds of danger. The first is typified by Khrushchev's critique of Stalin. This signalled an unprecedented split in elite ideology, amplified by the use of the press to conduct the debate. This dissensus was quite disorienting when a key basis for effective political leadership was a monolithic unity, based on an unswerving claim to truth. This is what Habermas would call a rationality crisis in the output of the political subsystem. The second danger is that the exercise of power over the economy and the sociocultural system is very visible, so that any failures in these subsystem outputs (either in material or normative terms) are clearly linked to the elite.

A further difference from Western crises is apparent to the extent that problems in the East went deeper and wider than elite collapse. Parallels with earlier transitions from authoritarianism in post-war Europe, southern Europe, and South America have of course sprung to the minds of observers. However, these parallels are limited. The main problem is that eastern Europe faces a contemporaneous restructuring of economy and polity,

THE TRANSITION AND SOCIAL MOVEMENTS

whereas these earlier political transitions took place against a background of relative economic continuity. Some would also add that there is a parallel third reconstruction of social and domestic life.

These models of crisis pay little attention to life beyond the elite. The revolutions of 1989 and 1991 are a justification of this to the extent that they were marked by elite collapse rather than the overthrow of governments by movements from below. Nevertheless, there was a very sharp upsurge of activity outside the corridors of government from the late 1980s, as it became evident that legitimacy was ebbing away from incumbent elites. It is towards the examination of this development that the rest of this chapter is directed. The question therefore arises of the relationship between elites and mass or social movements for change.

The transition and social movements

Sociological work on Western social movements has grown substantially, and now contains a number of clearly articulated models addressing the question of where social movements come from, what sustains them, and what effects they have. These questions have given rise to three contending models, respectively stressing the grievances felt by, resources available to, and the political opportunities facing social movement members. Defining what they are has been less extensively discussed, although it is necessary to face this question squarely in order to find and investigate new movements in eastern Europe. It is easier to say what they are not than what they are. For example, they are more sustained than specific protests, demonstrations, or riots, yet less institutionalized than political parties. Each of the three theoretical models in contention draws attention to a key characteristic, and in combination can provide us with a working definition (cf. Diani 1992):
  - Shared beliefs (sense of grievance)
  - Network of informal interaction (for marshalling resources)
  - Collective action (oriented to available political opportunities).

These elements in the definition will be useful when we consider below some different models of the striking pattern of movement activity that has developed in eastern Europe, and to which we can now turn in very summary form.

The nature of the political transitions in eastern Europe, and the place of elites and social movements in them, can be usefully divided into three phases: pre-transition, transition, and post-transition. We are here con-

139

THE TRANSITION FROM STATE SOCIALISM

cerned, in Habermas's terms, with the political "steering" mechanism. By contrast, changes in the economic or the sociocultural subsystems will be a very drawn-out process, possibly leading to the eventual removal of the boundary between transition and general social and economic change.

Observers from Russia, Hungary, and Estonia (Gyori 1988; Igrunov 1989; Yanitsky 1989; Szirmai 1991; Tyomkina 1991; Raudsepp 1992) have confirmed that a typical pattern of social movement development seems to have occurred in all three countries. This started with the pre-transition growth of "safe" movements in the early 1980s, or earlier, usually around environmental issues, and organized exclusively by intellectuals/scientists. Thus in Estonia, for example, by 1982 there was a widespread national awareness of ecological issues. Similarly in Hungary in the late 1970s and early 1980s, a number of ecological incidents had provoked the state into financing an environmental protection programme. By the mid-1980s this growth in awareness became focused in each place on a celebrated, and formative, issue through which the traditional state structure and its legitimacy was successfully challenged. In Estonia this was the 1987 campaign against phosphorite mining; in Hungary it was the 1988 campaign to stop the building of the Nagymaros dam across the Danube; and in the USSR, the campaigns against the Siberian rivers diversion (1986) and for the protection of Lake Baikal (1987).

Towards the late 1980s this situation mushroomed dramatically in the build-up to full transition, with myriad groups, associations, and movements appearing. Although green groups still played a leading rôle, the focus of this activity had clearly widened to include the whole of the old regime. Again intellectuals were predominant in this early political debate out of which the new parties would duly emerge. For example, survey evidence in Estonia (Jarve 1989) shows that there was a sharp drop in public concern with the environment compared to the nationality issue between 1985 and 1989, when the Law of Citizen Associations was passed. In Hungary this right had been granted a year earlier, from which point ecological activists began to be sucked into wider political developments. In Russia, in addition to the two big ecological struggles, many local groups in Leningrad and Moscow used ecological and "monument" preservation issues in 1986 and 1987 to test the limits of open political activities. These rapidly expanded into "political clubs" (Leningrad) and "social initiatives" (Moscow) in 1987 and 1988, and then into a popular front in both cities in 1988 and 1989.

This upsurge was frequently taken by both Eastern and Western observers to be a longed-for reawakening of "civil society". However, within a short

THE TRANSITION AND SOCIAL MOVEMENTS

space of time, often only one or two years, this level of activity subsided in the post-transition period as either political parties developed as alternative vehicles for the expression of these interests, or the cold realization set in that there were deeper "subsystem" difficulties than could be resolved through spontaneous civil action. Democratic forces in each country rapidly fell into division and dispute, and the euphoric notion of a collective civil society, at its height in 1989–1991, found that its very identity was dependent on the solidarity of opposition. The membership and level of activity of environmental groups has declined, and their focus has returned to specific ecological issues. However, in the harsh new economic environment, the costs not of pollution, but non pollution, are being more carefully weighed in terms of jobs and production. Moreover, as might be expected, movements around more mundane issues such as property interests, particularly housing, are beginning to emerge in the 1990s.

Why has this strikingly similar pattern emerged? There are a number of possible explanations. The first returns to Habermas.

First model: Szirmai (1991) has suggested that these movements played an important part in the changing bases of social order in the three transition phases. In each phase the significance of social movements lay in their relationship to the elite or elite factions. In the first phase they were tolerated, or more often officially sponsored, as a way of providing a means of identifying problems and assembling knowledge that the traditional party/state bureaucracy could not be relied on to do. In addition they could be used as vehicles for elite faction struggles, and in a more general way they were a useful (though of course also potentially dangerous) adjunct to the official ideology of citizen participation.

In the second phase, at the time when a full-blown legitimation crisis had erupted, the rapid growth of movements served for a time as an alternative avenue for channelling public concerns, mostly about one single overriding problem, the future of the political "steering" mechanism itself. We see here a rapid switch from social movements as conservers of the old order to social movements as lubricators of the birth of a new political order. Similarly, rather than acting as before as creatures of elite factions, social movements now served as the spawning ground of new elite faction membership, particularly with respect to the ideas, images, information, and concerns of sections of the population that each faction sought to represent.

In the third phase, where it is appearing, a new, if fragile, political order is settling down. The membership and activities of environmental movements have shrunk quite dramatically, and their focus has returned to more

141

THE TRANSITION FROM STATE SOCIALISM

mundane issues and specific grievances. However another significant area, housing, is now beginning to awaken as new property rights and principles of distribution are debated and implemented. Housing movements are beginning to take off, while environmental concerns fade in the scramble to shore up falling, even if environmentally unsound, industrial production. To the extent that the new order resembles liberal democracy, it is to be expected that social movements will come to a third kind of relationship with the elite(s), more familiar to the Western literature. Whether this is so forms an important question for future research. Thus relationships between movements, parties, authorities, intellectuals, grievances, and resources need to be examined carefully.

In sum, Szirmai suggests that while the shape, size, and focus of movements in the three phases was quite different, they were commonly involved as a key mechanism for the maintenance of social and political stability. In short, she suggests that the environmental movements were as much about stabilizing power as they were about ecology.

Second model: The problem with that kind of functionalist model is of course that it tends to assume what it also wishes to explain (the "function" of sustaining order). An alternative approach might be to examine the changing bases for social action, that is the interests articulated throughout the three different phases of movement activity, and the changing resources and opportunities available at each stage. Rather than search for order, we can examine the opportunity for expressing conflict (although of course functionalists have claimed this is important for order, too).

If we return to the three elements in our earlier definition, and examine them for each of the three phases, an alternative way of making sense of the pattern emerges.

The first point from Table 8.1 to notice is that there is a changing mix of grievances towards which movement activity is directed. Initially environmental concerns are pre-eminent, but with the regime itself as a very clear, if hidden, background issue. With mass mobilization, however, a complete change in psychological orientation takes place, clearly described by an Estonian colleague:

Table 8.1   Elements in the three phases of transitions.

	Pre-transition	Transition	Post-transition
Grievances	Environment + (regime)	Regime	Envinronment
Resources	Intellectual	Mass	Loss of leaders
Opportunities	Limited	Wide	Institutional politics

142

THE TRANSITION AND SOCIAL MOVEMENTS

> 1988–1989 was the peak of the so called "singing revolution" in Estonia. It was characterized by euphoric activation of people in numerous large scale public gatherings on various political and cultural occasions, as well as by strong self identification as a collective (national) subject. The phenomenon of joyful crowd arousal (the so called agoral phenomenon – see Biela & Tobaczyk 1987) could be observed on several occasions, manifested by voluntary participation, publicity, and mass scale (the size of individual gatherings could reach 300,000, i.e. about 30 per cent of the whole Estonian-speaking population). (Raudsepp 1992, 1–2)

Subsequently, however, with the regime changed, there is a return to a smaller and more discrete focus on green issues and, moreover, in a context of cold realism about the costs of environmental improvement.

At the level of resources, a repeated observation is the crucial rôle of intellectuals in the movements in the early phase. However, as mass mobilization occurs this source is overshadowed by the labour and finance available from large sections of the population. Subsequently, the transformation of this activity into political parties then spirited away many of the original leaders, leaving movements organizationally weakened in the post-transition stage.

Of course, little of this activity could have taken place without the opening up of new political opportunities. In terms of this third factor, we once again observe the gradual and then rapid widening of opportunities for political meetings, publications, and open debate. This has not, in contrast to the grievances and resources, disappeared in the post-transition phase, except in so far as politics has become institutionalized as a specialist activity for professional politicians.

This evidence seems to point to a variation in the significance of the three factors at different points in the process. The recent emphasis on political structures and opportunities in models of movement growth (Pickvance 1975; Bagguley 1992; Siisiinen 1992) has great relevance here. Clearly it was the opening up of political opportunities in the early to mid-1980s that stimulated the early activity, drawing on an existing yet stable level of grievances and resources. However, the subsequent rapid decline in activity seems to have been the result of the loss of key personnel resources, and a substantial change in public concerns. These factors vary in significance in eastern Europe, depending on the particular phase in the cycle of growth and decline.

THE TRANSITION FROM STATE SOCIALISM

Third model: One interesting conclusion that could be drawn from this kind of exercise is that the traditional debate in Western social movement theory, between grievance-driven and resource-driven movements, should not only be more sensitive to the structure of political opportunities, but could reconsider social movements as a kind of "collective thinking" by elites or elite factions. For example, Eyerman and Jamison (1991) have argued that in the field of Western environmental and civil rights issues (which have also been particularly significant in eastern Europe), social movements are most importantly the bearers of new ideas. Since "movement intellectuals" are occasionally the source of new scientific theories, but more often the site of new ideas in society, their activities should, they suggest, be a major focus.

Some commentators have stressed the rôle of intellectuals, Gyori (1988, 16–17) for example, describing Budapest as the home of a special concentration of researchers, students, artists, and professionals, with a rich network of personal connections. He describes the way in which social initiatives were spawned in the creative lifestyle and shared values of sections of this group, yet at the same time he recognizes that their "ghetto-like" separation from wider society makes their position potentially weak, unless they resonate with "wider social developments". Almost all observers of eastern Europe suggest that intellectuals, whether established intellectuals from the Academies or new intellectuals coming of age under *perestroika*, were the key site for new ideas and activities in the early to mid-1980s.

While external conditions for movement development are important in the first two models, the relative significance for the influence of intellectuals of "wider social developments" is crucial in this model. Intellectuals are very dependent on the moment when their time has come, since, like grievances, we might argue that there are always plenty of them about. However, returning to two of our earlier models of post-Stalinist social order, we can recall the unusually important position that intellectuals held in eastern Europe. Both the Konrád/Szelényi and Bahro models stressed that intellectuals were in a commanding position over the social order, and consequently any internal conflicts within the group would have significant consequences.

Once again it is not difficult to see how the remarkable cycle of growth and decay of movement activity already described might be explained by the movement of some intellectuals and their ideas from relative isolation to the mainstream, exemplified by the widely remarked career of Václav Havel. In particular their position as ideological articulators or construers of a consistent reality can be seen, for example, in the wide range of policy debates to be found on the future of social policy (Manning 1992).

THE POST-TRANSITION PHASE

Fourth model: A fourth model has been organized around the notion of civil society. From this point of view, the upsurge in movements was both the reaffirmation of a simple belief in the indestructibility of the human spirit in the face of oppression, and an explanation of the downfall of the regimes. The analysis rests on a clear dichotomy between the growing problems of statist social and economic development, and the growing strength of non-state society as it regained more and more areas of autonomy for social action.

There is a great deal of uncertainty about the utility of this concept, chiefly because it is so all encompassing. However, an important aspect is the relationship between personal or domestic life and political oppression. Ekiert (1991), for example, suggests that Western scholars have failed to appreciate the burgeoning of domestic freedoms in the post-Stalin era, and that it was here that fertile ground lay for the development of social movement activists. It was from this base that political society in eastern Europe was "resocialized from below" during the 1980s.

However, with the breakthrough into state transformation during 1989–1991, the direction and cohesion of oppositional civil society tends to break down, and the concept loses much of its utility. Offe (1991) has suggested that it might be better to think of three progressively deeper levels of politics, concerned at the deepest with "identity", moving up through "rules", and finally to "outcomes". The eastern European revolutions have touched the deepest level of national, regional, and ethnic identity. At the same time, debate within civil society about the nature of the rules to govern the new system, let alone the new distribution of outcomes that will result, is still continuing. Social movements in the post-transition phase are operating in different ways at all these levels.

The post-transition phase

The post-transition phase raises new questions about the place of social movements in the new political and economic context.[2]

There are a number of points to be made about the new era. The first concerns the relationship of social movements to elites. It was argued earlier that both order and crisis in eastern Europe have been intimately bound up with elites and elite fractions; moreover, elites again figured as a central concern in different models of the pattern of social movements of the past decade. While some observers (e.g. Hahn 1991) have been concerned to

145

demonstrate that the cultural requirements for political involvement exist among ordinary citizens, it remains the case that elites, their knowledge, recruitment, and resources will continue to be crucial to understanding social movement changes.

A second point concerns the economic difficulties that have accompanied the transition. Of the three countries, Hungary is, as a result of both earlier and more gradual economic liberalization, in the best position for future economic development. Current economic indicators suggest that Hungary's debt burden and growth rate do not look catastrophic (Clarkson 1992). By contrast, Russia's situation is chaotic, while Estonia is still in the process of disentangling itself from the consequences of its Soviet past. In fact Estonia has always been used as a kind of economic experiment, which, together with its cultural and other links with Scandinavia, suggests that the economic future is less bleak. Economic reconstruction will thus inevitably cast a long shadow over the political changes with which we are concerned.

A third point concerns the rôle of civil society. The solidarity generated during the transition has given way to divisions – between parties, ethnic groups, regions and, in time no doubt, economic classes. This, Hirst (1991) suggests, may well endanger the fragile democracy that is emerging. In the absence of legitimate central authority, dissensus may make not only political but also economic change less effective. It seems inevitable that post-transition eastern Europe will continue to be heavily statist (Weitman 1992); indeed, although the administrative capacity of the state at both national and local levels is as yet poor (Rice 1992), it is difficult to imagine any other agency through which the conflicts of civil society can be resolved.

Notes

1. I would like to acknowledge the work of my colleagues associated with this ESRC-funded project at the University of Kent at Canterbury: Chris Pickvance, Katy Pickvance, and Sveta Klimova, and the work of our colleagues in Estonia, Russia, and Hungary.
2. Our future work will examine contrasting explanations of eastern European developments in terms of Western social movement theory, compare the special rôle of environmental movements with the more mundane area of housing movements (which will expand rapidly as new forms of property rights emerge and housing prices change), ascertain the propensity of the general population for political involvement and action, and examine the changing differential impact of national contexts on social movements.

146

References

Abercrombie, N., S. Hil, B. S. Turner 1980. *The dominant ideology thesis*. London: Allen & Unwin.

Bagguley, P. 1992. Social change . . . a critical analysis of new social movements. *Sociological Review* **40**, 26–48.

Bahro, R. 1978. *The alternative in eastern Europe*. London: New Left Books.

Biela, A. & J. J. Tobaczyk 1987. Self-transcendence in agoral gatherings. *Journal of Humanistic Psychology* **27**, 390–405.

Brown, A. 1984. Political power and the Soviet state: Western and Soviet perspectives. In *The state in socialist society*, N. Harding (ed.), 51–103. London: Macmillan.

Clarkson, T. 1992. Hungary: an eastern economy ready for development? *European Research* **3**, 22–4.

Diani, M. 1992. The concept of a social movement. *Sociological Review* **40**, 1–25.

Ekiert, G. 1991. Democratic processes in east central Europe. *British Journal of Political Science* **21**, 285–314.

Ellman, M. 1989. *Socialist planning*. Cambridge: Cambridge University Press.

Eyerman, R. & A. Jamison 1991. *Social movements, a cognitive approach*. Oxford: Polity.

Gyori, P. 1988. New social initiatives – conflicts and coexistence of the state and society. Paper presented at the conference on Voluntarism, NGOs, and Public Policy, Jerusalem, 22–24 May.

Habermas, J. 1976. *Legitimation crisis*. London: Heinemann.

Hahn, J. W. 1991. Continuity and change in Russian political culture. *British Journal of Political Science* b21, 393–422.

Hirst, P. 1991. The state, civil society, and the collapse of Soviet communism. *Economy and Society* **20**, 217–42.

Igrunov, V. V. 1989. Public movements, from protest to political self consciousness. Paper presented at the ISA conference, Moscow.

Jarve, P. 1989. Is Perestroika changing Estonians' views and behaviour? Paper presented at the Tenth Biennial Meeting of the International Society for the Study of Behavioural Development, July 9–13, Jyvskyl, Finland.

Konrád, G. & I. Szelényi 1979. *The intellectuals on the road to class power*. Brighton: Harvester.

Lane, D. 1987. *Soviet labour and the ethic of communism*. Brighton: Wheatsheaf.

Lewis, P. 1984. *Eastern Europe: political crisis and legitimation*. London: Croom Helm.

Mann, M. 1970. The social cohesion of liberal democracy. *American Sociological Review* **35**, 423–39.

Manning, N. 1992. Social policy in the former Soviet Union. In *Eastern Europe in the 1990s*, B. Deacon et al. (eds), Ch.2. London: Sage.

Mason, D. S. & S. Sydorenko 1990. Perestroika, social justice, and Soviet public opinion. *Problems of Communism* **39**, 34 43.

Offe, C. 1991. Capitalism by democratic design? *Social Research* **58**, 865–92.

Pickvance, C. 1975. On the study of urban social movements. *Sociological Review* **23**, 24–49.

Raudsepp, M. 1992. Unpublished working paper on social movements in Estonia.

Rice, E. M. 1992. Public administration in post-socialist eastern Europe. *Public Adminis-*

THE TRANSITION FROM STATE SOCIALISM

tration Review **52**, 116–24.

Rigby, T. H. 1991. *Political elites in the USSR; central leaders and local cadres from Lenin to Gorbachev.* London: Edward Elgar.

Skilling, H. G. & F. Griffiths (eds) 1971. *Interest groups in Soviet politics.* Princeton, New Jersey: Princeton University Press.

Siisiinen, M. 1992. Social movements, voluntary associations, and cycles of protest in Finland 1905–1991. *Scandinavian Political Studies* **15**, 41–60.

Szirmai, V. 1991. Paper presented at the ESRC workshop on the social movement project, University of Kent at Canterbury, October.

Tyomkina, A. 1991. Political movements of Perestroika. Unpublished paper, Leningrad.

Weber, M. 1968. *Economy and society.* Vol. 1. Totowa, New Jersey: Bedminster.

Weitman, S. 1992. Thinking the revolutions of 1989. *British Journal of Sociology* **43**, 11–24.

Yanitsky, O. 1989. New social movements in the USSR and the process of decentralisation. Unpublished paper.

Zaslavskaya, T. 1989. *A voice of reform.* Armonk: M. E. Sharpe.

Zaslavskaya, T. 1990. *The second socialist revolution.* London: Tauris.

Chapter 9

Intellectuals and democratization in Hungary

András Bozóki

This chapter analyses the political rôle of the Hungarian critical intelligentsia in the recent past and after the change of system, employing the methodology applied by Konrád and Szelényi in *Intellectuals on the Road to Class Power* (1979). Here, the critical intelligentsia is the group of intellectuals who are related to existing authority first and foremost on an ethical-normative basis. Konrád and Szelényi describe the intelligentsia as a schizophrenic actor, characterized equally by "telos" and "techné", by teleology and rational knowledge (1989, 31–9); for the first time in history there has emerged a social actor with the opportunity to organize itself into a class and, with the development of bolshevism, to ascend to power and not only to figure as an estate (as in pre-capitalist societies) or a stratum (as in market societies). Konrád and Szelényi defined the intelligentsia as the owners of transcontextual knowledge, knowledge independent of situations, who legitimize given social status exclusively by their knowledge. Thus when we speak here of the critical intelligentsia, we mean a group of intellectuals who reflect upon political conditions from a moral-universal perspective.

The intellectual as "rational redistributor"

Konrád and Szelényi wrote when the Stalinist phase of state socialism was being replaced by the post-Stalinist phase, at a time when the dictatorship, while still maintaining the demand for the centralization of authority, became more lenient and less concentrated. Under Stalinism the bureaucracy successfully and often brutally repelled the power aspirations of the intelligentsia but, by the time of post-Stalinism, that bureaucracy had lost legitimacy and needed intellectuals who could by their professional knowledge

INTELLECTUALS AND DEMOCRATIZATION IN HUNGARY

legitimize the existing system and strengthen the basis of bureaucratic authority.

Such regimes differed from authoritarian regimes in that they tried to base their rule not upon naked violence, as did some Latin American dictatorships, but upon the technocratic rationality produced by the intelligentsia. In Hungary the first sign of the softening of the system was that the communist party bureaucracy made efforts to reintegrate into society intellectuals either condemned or marginalized after the revolution of 1956. In the wake of economic reforms, the way was opened for the intelligentsia to return to considering their justification of decision-making by techné. Since the bureaucracy had not then abandoned the idea of a "planned", governed society, Konrád and Szelényi were justified in supposing that the intelligentsia occupying the positions of "planning" would not be satisfied with a modest contribution to the technocratic legitimation of the system. Accordingly, they assumed that the intelligentsia would acquire class power as "rational redistributors" and by hiding their teleological aspirations behind professional knowledge. With hindsight it is clear that Konrád and Szelényi overestimated both the internal cohesion and innovative capacity of the state-socialist system and the strength of the intelligentsia.

As Szelényi acknowledged in a paper written in 1986, bureaucracy proved to be more "stubborn" in the struggle for the preservation of power than he and Konrád had supposed (Szelényi 1990, 68–77). First, the party bureaucracy repressed the philosophers who were challenging the ideological legitimation of the system and wished to restore its original Marxian bases; then even the reformist technocrats were pushed into the background. All this had an international context. The suppression of the "Prague Spring" of 1968 and the repression that followed indicated that the Soviet leadership under Brezhnev recognized the system's lack of legitimacy and rejected the option of humanizing it. The "counter-attack of the bureaucratic estate" proved successful, and the bureaucracy looked for new allies to pacify society.

The bureaucracy made further concessions but not, as might have been expected on the basis of its earlier behaviour, to the intelligentsia; instead, and despite recurrent, increasingly merely rhetorical campaigns against the *petite bourgeoisie*, it extended tolerance to small businesses and the "second economy", a direction from which no rival ambitions were apparent. Thus did the pragmatic Kádárist bureaucracy sacrifice the remnants of teleological ideology on the altar of social peace. Where the party bureaucracy is no longer Marxist, the reform intelligentsia can no longer be revisionist. Where

THE INTELLECTUAL AS REFORMER

there is no "telos", the intelligentsia may withdraw into the trenches of technocracy, but it cannot be the agent of rational distribution. The intelligentsia was able to remain in the proximity of authority partly as an estate and partly as a social stratum, but the dream of class power, if ever there was one, evaporated.

The intellectual as reformer

The end of revisionism (Rupnik 1979) further fragmented the already divided critical intelligentsia. Four significant groupings can be identified.

Technocrats and meritocrats

Those social scientists who managed to retain their jobs turned towards their disciplines and, in the reform period renewed in the early 1980s, expressed their criticisms in their professional languages. It is difficult in retrospect to determine how sincere were arguments advanced in the professional and reform debates; some had certainly believed that the system could be reformed, and advocated a kind of self-managing socialism, whereas others proposed "market socialism" as a combination of planned economy and market redistribution, either out of conviction or as a kind of Trojan Horse. A contemporary analysis (Gombár 1983) revealed that the majority were unambiguously moving in the sphere of leftist thinking, and worded their criticism from that position. The reformist economists, enabled by their networks and their empirical research to see the condition of the economy, were the decisive figures. They could rely on the hidden support of politicians who, though pushed into the background by the anti-reform policy of the 1970s, lost little of their authority. In this shelter there grew up by the 1980s an entire new generation of reform economists which, due to their knowledge of foreign languages, schooling, and connections, appeared to be more competent than the party bureaucracy. It is not accidental that it was this group that, after the change of system, despite the mistrust of the new political leadership, produced (though in smaller numbers than their professional knowledge would suggest) the heads of banks, advisers of parties, and leading officials of the administrative institutions. Also worthy of mention are sociologists who, as disciples of the exiled Istvan Kemeny and Ivan Szelényi, dealt with issues of social and regional inequalities, of the "second economy", and poverty. The professional war of independence of political science was

INTELLECTUALS AND DEMOCRATIZATION IN HUNGARY

also waged in the 1980s. The discipline had grown out of, but had turned against, vulgarized Marxist scientific socialism. Its decisive personalities temporarily acted as informal advisers to reformist politicians, mostly to Imre Pozsgay, but the younger ones to Miklós Németh. These groups represented professional rationality within the domain of officialdom, but they never for a moment gave up asserting the teleological ethos in politics (Kovács 1984; Kovács 1990). By the end of the decade they were joined by jurists, constitutional lawyers in particular, who, as well as influencing the decision-making process and giving legal advice to the nascent parties, criticized bills that could not be harmonized with the principles of a state based on the rule of law; they also tried to democratize the Patriotic People's Front, or were working on a new constitution. In 1988 an Independent Lawyers' Forum was founded, and its members subsequently rendered practical assistance to the organization of the Opposition Round Table.

The relative flexibility of the Kádár system is indicated by the fact that it was able to keep these groups within the orbit of the official system of institutions until the mid-1980s, and quite a number of them until as late as 1989. As the change of system approached, it became increasingly uncertain whether it was the politicians moving the intelligentsia or the other way round. The specialist intellectuals, promoted to be politicians or advisers, and successfully used in 1987 by the then Prime Minister Károly Grósz to legitimize himself and his programme, gradually turned away from Grósz after the fall of Kádár, costing him first his premiership and then his position as Secretary-General of the party.

By the late 1980s the normative models of these pressure groups of the reform intelligentsia had evolved. Earlier the economists were speaking about the harmonization of plan and market, the sociologists were preoccupied with the transformation of the inner workings of the redistribution system, the constitutional lawyers were talking about socialist constitutionalism, and the political scientists discussed democratic socialism, corporate pluralism or a new compromise. By the late 1980s the picture had changed. For the economists, the self-regulating market economy based on private property became the normative model; for the sociologists it was the welfare state, for the constitutional lawyers a state based on the rule of law, and for the political scientists a representative democracy based on a multiparty system.

THE INTELLECTUAL AS REFORMER

The "popular" critical intelligentsia

Another group of intellectuals was the circle of so-called "popular" writers. Anti-bourgeois and anti-urban, they regarded the politics of left and right as irrelevant and focused instead on issues of "national destiny", the problem of the collective identity of the nation and the dimensions of social inequality. In the spirit of opposition to the elite, they undertook the representation of the socially disprivileged, identified with "true" Hungarianness, and described the elite of the day as "alien" to the real interests of Hungarians. For a long time they rejected open opposition to the regime but, despite tactical co-operation with different official and unofficial groups, they worked on the development of an autonomous political stand and criticized the system on a moral basis, saying that it refused to see the root of the crisis in the crisis of national values and morals. The group's members mostly occupied decisive positions in cultural life, particularly in literature, and believed that it was worth co-operating with anybody in the interests of national destiny, even, if necessary, with the urban opposition or with certain groups of social scientists outside the urban opposition, and even with reform communists.

The normative model of this group is "the people", building itself from small communities and identifying itself primarily with national values (and less with individual or supranational ideas), with a mission to create a kind of "Hungary of gardens", a middle-of-the-road programme rejecting capitalism as well as socialism. Its historical outlook is romantic, opposed to modernization, and regards freedom not as negative but as a joint acceptance of values oriented towards a goal set by individuals and communities. Freedom is not an objective in itself, but the nation is.

The "urban" intellectual opposition

The group of philosophers, historians, and sociologists, most of them previously dismissed from official posts, who defined themselves as the "democratic opposition", appeared as the open opposition to the Kádár regime in the 1980s. The ideas of this group, mostly consisting of people who lived in Budapest and were linked through personal networks, went through two stages of development. First, they went from Lukács to Bibó (in the 1970s), and second, from Bibó to modern liberalism (in the eighties). The leading representatives of the group broke away from George Lukács' revisionism in the early 1970s and increasingly espoused the democratic humanistic political ideology, which amalgamated liberalism and socialism, of the po-

153

litical thinker István Bibó. This was also a kind of middle way. The group's ideology crystallized only gradually because of its political strategy of breaking out of the urban intellectual "ghetto", and because of its heterogeneous composition. The normative model of human rights, elaborated by János Kis, represented the common denominator that could be accepted by the "anti-politicians" of the new left, by the social democrats, the liberals, the erstwhile anarchists turned conservative liberals, the socialists, and the plebeian radicals of 1956.

The group gradually shifted from its radical stance to a liberal one. The party created in the autumn of 1989 by the core of the group, the Alliance of Free Democrats, was not a social democrat or bourgeois radical but a liberal party, mostly under the pressure of its younger members and economists. The party stood for rapid capitalist development, spontaneous privatization, and the Western model of modernization. Perhaps the group believed more than others in the possibility of establishing bourgeois democracy in Hungary relatively quickly, by one or two "big leaps". It can be regarded as the representative of modern rather than conservative liberalism in so far as it follows liberal (and not conservative) principles in social as well as economic policy.

The group has undergone changes not only in its ideology, but also in its form and its relationship to politics. Between 1977 and 1981 one can only speak about a cultural, or more precisely, "lifestyle" opposition, about the challenging form of behaviour of a group of Budapest intellectuals. It was gradually accompanied by the appearance of the first samizdats, the foundation of the Fund Supporting the Poor (SZETA), the flying universities, and acts of solidarity manifested in petition campaigns. In 1982 the group came to a crossroads after the introduction of the Polish state of emergency. Simply making a moral existential break with the system, and being an "opposition" irritating to the party bureaucracy by its sheer existence, was not enough. From 1982 onwards the group, retaining the elements of cultural opposition, increasingly made efforts to offer a programme, to find allies, to become a political opposition. Based on the example of the Polish opposition (Michnik 1987), they set out on the road of the Polish critical intelligentsia but in a country not characterized by Polish conditions. They were realists enough not to become revolutionaries, and their circle was not to become a revolutionary sect. Recognizing that their social base was modest, they tried to follow a "popular front" evolutionist strategy, increasingly opening up towards the society in the spirit of radical reform.

THE INTELLECTUAL AS REFORMER

The "mediacracy"

Finally, reference should be made to the rôle of journalists among the critical intelligentsia. The journalists were basically loyal to the system until 1987. If an intellectual wanted to publish journalism, he or she had hardly any alternative; only certain literary and social science periodicals would allow the publication of papers critical in spirit. The party bureaucracy was eager to keep the critical voices of the press isolated and adequately counterbalanced, and not to allow the papers to represent other political viewpoints. The limits of tolerance varied with the changing political situation; some editors were able to sense the limits of censorship with great skill, but most were careful to avoid risks. One refreshing exception was the economic weekly *HVG*, speaking the language of the younger generation of technocratic intelligentsia within the constraints of the official line, and depending on its readers understanding by allusions and "reading between the lines".

The appearance of samizdat journals established an alternative point of reference for readers of the "official" press. The voice of democratic opposition was amplified primarily by Radio Free Europe, which introduced samizdats to a multitude of listeners. All this influenced the official press and encouraged some magazine editors openly to confront the authorities. Even though these editors lost, such scandals forced the representatives of cultural policy to give embarrassing explanations and challenged the (already increasingly shaky) belief in the omnipotence of the party bureaucracy.

The rigid borderline separating the two kinds of press began to weaken during the 1980s, and a "grey zone" appeared, manifest in university newspapers, magazines, and low-circulation periodicals, which popularized or expanded ideas expressed by that part of the press not controlled by the *nomenklatura*. Meanwhile, the three major camps of the intelligentsia penetrated the spheres of university students and the local press by public lectures delivered at the invitation of newly organized clubs and circles. An increasingly free flow of critical ideas began.

This was the state of affairs when Gorbachev's *glasnost* reached Hungary. The younger generation of journalists must have felt as fish thrown to the shore, and returned to the water. The "explosion" reached the dailies, the broadcasts of radio and television for the intelligentsia, and subsequently even the political programmes. The "revolution of words" was accomplished, critical rationalism was victorious, and the critical intelligentsia as communicator or as "intermediary" inflicted humiliating defeat in the sense of "telos" as well as "techné" on a bureaucracy that knew only the old style

155

INTELLECTUALS AND DEMOCRATIZATION IN HUNGARY

of discourse. The "culture of critical discourse" (Gouldner 1979) replaced party jargon and evolved the alliance of the new "politocracy" and the mediacracy (Konrád & Szelényi 1991). The normative model that inspired the journalists and media experts was unambiguously the mass communications practice of open Western societies.

Intelligentsia and revolution

If 1989 was a revolution, it was primarily a revolution achieved by the force of free ideas made public. Yet 1989 was not only a revolution of the intelligentsia; a "quiet revolution" (Konrád & Szelényi 1991) had been going on for several decades in the daily life of society, and there was a tenacious insistence upon certain bourgeois values that reached not only most of the critical intelligentsia but also the second generation of the techno-bureaucracy inside the party. The influence of bourgeois values meant not that intellectuals in and out of power became bourgeois but rather that, considering themselves the representatives of "civil society", they began to behave as civilians (Arato 1991).

An intelligentsia producing ideology, expressing ideas in the language of the age, and capable of handling the media, had won a decisive battle against the bureaucracy of the old order. As with the collapse of the post-Stalinist system, not only did the third stage of socialism fail to appear, but socialism as a system collapsed. The intelligentsia had not been victorious as an organized class but as the "vanguard of the building of capitalism" (Böröcz 1990). Wishing to modernize and westernize, it accomplished victory as an *ad hoc*, heterogeneous coalition of intellectual strata, estates, and "tribes".

The older generation of the bureaucracy and political leadership had disappeared, and the technocratic and critical intelligentsia was unable to find either strong allies or strong adversaries in the "classless" society of the post-Kádárian world. The evolving vacuum practically sucked it into politics. A rapid process of party formation started under the leadership of intellectuals, and pluralization took place by the reconstruction of the fragments of political traditions (Vajda 1992, 67), by the recreation of tradition. While in the early 1980s many people thought that the economic rearrangement launched by slow embourgeoisement would not lead to democracy (Szelényi 1990, 93), in reality democracy evolved more rapidly than capitalism. After the change of system, the coalition of intellectuals characterized by estates, tribes, and strata seemed to fall apart.

156

THE INTELLECTUAL AS POLITICIAN

The intellectual as politician

From the end of 1988 onwards, the intelligentsia found itself in the front line of the nascent parties. The emerging political vacuum encouraged it to represent democracy not only theoretically, or as citizens, but to participate in its practical realization as well. Many interpreted the politician's rôle as a mission or at least as a response to an exceptional historical challenge. Who else should "shape history" if not those who had a plan, an idea, a normative model of it? Initially some critical intellectuals wandered among the new parties like a modern Odysseus, as if they found it difficult to resist the lure of the siren voices of transcendence, but the majority put wax in their ears and tied themselves to the masts of particular parties; as it was then mostly ex-communists who called themselves independents, the critical intelligentsia did not want to taint themselves by open declarations of independence.

Intellectuals in the parties

In the year of "democratic change" perhaps only two parties could say that they were not, at their core, intellectual formations: the Social Democratic party (MSZDP) and the Independent Smallholders' party (FKGP). Some representatives of the critical intelligentsia did appear among the social democrats, but they all failed, the supporting advisers left, and subsequently or simultaneously, the party itself failed. The elite of the Smallholders' party was recruited first and foremost among rural cultivators and surviving Smallholder politicians of the pre-communist era; the small number of intellectuals joining them later had never belonged to the critical intelligentsia of the Kádár regime. The situation was similar in the case of the Christian Democratic People's party (KDNP), with the difference that the intelligentsia was more dominant in the core of the party. This group consisted of those elderly, mostly Catholic intellectuals who had not opposed the Church's policy of collaboration with the regime, and partly of younger critical intellectuals who were close to the lower clergy, but initially the leadership of the party clearly came from the older generation (Such 1992).

FIDESZ, the radical-liberal party of urban youth, came to the scene as a curious intellectual-semi-intellectual formation. This group of college-educated youth of mostly rural origin, representing the radical generation of young critical intelligentsia, was the first to form its political organization openly (in March 1988). It was "intellectual-semi-intellectual" because, though the core of FIDESZ was university educated (some had even studied

INTELLECTUALS AND DEMOCRATIZATION IN HUNGARY

in Western universities), the majority, entering politics directly from university, had no time to be socialized into an intellectual rôle. With few exceptions, they did not develop the intellectual ethos that characterized and shaped the political behaviour of older generations. This, together with the fact that these young people had not sensed the rigid resistance of the bureaucracy and the irremovable taboos at the time of disintegrating Kádárism, explains why FIDESZ's criticism of the system has been pragmatic almost from the outset.

The fact that the aspirations propelling FIDESZ to become a party were those of a politician and not of an intellectual (Róna-Tas 1992) is explained by the dual mobility of the core of the party; primarily lawyers and economists, these were people who were rapidly intragenerationally mobile from country towns to the capital, from non-intellectual families to the intelligentsia. One shade farther from the decision-making centre are those born into intellectual families and whose mobility was only regional. Finally, there are those, located in the outer circle of the political core, who were born into intellectual families in Budapest and themselves set out on intellectual careers. The old intellectuals of the earlier democratic opposition who joined FIDESZ are not politicians but have taken up advisory rôles. With inevitable exceptions, the young people of FIDESZ are young first or second generation intellectuals for whom catching up with the social hierarchy is a primary criterion of success.

In 1989 the "politocracy" of the intelligentsia found its political representation mainly in the largest liberal party, the Alliance of Free Democrats (SZDSZ), where it worded the radical programme of systemic change. If there was any representation of the intellectual behaviour called "political capitalism" (Staniszkis 1991), then it was primarily apparent in the liberal core of the SZDSZ. It was in this party that the sympathizers of the earlier democratic opposition met a major group of earlier reform economists turned liberals and the leading figures of 1956 who had been followers of Imre Nagy. Already in the 1980s, these mainly Jewish Budapest intellectuals had understood each other better than any of the "popular" groups of intellectuals, partly because of the similarity of their objectives and partly because they shared modern Western-oriented attitudes. The more heterogeneous company of reform economists and the apparently more united urban opposition saw each other not as enemies but as strategic allies, whereas the relationship between the urban opposition and the group of "popular" writers can be described as rather an occasional tactical alliance tinted with rivalry. The intelligentsia of the SZDSZ entered politics after successful professional

THE INTELLECTUAL AS POLITICIAN

careers without being absolutely sure whether they wanted to be engaged in it and, if so, for how long, and many of them continue to be ambivalent towards the professional politician's rôle.

Some attempts at co-operation by the "popular" and urban groups proved successful, but it was the first manifest sign of the pluralization of Hungarian politics when they came forwards as separate movements. The "popular" group complained that the urban opposition had prepared a programme without consulting them (Kis et al. 1987), whereas the urban group said that the "populars" entered an alliance with the reform communists in power while the urban group was evolving its political movement (Agócs & Medvigy 1991). The two ideological traditions of the Hungarian intelligentsia, established in the 1920s and 1930s, were again separated in a time of systemic change.

The "popular" critical intelligentsia was organized in the Hungarian Democratic Forum (MDF), which, with its claim to be the "calm force" and a programme promising a less painful economic transition, became the winner of the first free elections. The circle of founders consisted mostly of writers, historians, and other arts graduates from Budapest and the countryside; some practising lawyers of the Independent Lawyers' Forum and some less eminent reform economists joined them only later. Initially, the party was dominated by the plebeian-Protestant ethos that advocated a leftist middle-of-the-road position, promoted co-operation with the popular wing of the reform communists, and for this purpose defined the MDF as "neither pro-government, nor opposition". However, it became clear by the second part of 1989 that it was impossible, with this fellow-traveller policy, to participate in the elections with any hope of victory. The party's founders were forced to make a pragmatic turn as they sensed the growing anti-communist mood of the public. Thus an intellectual active in politics (Zoltán Bíró) was replaced as chairman of the MDF by an intellectual politician (József Antall). The correctness of this choice was justified by subsequent events: after the plebiscite of 1989, Antall's tactics proved successful in the face of SZDSZ as well as the communists (Kolosi et al. 1992). Yet the ideological intellectual core of the MDF saw and still sees in Antall a politician who came from outside and removed its authority.

However, according to the politicians who had come from the "popular" intelligentsia, an outsider, representing a different, gentlemanly-conservative set of values, can keep his position until he is obviously successful. Economic transition accompanying systemic change inevitably causes social dislocation, and the popularity of the government decreases. Thus the "popular"

159

INTELLECTUALS AND DEMOCRATIZATION IN HUNGARY

intellectuals, many of whom considered politics as a mission and not as a task, and regarded their rôle as the solution of the "issues of national destiny" and not the development of daily consensus, found an opportunity to reunite against the "helpless government" by "rightist popularism" with the people as they imagine them and not as they really are. The August 1992 paper expressing extreme rightist views (Csurka 1992) is not only the document of the struggle between politicians of different principles, but represents an attempt to reclaim power by the ideological group of intellectuals incapable of adjusting to professional politics. With Csurka's paper "the intellectual . . . has again set out on his irresponsible adventures, driven by the aesthetic ambition to perform his 'grandiose' political work of art instead of 'base life'." (Fehér & Heller 1992, 202)

The state party, the Hungarian Socialist Workers' party (MSZMP), was an interesting conglomerate of intellectual politicians and a "mass party of intellectuals" and an "elite party of the workers". One of the most important lines of division was generational and divided the party between old cadres and "Young Turks". The old cadres were not intellectuals, though some of their younger representatives called themselves economists or historians. Those with diplomas of higher education had acquired them either at party schools (at the Lenin Institute or at the party college) or in the Soviet Union. It was in the later 1960s that intellectuals began to join the party in larger numbers. For the majority of intellectuals the party membership card was needed to smooth progress in their professional careers and not because they wanted to become politicians, yet some younger intellectuals, given even this opportunity via the Young Communist League (KISZ), used it as a springboard. The communist party leadership preferred the ideologically less polished technological intelligentsia; thus did young technical intellectuals come to occupy the leading ranks of the ruling estate (Nyírö 1989). Those who were unable to achieve this filled the ranks of the techno-bureaucracy, at a distinctly higher level of skill than the old cadres. As politicians, they bore no trace of critical attitude, and faithfully supported the Kádárian gerontocracy until May 1988.

Kádár's generation was overthrown in May 1988 by a curious *ad hoc* coalition. It consisted of communists of the old kind, who were ready to subordinate certain taboos to the interest of acquiring power, the earlier technobureaucrats of the KISZ, sensing danger and wishing to quit the sinking vessel in time, the reform communists who had been "pushed into parking" because of their earlier intellectual deviance, and the young career technocrats, who were mostly economists and represented the interests of economic ef-

THE INTELLECTUAL AS POLITICIAN

ficiency. The changing of the guard took place under the banner of "reform" of unspecified content (Schöpflin et al. 1988).

Imre Pozsgay played a key rôle in gradual liberalization and, as a Hungarian Gorbachev, in a matter of months he extended freedom of the press. He started to negotiate with the intellectuals who had been organizing the germs of political parties, and accomplished a symbolic but very significant political breakthrough when he declared, on the basis of the "investigation" of a committee of intellectuals set up by him, that 1956 was a "popular uprising". It was in the debate of the Central Committee, following the removal of this taboo, that the hitherto heretical idea of a multi-party system was accepted. As Pozsgay primarily approached the "popular" opposition intellectuals, the leftist intellectuals organizing themselves in the New March Front were trying to find their mentor in Rezsö Nyers, whereas the urban-liberal groups regarded both with suspicion. The technocratic and ideological reformers, who were gradually coming to the foreground in the MSZMP, needed only Grósz to get round the followers of the old system inside the party. Miklós Németh, replacing him as Prime Minister, not only legitimized himself with a good team of professional intellectuals, as Grósz had done, but by the fact that he had also been a reformist expert before becoming a politician. Németh did all he could to separate from the MSZMP the government of "experts" he led, in order to save the professional intellectuals turned politicians from the stigma of collaboration with communists of the old kind.

The appearance of the critical ideological intelligentsia within the MSZMP is related to the organization of the reform circles. The reform circles set up from early 1989 onwards included rural intellectuals who felt cheated and turned against the half-hearted policy of the Budapest Party Committee. They realized that they had been on the losing side and that their only possibility was the radical renewal of the party in the spirit of "democratic socialism". Two figures were typical of the new group: the first, a rural secondary school teacher marginalized himself and did not even join the successor party of the MSZMP, the Hungarian Socialist party (MSZP), set up in October 1989, and could next be seen as a spokesman of the Democratic Charter from December 1991 onwards; the second, a lecturer in the Department of Scientific Socialism at Szeged University, advocated a more moderate, "popular-democratic" socialism and, on that platform, became an MSZP member of parliament in the spring of 1990. Reflecting the earlier ideas of the reformist political scientists who had abandoned the idea of "democratic socialism" and were oriented instead towards social democracy, the reform circles soon became politically radical; at their national meeting in April

INTELLECTUALS AND DEMOCRATIZATION IN HUNGARY

1989, they saw no chance for the internal democratization of the party, and most stood for a split. As at that time neither Pozsgay nor Nyers was ready for the split, the disappointed intellectuals concentrated their efforts on preparations for the autumn party congress. By that time, however, events had begun to move so fast that their victory seemed to be highly probable, and an increasing number of conformist/careerist party members rushed to join their ranks. By the time the movement, under the name "Reform Alliance", accomplished a breakthrough in the October party congress, the group had been so much diluted that this victory itself disillusioned many intellectuals who initially participated in the reform circles (Bihari 1990).

The communist party's successor, the Hungarian Socialist party, deleted the word "worker" from its name and by the new name rid itself of reminders not only of the state party but also the contradiction between its declared objective and its sociologically demonstrable intellectual composition. Pragmatic "techné" was victorious over ideological "telos"; in the MSZP led by Gyula Horn, the intellectual was needed as a diligent expert politician and not as the "conscience of the nation". The remaining members of the reform circles became professional bureaucrats, and Pozsgay left the party in the autumn of 1990. In the meantime initial uncertainties in the party's self-legitimation made it necessary to include among its representatives such "ornamental intellectuals" who demonstrated the "social roots" of the MSZP, and it was made possible for them to express their intellectual identity by initiatives outside the party without endangering its internal stability.

It is of particular interest that it was the MSZP, an increasingly social democratic party of intellectuals, that, because there was a sudden vacuum on the political left, became a major political beneficiary of dissatisfaction with social impoverishment, growing unemployment, and a steadily weakening protective social net. This party of intellectuals found itself in the paradoxical position of trying to become a leftist "blue-collar" party representing wage and salary earners.

Intellectuals at the negotiations:
the Opposition Round Table and the trilateral talks

The historic meeting of intellectuals turned politicians was organized in the spring of 1989 at the Opposition Round Table and subsequently, in the summer of the same year, at the trilateral negotiations, where the political realization of the change of system and the basic principles of the new set-up were discussed. On the opposition side it then became clear who among the poli-

THE INTELLECTUAL AS POLITICIAN

ticking intellectuals were going to become politicians and who were those budding politicians who continued to think as intellectuals. It was an exceptional moment; the emergent and the decaying "political classes" faced each other in the negotiating chambers of Parliament.

The top delegation of the MSZMP, headed by Pozsgay, was composed of techno-bureaucrats who had entered the party in the 1970s and moved clumsily in the medium of democratic debate. The topmost representation of the MSZMP at the negotiations was a politically suicidal undertaking, and it is not accidental that Németh and representatives of his government of "experts" did not attend. The situation was different at the lower, expert levels, where the participants were mostly not party bureaucrats but younger technocrats from the ministries who utilized all sorts of gestures to detach themselves from their rôle and to indicate to the opposition that they had not volunteered but were delegated by the party. The new parties were struggling against an enormous shortage of cadres, and the MSZMP technocrat who could call attention to his expertise was able to "save himself" and even to lay the foundations of a career in the public administration of the new system. It was mainly at the political negotiations that the stakes were high; the negotiations on the economy, by contrast, were conducted by people who knew each other well and who had been discussing these issues for a long time. With some irony one could even say that the discussions on the economy were conducted between two groups of reform economists: those who had left the MSZMP in time, and those who had failed to do so. The modernizing economists of the MSZMP and the Opposition Round Table were more in agreement than was either group with the experts of the Third Side in the trilateral negotiations, which also included representatives of the earlier intelligentsia, opposed to reform.

The Opposition Round Table (EKA) was a far more colourful and mixed company than the delegation of the MSZMP; it gathered a large number of intellectuals, academicians and students, film directors and museum directors among them. The dominance of intellectuals in the humanities was conspicuous. The Opposition Round Table was a meeting place of generations, each with a different political socialization, past experiences, historical references, and political culture: the oldest sat alongside members of the postwar generation, the people of 1956, the "great generation" of 1968, and the generation of the late Kádár regime and systemic change.

As far as the political background is concerned, those who had personal experience of the operation of the institutions of the short-lived democracy after 1945 could be isolated from those whose experience was primarily that

163

INTELLECTUALS AND DEMOCRATIZATION IN HUNGARY

of movements and opposition, and from those who had neither. The extent of integration into the previous regime was related to political background and ranged along a scale from a former state prosecutor to members of the opposition who had been dismissed from their jobs for political reasons.

Despite some descriptive accounts (Bruszt 1990; Richter 1990; Szalai 1990; Sajó 1991; Bozóki 1993), little is known about the events of the trilateral talks and about the motivations of the participating intellectuals. Nevertheless, this extremely heterogeneous group reached a consensus about constitutional democracy, even if there remained serious differences about details of its realization.

A test of the intellectual's rôle

In the new political field emerging in the wake of the trilateral talks, four types of intellectuals and intellectual attitudes could be distinguished according to the individuals' attitudes to politics and to becoming politicians: the "professionals", those having a "sense of mission", the "brooding", and the "people of rapid retreat".

The first category consists of the "natural" politicians. It soon became apparent that for a large group of intellectuals the intellectual profession they had been pursuing was only a detour, a parking place. For them, politics did not mean something shameful or "lowly"; they lacked the characteristic intellectual's arrogance towards politics, felt they were born for politics, and admitted it. They easily and rapidly identified with the politician's rôle and sought quickly to raise it to a professional level.

The second group consisted of intellectuals taking part in politics with a sense of mission. It is not evident why they took part in politics, and they had to justify it even to themselves. However, self-legitimation is easy as "we live in extraordinary historical times", and if the homeland and duty call, "all of us have to go". Many of them felt that the present was a direct continuation of their earlier existence as critical intellectuals; after all, if they had been fighting for the nation and for democracy, they couldn't stop half way, just as their ideas seemed about to materialize. Quite a number had a politician's constitution even when they were prophetic or ideological intellectuals, but they did not admit it even to themselves. They did not start to take up politics as writers so that they might write freely, but they had been writing so that they might freely take up politics. However, neither politics nor writing was a goal in itself; both were subordinated to a higher ideal, to a moral, "metapolitical" objective. The group was not homogeneous and did not consist

164

THE INTELLECTUAL AS POLITICIAN

only of extremists or populists. Most came from the earlier group of "popular" writers, but there were also members of the earlier opposition, committed advocates of 1956 among them, and people who wished to atone for their earlier lapses and mistaken compromises by joining the service of democracy.

The third group consists of intellectuals brooding over their political activities. They were the people for whom the morally elevating power in itself is an insufficient justification for acceptance of the politician's rôle. Initially they had daily to answer the question why were they engaged in politics, and after some time they would have to decide what they actually wanted. Some attempted the impossible: to make the one consistent with the other; by piling up intellectual and politicians' jobs, they tried "rationally" to divide themselves and soothe their consciences. Many are highly popular among voters because it is clear that they are not power-hungry. They do not want to be politicians at any cost; they are not much disappointed if their destiny lets them continue their intellectual calling. Yet with the progress of the professionalization and bureaucratization of parties, they became increasingly irritating for many within their party, and sooner or later became an "alien body". Some were pushed out or voluntarily gave up politics, but the vast majority "submitted themselves to their fate" and willy-nilly became professional politicians. However, cases of compromise also occurred when people retired from the front-line of politics but "left a foot in the door" and, alongside their main vocation, remained members of various non-executive bodies of their party.

If the politician is defined as somebody who "is able to make unprincipled compromises" (Vajda 1992, 66), then neither the members of the second nor the third group are real politicians. Neither those having "a sense of mission" nor those who "brood over politics" are able to make unprincipled compromises, and their attachment to the transcendent justification of political action is always, potentially, a threat to democratic politics.

The fourth group, the "people of rapid retreat", are intellectuals interested in politics who regarded flirtation with practical politics as a passing adventure, a short detour deriving from the exceptional situation, and who, as soon as they felt that the situation had changed, returned to their old vocations. Some may have been attracted by politics but realized that constitutionally they were not suited for it and quickly drew the necessary conclusions. However, they did not lose interest in politics, and later functioned as advisers or turned up as signatories of the Democratic Charter.

Hungary reached the age of democracy with the free elections, but the

165

INTELLECTUALS AND DEMOCRATIZATION IN HUNGARY

rôle conflicts between the intellectuals' and politicians' identities were resolved only slowly. "Commuting" between these rôles continued for a long time, and the intellectuals enjoyed this masked ball far more than the professional politicians.

Learning the politician's rôle was easier in the "historical parties" (FKGP, KDNP) than in the ones that had grown out of the movements of the 1980s (SZDSZ, FIDESZ, MDF) because the former did not consist of critical intellectuals but of "grand old men" and middle-aged careerists, while the professional politicians of the MSZP were able to integrate the newly arriving intellectuals; those who could not make the necessary adjustment left the party of their own accord.

In the parties in which critical intellectuals were present in larger numbers, the issue of party or movement caused serious problems. There are some intellectuals who still regard the foundation of the SZDSZ in November 1988 as a kind of "coup" after which the Network of Free Initiatives, operating on the basis of the earlier principles of decentralization, continued for a short time. The SZDSZ tried to overcome the problem by becoming a party of action but, though this produced initial successes, it later led to crisis. Finally the party leadership of intellectuals whose past was identical with the movement was confronted with the increasingly dissatisfied members of the "movement" it generated.

The conflict between "movementism" and "professionalism" appeared in FIDESZ as well as in MDF. After a minor conflict at its congress in June 1990, the movement wing of FIDESZ launched a sharp attack against the party's parliamentary elite. However, the party leadership did not make concessions to the "movementists" and, justified by the subsequent successes of the party, ultimately they were able to squeeze out the dissident faction.

When led by Zoltán Bíró, MDF did not want to become a party, because its founders did not want to "degrade" it to represent partial interests instead of the comprehensive "cause of Hungarians". After long disputes the March 1989 meeting of MDF tried to dissolve tension by declaring that it was a party as well as a movement. The MDF was shaped into a party by József Antall, but the grey party soldiers brought by him were intellectually no match for the founders, and discredited the party by their mistakes in government. The figure of greatest authority in the "popular" camp, Sándor Csoóri, could be pacified by Antall, who offered him the Presidency of the World Federation of Hungarians, within which Csoóri could freely organize a "movement" influenced by MDF but not of it. By this gesture the Prime Minister let part of the spirit of the intellectual movement out of the bottle of MDF. Other

THE INTELLECTUAL AS POLITICIAN

"popular" intellectual politicians, making politics with a "sense of mission", were not satisfied by this solution, but wished to transform MDF in accord with their own transcendent principles. This moment was utilized by István Csurka and his circle to launch an attack against the professional politicians of the party and, through them, against the democratic system, thereby causing the gravest crisis in the history of MDF.

The rôle conflicts of critical intellectuals turned politicians are among the causes of the disturbances generated by the "movements" within these parties. The development of a political situation that pushes the movements and their ideologists out of the parties seems to be a significant step towards the stabilization of the party system, but it also calls attention to the occasionally weak legitimacy of the system of democratic institutions as well as to the weaknesses of the organizations of interest representation.

The SZDSZ and the liberal intelligentsia

The liberal intelligentsia, considered by many to be the real heir of the change of 1989, was pushed into parliamentary opposition after the elections. The coalition that came to power consisted not only of groups who had been actively in confrontation with the Kádár system, but in large part of those whose major strategy had been survival in the system, and whose values had been closer to pre-communist Hungary, to the traditional, paternalistic, state interventionist policy of the "gentlemanly middle class". It soon occurred to the intellectual leadership of SZDSZ that the party might have to become the opposition to the system instead of the government, because the centralizing objectives of the government and the anti-parliamentary, populist rhetoric of the extremists of MDF might lead to the creation of a new nomenklatura, to the seizure of political power over the economy, and to the consolidation of a seemingly democratic but essentially semi-authoritarian regime. The recurrence of the idea of opposition to the system also indicated that only with difficulty did the opposition part of the "politocracy" of 1989–1990 find its place, not only in the new system, but also in the new political elite. The party's membership and some of the public did not understand why the party, successful earlier with strong anti-communist rhetoric, concentrated only upon institutional rather than personnel changes, and why it turned not only against the new government but at times also against the new power system as well. In 1991 its erstwhile intellectual sympathizers turned away from SZDSZ, and the popularity of the party rapidly decreased.

INTELLECTUALS AND DEMOCRATIZATION IN HUNGARY

The political heirs of the earlier democratic opposition advocating liberal principles of economic policy were also adversely affected by the fact that many representatives of the "new technocracy" who had been members of the MSZMP easily found their way into the new hierarchy and established contacts with the first representatives of the slowly emerging "new bourgeoisie". Though the MDF, leading the governing coalition, advocated the creation of a "Hungary of owner-cultivators", a national middle class and a national bourgeoisie, after serious internal political struggles it compromised in the economic sphere with the "new technocracy" that had growing influence during the last phase of the Kádár regime and was now loyal to the MDF. Under the pressure of its populists, MDF tried quite militantly to realize its original programme, hesitating between the tolerant policy of embourgeoisement and interference intended to create a bourgeoisie, and often arbitrarily alternating between the two. In official politics, the space for the oppositional "politocracy" of 1989 gradually narrowed.

In the 1980s, opposition intellectuals had a "movement" way of life, and their independence made them suited to becoming the most consistent critics of the Kádár regime. Their brave behaviour served as a model to Hungarian journalists during the period of transition, and in the autumn of 1989 they were able to mobilize successfully for the abolition of the privileges of the communist party and, by forcing a successful plebiscite, to hinder the early presidential election proposed by those in power. In October 1990 they openly supported the taxi-drivers' blockade and thus played a rôle in preventing the government from employing violence against the drivers (Bozóki & Kovács 1991). The democratic opposition was able in the 1980s, in the rather isolated and limited political media they created, to insert political society in the Tocquevillian sense between the state and society. In 1988, early in the political changes, they established the Network of Free Initiatives, a political organization that did not resemble a party, with the purpose of creating a co-ordinated co-operation among the politically active informal groups of society. SZDSZ has outgrown the Network, but its leaders retained their "movement" attitude for a long time, and the new party was successful so long as it was able to interpret politics in movement terms; but when the taxi-drivers' blockade offered the opportunity, the party was unable to mobilize the public. The slow professionalization and bureaucratization of the political elite left less and less scope for the earlier manifestations of the critical intellectual attitude. It was a painful defeat for the leadership to realize the changing situation, that in parliamentary democracies circumstances force a transition from an anti-political language to an expressly

THE INTELLECTUAL AS POLITICIAN

political usage (Garton Ash 1991), and a significant part of the intellectual circle around the leadership was disillusioned with politics. The party leadership as well as the liberal intelligentsia were dissatisfied with the new situation, because they felt that the principles they so successfully represented in 1989 were being dissipated.

Critical intelligentsia and the press

After the elections of 1990, the press, liberated only a year earlier, became one of the most important spheres of mobility for the old critical intelligentsia. Never before had so many interesting articles been published in Hungarian periodicals, yet most of the intelligentsia was reading not the periodicals but the dailies, and watching political programmes on television. The intelligentsia was in a feverishly politicized state.

The magazines founded by intellectuals close to the different parties varied in their relationships with their parties. *Magyar Fórum*, representing the populist trend of MDF, was acquired by politicians with a "sense of mission". "Brooding" politician-intellectuals edited *Kis Ujság*, which differed from the FKGP party line, and *Beszélő*, which became a weekly, concentrating primarily on social problems. *Magyar Narancs*, sympathetic to FIDESZ, was edited not by politicians but by "people of rapid retreat", and consequently the paper acquired greater independence from the party. The liberal periodicals soon developed good relations with the society of Budapest journalists, while the journalists and politicians close to the "popular national" line experimented with the setting up of a new journalists' association. This experiment did not meet expectations and, despite the papers founded or reorganized by the government, the vast majority of journalists viewed the activities of government critically. The majority of journalists felt that their own independence was endangered by the removal of the presidents of radio and television, who had been appointed by the consensus of the parties; when the government launched the "media war" (Farkas 1991; Sükösd 1992) against them, most journalists sympathized with the President of the Republic, counter-balancing the government, and with the opposition parties.

Pokol (1992) finds it characteristic of the Hungarian situation after 1990 that the media, instead of really becoming independent, have again been intertwined with politics, but this time with the opposition parties, and believes that the uniform intellectual culture manifest in this interrelationship does not suit the logic of a competitive party system and may become an obsta-

INTELLECTUALS AND DEMOCRATIZATION IN HUNGARY

cle to political modernization. Like the intellectuals, most of the press experienced the liberation of 1988–1989 as a kind of moral revolution. The journalistic profession was radically rejuvenated, and its old members also tried to renew themselves and to forget the submissive practice of earlier decades. Intense competition for readers began and, under the conditions of democracy, news value, attractiveness, and sensation have become decisive. Newspapers survive either by giving information that would resist any challenge, or – characteristically – by "exaggerating" the events, by presenting the paradox of events in bold relief. Criticism attracts more readers than apologetics, and so it is a consequence of the nature of democracy that the majority of the press has gone into "opposition".

The boundaries within the never uniform culture of the critical intelligentsia have become sharper. Organized between the governing coalition and the political opposition respectively, it has become more apparent that the normative models of these groups are different. In this respect the parties and persons forming the governing coalition as "natural allies" can be divided into two groups. One consists of the tendency exemplified by Prime Minister Antall, the normative model of which is the Western social market economy and democracy based on a multi-party system, but employing a language and a set of symbols linked to the old days. The language of this group is that of modernization by restoration, expressing the conservative values of a return to democracy. Those politicians of the governing party who had been critical intellectuals and have retained their critical attitude were not modernizers either; their criticism of the Kádár regime had not been modernistic but was built on a *Gemeinschaft*-based romantic anti-modernism.

These factors have greatly contributed to the growing sympathy of the press with those opposition parties that adopted the normative model of modernity and did not express it in archaic symbols and usage. Two kinds of historical outlook are involved: to the first, communism broke the flow of Hungarian history four decades ago and now the "waistcoat has to be buttoned from the button up to which it was unbuttoned"; to the second, communism was, despite its catastrophic effects, a distorted modernization that brought about changes in the structure and values of the society that make impossible a return to pre-communist conditions. From this perspective, existing, post-communist conditions should be accepted as the basis when Western normative models are adopted. This latter view was, more or less, the interpretation of the changes of 1989 by the press and the opposition parties; though the political transition has been completed at the level of the

CONCLUSION

transformation of institutions, the "cultural fight" between the normative models, to which the intellectuals "turned" politicians are particularly susceptible, continued.

All these causes have produced the conditions described by Pokol (1992) as the "interpenetration" of liberal intellectuals, politicians and the press, where intellectuals' shaping of politics is counter-productive to the functional differentiation of modern political life. Historical reasons apart, the critical intelligentsia outside the parties, in so far as it does not wish to give up its influence, may also be "blamed" for the maintenance of a close relationship often accepted even by opposition politicians who feel that, without the legitimation offered by the intelligentsia, their own legitimacy is weak. The long-term strengthening of the system of political rotation is a necessary condition for the full separation of the functional rôle of the press and the system of political institutions. Until it happens, neither actor is interested in winding up the alliance, though the intelligentsia, following its universalist inclinations, has become dissatisfied with the opposition parties as well. The recent recurrence of its activism in movements is a sign that its retreat from the parties to "political society" has begun.

The critical intelligentsia had to elaborate new forms of activity, a new strategy of interest articulation alongside the different yet equally closed orientations of politicians' professionalism and civilian vocation. It needed a strategy that did not lock up the politically active intelligentsia in the various professional fields, but left open an outlet and allowed opportunities for the self-realization Szelényi and Konrád called "generic-transcendent".

Conclusion

The fundamental experience of the middle-aged generation of the Hungarian critical intelligentsia has been the dissolution of the Kádár regime and the untrustworthiness of the stability of institutions. They have therefore adopted a concept of democracy that is not based on acceptance of the procedural rules of democracy, on faith in the workability of "formal" representative democracy, but on an acceptance of democratic political culture. For them, democracy consists in substantial content more fundamental than rules of procedure. The smaller part of the critical intelligentsia has adjusted to the political elite of the new democracy, but the major part has been gradually squeezed out. Initiatives such as the Democratic Charter offered them space.

INTELLECTUALS AND DEMOCRATIZATION IN HUNGARY

The Democratic Charter was issued by liberal and leftist intellectuals in September 1991, and summarized the criteria for democracy in the different fields of the society in 17 points, worded by such well known writers as György Konrád and Mihály Kornis. The declaration was signed by 5000 people within two months, and though the appeal was explicitly not directed against the governing coalition, it was so interpreted by the head of government. Consequently, signing or not signing the appeal has become a direct political issue and even a matter of confidence, and so the representatives of the governing coalition and their supporters have not joined it. The Charter has simplified political discourse to a choice between the government and opposition.

In late November 1991, when Prime Minister Antall removed the President of the Hungarian National Bank because he had signed the Democratic Charter, all three opposition parties demonstratively joined the Charter to protest against the assessment of those with responsibility for the economy according to their political reliability rather than their achievement. In early December, more than half the signatories of the Charter held a meeting in Budapest, where the participants unanimously declared the Charter a movement and elected its spokesmen. In the next two months the number of signatories of the Charter grew to 20,000. On 15 March 1992, the national holiday, the Charter for the first time called upon its followers to take to the streets, and held a mass demonstration of 20,000 people in Budapest.

The Charter has no formal membership and does not wish to become a party, but it intends to remain the representative of the cause of democracy within civil society. Because of its popular front character, it includes even leftist intellectuals – the erstwhile members of the communist party (MSZMP) – against whom the majority of the participants of the movement stood in 1989.

While this initiative promoted the strengthening of the demand for democratic political discussion and thus contributed to the survival of the political society evolved in 1989, it has also become a curious "counter-attack of an estate". The critical intelligentsia, unable to organize itself into a class or to act as the advocate of certain social strata, has performed its historical mission by organizing the democratic change, when it filled the vacuum created by the collapse of the old *nomenklatura*.

Can the intelligentsia retain the power it acquired in an exceptional historical situation? The post-election events and the organization of the Democratic Charter suggest not. Now the critical intelligentsia is returning to its pre-1989 rôle: it is becoming a "mediacracy", shaping educated public

REFERENCES

opinion, and a "meritocracy" in the universities and research institutes. After an excursion into professional politics, a large number of intellectuals return to the scenes of the politics of "movement", but their voices are no longer likely to be decisive; they will be lost in the noise of the struggle of social interests in the new democracy. The programme of the intelligentsia as a "political class" is not going to be realized, and after the systemic change the task of the earlier "politocracy" would again be to create a "political society" in the Tocquevillian sense of the term, between the state and society, by articulating the opinions of groups active in politics. The Democratic Charter and other new extra-parliamentary initiatives have offered an opportunity to the politically active intelligentsia to find its way back to a rôle of its own. But, to be able to perform this rôle, it has to emerge from the earlier political organizations of the "estate" type and, emerging from the prophetic rôle of the "nation's conscience", it has to become a modern social stratum. The critical intelligentsia of the post-communist society can be the advocate of democracy if it becomes democratic in its mentality and daily political routine.

Acknowledgement

Translated by Vera Gàthy.

Abbreviations of Party names

FIDESZ	Federation of Young Democrats
FKGP	Independent Smallholders' Party
KDNP	Christian Democratic People's Party
MDF	Hungarian Democratic Forum
MSZDP	Hungarian Social Democratic Party
MSZMP	Hungarian Socialist Worker's Party
MSZP	Hungarian Socialist Party
SZDSZ	Alliance of Free Democrats

References

Agócs, S. & E. Medvigy (eds) 1991. *Lakitelek, 1987. A magyarság esélyei*. Budapest: Antológia-Püski.

Arato, A. 1991. Revolution in east-central Europe: interpretations. In *Demokratikus átmenetek*, G. Szoboszlai (ed.), 112–36. Budapest: MPT.

Bihari, M. 1990. *Demokratikus út a szabadsághoz*. Budapest: Gondolat.

173

INTELLECTUALS AND DEMOCRATIZATION IN HUNGARY

Böröcz, J. 1990. A kapitalizmus építésének élcsapata. *Magyar Nemzet*, 25 October, 7.

Bozóki, A. 1993. Hungary's road to systemic change: the Opposition Roundtable. *East European Politics and Societies* 7(2), 276–308.

Bozóki, A. & É. Kovács 1991. A pártok megnyilvánulásai a sajtóban a taxisblokád idején. *Szociológiai Szemle* 1(1), 109–126.

Bruszt, L. 1990. 1989: The negotiated revolution of Hungary. *Social Research* 57, 365–87.

Csurka, I. 1992. Néhány gondolat a rendszerváltozás két esztendeje és az MDF új programja kapcsán. *Magyar Fórum* 20 August 20 9–16.

Faragó, B. 1986. *Nyugati liberális szemmel*. Paris: Magyar Füzetek Könyvei.

Farkas, Z. 1991. Állóháború. In *Magyarország politikai évkönyve*, 207–12. Budapest: Ökonómia Alapítvány – Economix Rt.

Fehér, F. & A. Heller 1992. *Kelet-Európa "dicsöséges forradalmai"*. Budapest: T-Twins.

Garton Ash, T. 1991. *A balsors édes hasznai*. Budapest: Századvég.

Gombár, C. 1983. Van-e, 's ha van, milyen a politikai tagoltság ná-lunk? In *Politika és társadalom. A Magyar Politikatudományi Társaság Evkönyve*, G. Szoboszlai (ed.), 32–66. Budapest: MPT.

Gouldner, A. 1979. *The future of intellectuals and the rise of the new class*. London: Macmillan.

Kis, J. 1992. Gondolatok a közeljövöröl. *Magyar Hírlap* 24 December, 11.

Kis, J., F. Köszeg, O. Solt 1987. Társadalmi szerzödés. *A Beszélö különkiadása*.

Kolosi, T., I. Szelényi, S. Szelényi, B. Western 1992. The making of political field in post-communist transition: dynamics of class and party in Hungarian politics, 1989–90. In *Post-communist transition: emerging pluralism in Hungary*, A. Bozóki, A. Körösényi, G. Schöpflin (eds). London: Pinter; New York: St. Martin's Press.

Konrád, G. & I. Szelényi 1979. *Intellectuals on the road to class power*. New York: Harcourt Brace Jovanovich; Brighton: Harvester.

Konrád, G. & I. Szelényi 1989. *Az értelmiség útja az osztályhatalomhoz*. Budapest: Gondolat.

Konrád, G. & I. Szelényi 1991. Intellectuals and domination in post-communist societies. In *social theory for a changing society*, P. Bourdieu & J. Coleman (eds.). Boulder: Westview Press.

Kovács, J. 1984. A reformalku sürüjében. *Valóság* 3, 30–55.

Kovács, J. 1990. Reform economics: a classification gap. *Daedalus* 27(2).

Michnik, A. 1987. A new evolutionism. In A. Michnik, *Letters from prison and other essays*. Berkeley & Los Angeles: University of California Press.

Nyírö, A. 1989. *Segédkönyv a Politikai Bizottság tanulmányozásához*. Budapest: Aula.

Pokol, B. 1992. Political culture and the intelligentsia in Hungary. Paper presented at a conference on Political Culture in Eastern Europe, Oberjoch, Germany, August 23–28.

Richter, A. 1990. *Ellenzéki Kerekasztal*. Budapest: Aula.

Róna-Tas, A. 1992. FIDESZ – Mi DESZ? Nemzedékek és pártok. In *tiszta lappal. A FIDESZ a magyar politikában, 1988–1991*, A. Bozóki (ed.). Budapest: FIDESZ.

Rupnik, J. 1979. Dissent in Poland, 1968–1978. In *Opposition in eastern Europe*, L. R. Tökés (ed.), 60–112. London: Macmillan.

Sajó, A. 1991. Round Tables in Hungary. Unpublished manuscript.

Schöpflin, G., R. Tökés, I. Völgyes 1988. Leadership change and reform in Hungary. *Problems of Communism*, August–September.

Staniszkis, J. 1991. *The dynamics of breakthrough in eastern Europe: the case of Poland*. Berkeley

REFERENCES

& Los Angeles: University of California Press.

Such, G. 1992. Christian Democrats: too meek to inherit. *East European Reporter* **5**(6), 18–19.

Sükösd, M. 1992. The media war. *East European Reporter* **5**(2), 69–72.

Szalai, E. 1990. Utelágazás. *Valóság* **32**(12), 33–52.

Szelényi, I. 1990. *Uj osztaly, allam, politika*. Budapest: Europa.

Vajda, M. 1992. *A történelem vége? Közép-Európa, 1989*. Budapest: Századvég.

Chapter 10

State and society in Poland

Mira Marody

In this chapter I focus on the way in which habitual expectations, attitudes, and patterns of action shaped during the years of the communist regime affect current developments in Poland. The concepts of state and society play an important rôle in this analysis, mainly because of the logic of the reforms now being introduced. The primary objective of these reforms is the transformation of general systemic principles, the underlying assumption being that "capitalist" institutional structures – a market economy and a democratic political system – will produce a "capitalist" society – a competitive society that should emerge as a result of the institutional changes.

The new systemic rationality can be summarized in the phrase: "as little state involvement as possible". In the economic sphere it means, first of all, the withdrawal of governmental subsidies for plants, enterprises, and agriculture and, at a later stage, privatization of the economy. In the social sphere it means giving up the idea of a "protective state". In both cases a belief in the effectiveness of an "invisible hand" has replaced the former belief in the necessity of statist interventionism. Impersonal political, economic, and social mechanisms are meant to take over those functions that under the communist regime were realized through the decisions of the state or, strictly speaking, of those representing its political and administrative authorities. The rôle of government should, therefore, be limited to the preparation of institutional structures for these mechanisms.

In other words, there is a tendency to think that now, when the communists are out of power and the necessary institutional changes have been introduced, to become a competitive society depends only on the goodwill of Poles. Such an expectation neglects the fact that communism was not only a specific type of political regime but also a peculiar type of social system that introduced its own institutional structures in all spheres of social life. They

SOCIAL HABITS

have been shaping social practice and social experience since the late 1940s. Habitual ways of coping with social reality that emerged as a result of this experience have been internalized deeply enough to become a natural and obvious mode of being for individuals. In collision with a new systemic rationality they may, therefore, produce results quite different from those assumed by reformers. In this sense, the knowledge of social habits shaped over the years of the communist system may prove to be of the utmost importance in our understanding of current developments.

Social habits

The most essential factor in forming social practice and its related expectations of the state was that at the beginning of the post-war period, Polish society was furnished with a system of institutions and principles of functioning that were not a natural result of social processes. Rather, they were designed according to a doctrinaire vision of a perfect society. The communist society intended to be the embodiment of all the fundamental ideals of humanity – equality, justice, freedom, abolition of exploitation, respect for human dignity, and total fulfilment of social needs. The blueprint for such a society was to legitimize the communist regime, and the party, holding all power in its hands, became the main executor and guardian of that design. The requirements imposed upon society were, over time, limited to only one: that it should not disturb the work of implementing the Design (Marody 1991b).

Thus, the peculiar political contract binding the state and the society was based on a division of rôles according to which the people were meant to profit from the goodness of the system thus created while leaving all the executive decisions to the prerogatives of the authorities representing the state. Narojek (1986) calls this a "nationalization of the initiative of social actions", by which he means the communist party's assuming complete, unshared control of social life. Politics, perceived as an exclusive domain of the authorities, became a main tool for running society (Marody 1990).

When speaking about a contract, I do not mean that the division of rôles was accepted willingly on the part of society. Rather, it was imposed on it by the communist regime during years of painful social training. The sphere of politics was always most diligently guarded and controlled by the authorities, and any attempts by "unauthorized" persons to get into it were most speedily and severely punished. It made politics into a kind of negatively sacred area whose influence radiated upon all spheres of social life, but the borders of which were crossed rarely, reluctantly, and only in situations of extreme necessity.

Nevertheless, the expulsion of society from the sphere of politics was not only achieved by sheer physical coercion. There was also a kind of implicit consensus and hidden agreement binding both sides of the rulers–ruled relation. The terms of the agreement contained the promise of a better life, which was to be created *by* the authorities *for* society (Marody 1987).

The results of sociological surveys conducted in Poland in the 1980s clearly show that the complaint of "unfulfilled promises" was the reason most often given for lack of obedience to the state powers. In the popular perception this was the main cause of social disorders, far more important than, say, frustration with the incompetence and corruption of the administration, or its repressiveness (Marody et al. 1981; Rychard & Szymanderski 1986).

Although the initial division of rôles had at its roots a vision of an ideal system, it formed social practice in quite a real way for the next 45 years. Its consequence was the emergence of certain habitual beliefs, attitudes, and expectations that began to influence people's behaviour not only in the sphere of politics but also in other spheres of social life. Three of them seem of particular importance when we try to analyse *present* conditions of post-communist societies.

The first is a set of particular expectations of the state and, representing it, the authorities. During the whole period of the communist regime, the state was identified with politics, which was above all a source of threat to the average person. It was a direct threat that struck at those who, purposefully or unknowingly, crossed its borders. It was also an indirect threat in that political decisions of the authorities regulating all manifestations of social life were subordinated to a rationality different from that of the average person and, as such, they introduced an element of unpredictability and uncertainty into a social reality to which people had somehow grown accustomed.

On the other hand, politics during this entire period was also a source of hope: a hope for a better life, which would be delivered by the authorities to society; a hope that was diminishing under the experience of everyday life, but re-emerging with amplified strength every time there was a change of governing personalities; a hope that not only turned politics into the fundamental tool for the distribution of all social goods but also their fundamental source. In this sense, the politics of the state took the place in social consciousness of economics as the basis of social affluence.

If in the communist system, politics was, although negatively, neverthe-

SOCIAL HABITS

less the sacred area, then people's attitudes to it most closely resembled the disposition of the disciples of the cargo cult.[1] In both cases, we are dealing with expectations of gifts from outside the people's world, controlled by powers whose behaviour is capricious and fear-instilling. In both cases, there is an emphasis on just distribution and also an identical lack of interest in the processes necessary for the creation of the desired goods or states of social reality. First, the basic category on which the behaviour in the sacred area is based is, in both cases, the category of faith: a faith in ancestors who are sending ships and planes with cargoes or, correspondingly, a faith in political leaders promising quick implementation of "normal life".

Secondly, the division into those "authorized" to make decisions concerning social life and those without any such right resulted in a re-definition of basic dimensions of social space in which individuals acted. The social versus individual distinction predominant in Western societies was replaced with the public versus private one in the societies of real socialism.

Many authors have pointed to the crucial importance that the division into "authorities" and the "society", "them" and "us", played in the countries of the former communist bloc. It was perceived as the main dimension of social integration and has promoted the development of negative solidarity, the base for which was a general social interest put against the "selfish" interests of those in power. We must remember, however, that this division was far from precise and was difficult to make in everyday life. On the one hand, in the system in which every job position was an element of the multidimensional structure of the state, everybody became involved to a greater or lesser degree in the implementation of the communist design. On the other hand, the rationality of the system was so different from the everyday rationality of individuals (Marody 1991b) that people had to find a way to combine them. The public versus private distinction was a solution to the problem.

At first the distinction marked a difference between two spheres of social life, one controlled by the communist state and the other in which individuals could make their own decisions. As functionaries of the state, citizens were expected to act according to the systemic rationality that was aimed at realization of the Design, whereas in their private activity they could have goals different than the ultimate goal of the system. However, with the passage of time, the separation of public and private rôles resulted in the emergence of two separate sets of behavioural attitudes, neither of which had much in common with the rationality of the Design (Marody 1988).

In general, the attitudes connected with public rôles can be described as governed by the principle of minimizing one's effort. Because its rationality was different, acting in a public rôle was perceived as hazardous, so the most popular strategy connected it with an attempt to avoid responsibility by waiting for the decisions of persons higher in official ranks. "Public"-related attitudes had a distinct defensive character; they were conducive to formulating "negative" goals of activity such as: not to suffer losses, not to expose oneself to danger, not to provoke undesirable effects, not to let others succeed. "Private"-related attitudes had, on the other hand, an expansive character; actions were motivated by the hope of success, ambition, and curiosity, as well as greed. For "public" attitudes the attitude of "learned helplessness" was most characteristic, whereas for "private" ones it was the readiness to take risks.

Thus, the division of rôles on the "macro" level had as its counterpart the division into "public" and "private" standards, which governed individual activity on the "micro" level. Acting "for the system" became axiologically separated from acting "within the system". The system and, representing it, the state, was perceived as alien, "not mine", a source of threat rather than a guarantor of rules that could be used to defend one's rights. Retreat into private life was, in a sense, a natural consequence.

Last but not least, the public versus private distinction that arose from the initial division of rôles has changed not only the individual behaviour but also the patterns according to which it was "socialized". By "socialized" I mean here widespread patterns of individuals' co-operation or the ways through which common, supra-individual goals, rules, and interests are being established among the population. There were two such basic patterns that emerged as a result of confrontation of human aspiration and needs with the systemic changes introduced by the communist regime.

The first arose from adaptation processes. It copied the family matrix as the basic standard for co-operation of individuals on all levels of social reality. Personal ties and personal loyalties became the basis on which common goals and interests were established. It divided the society into small, informal groups fighting against each other for access to the resources of the state. It involved "ethical dualism", which allowed individuals to suspend moral norms in contacts with members of out-groups and to consider the claims of such groups as illegitimate and threatening to the well-being of one's own group.

The second pattern of socializing individuals' behaviour arose from social protests. It generated the feeling of unity and solidarity in response to threats perceived as external. The society-at-large, very often identified with the nation, became the basic reference group, and the state, or rather its leaders, the main enemy. Individuals unified in an effort to dismiss the threat, suspended their everyday goals and ways of behaviour. The place of those goals was taken over by a general social interest identified with an ideal vision of "normal life". Social behaviour was meant to be governed by basic norms of human solidarity, appealing to moral rather than legal obligations.

The first pattern of socializing transformed the society into an aggregate of primary informal groups, whereas the second resulted in a short-term feeling of unity that disintegrated in a collision with the reality of everyday life. Both undermined the existence of the state as an entity subordinating the activity of individuals to the generally observed norms and rules of behaviour. The first did so by attempts at "re-privatizing" them, the second by trying to replace them with moral norms. Both also eliminated the need for individuals to create new institutions of social life. The first did so by directing people's attention to the possibilities of individual and collective "setting oneself up" in the existing institutional order, the second by restricting their political activity to the search for better leaders, promising the quick implementation of "normal life".

To summarize the habitual expectations, attitudes, and beliefs of Polish society towards the state, it can be said that the "to obey or to rebel" alternative created the basic pattern of popular reactions in this area, developed under the communist regime. Neither part of this alternative left room for an autonomous functioning of the society; both made social behaviour of individuals dependent, directly or indirectly, on the decisions of the state.

The transition to what?

All the above-described expectations, attitudes, and beliefs became internalized deeply enough to survive the change of political system (Marody 1991a). Their persistence is now additionally reinforced by structural characteristics of Polish society that make difficult the spontaneous emergence of alternative democratic patterns of social behaviour.

First of all, the idea of democratic competition presupposes the existence of social groups whose different interests influence the choice between alternative goals and ways of social development. I would stress here the word "social", which means that group interests should be a derivative of social structure, with the latter reflecting the basic mechanisms of societal differentiation. In the case of post-communist Poland, the problem, however, is that all significant social groups owe their existence to the policies of the former communist state and do not have any "objective" interests independent of the state, be it communist or post-communist (Ost 1990; Mokrzycki 1992). The economic relations of each social group with the rest of the society were and still are mediated by the state, and their interests can be defined only *vis-à-vis* state policy and not *vis-à-vis* one another. Until now, even the interests of the emerging group of private businessmen depend mostly on state decisions; private enterprises are flourishing mainly in those areas where state regulations are so imprecise that they allow entrepreneurs to make money without engaging in productive activity.

The conflicting character of present social interests in Poland stems from the fact that each group competes with all others for access to social resources distributed by the state and not from competing programmes of how to produce these resources, which they could negotiate among themselves. Under such circumstances, the state and the authorities representing it are still perceived as the only group responsible for goals and ways of social development, and this reinforces the old division into those who take part in politics and those who do not (Marody 1991a).

The informal, spontaneous ways of socializing individuals' behaviour that have been formed in Polish society during the years of coping with social reality controlled by the communist regime, also seem a poor basis for the emergence of groups able to articulate their interests in social terms, i.e. in terms of common characteristics of individuals' social positions. Groups formed as a result of adaptation processes were based on personal ties and loyalties rather than on structural characteristics connected with social differentiation of interests. They reflected situational alliances between individuals occupying different social positions, and were oriented towards the "re-privatization" of the part of the state's power, rules, and/or resources that was controlled by the particular members of a group. In the case of the second pattern of socializing, which arose from social protests, the society-at-large became the main group of reference. The interests of individuals were diluted in a general societal interest defined in terms of abstract values.

Both patterns prevent the emergence of groups based on *social* differentiation of individual interests. The first does so by facilitating the emergence of common interests across the social structure and at the same time by constraining them to local groups, the second by subordinating individual and group interests to a general societal interest. In the first case, group interests are differentiated but cease to be "social", in the second case they are "social" but cease to be differentiated. Both patterns of socializing also pro-

THE TRANSITION TO WHAT?

mote the definition of individual interests *vis-à-vis* the state. The first does so by making people sensitive to all the opportunities created by state regulations that allow a "transfer" of the state's assets for the individual or group benefit, the second by defining societal interests in opposition to an "unjust" state's policy.

The existence of informal ways of socializing individuals' behaviour not only prevents the emergence of groups able to articulate their interests in terms of social structure but also reinforces the habitual division into "public" and "private" spheres of action, with the latter expanding to an enormous degree. What is not controlled by the state – and according to the new rationality almost nothing is – becomes "private" and is regulated by rules and norms specific to a given informal group. This phenomenon strongly affects chances for the emergence of other characteristics of democratic order.

The prospects for a successfully functioning democratic society are not determined only by the existence of social groups able to define their interests independently of the state. A democratic order requires compliance on the part of all significant interest groups to both the institutional arrangements regulating the negotiation of conflicting interests and the outcomes produced within this regulated competition. As many authors have pointed out, the essential difference between the authoritarian and democratic systems is that the former are characterized by uncertain institutions and (at least for strategic groups) certain outcomes, whereas the latter are based on the certainty of political rules and uncertainty of political outcomes (Bounce 1990; Bielasiak 1992). Thus, the successful functioning of a democratic system requires, on the one hand, the recognition of formal-legal procedures as the only basis for resolving social conflicts and, on the other, the readiness of all significant social groups to engage in give-and-take interactions, the outcomes of which are not known in advance. Both conditions are in opposition to the social habits shaped in Polish society during the 45 years of the communist regime.

There is still a strong belief that the state and the authorities representing it are in power to change any institutional decision that opposes a commonsense understanding of justice, and that using this power depends only on their goodwill. Moreover, in Polish society the popular understanding of justice is strongly connected with an orientation towards "consensus and interpersonal harmony", "law and order" (Jasinska-Kania 1988). One can expect, therefore, that even with established institutional arrangements (the conditions for which have not been yet accomplished in Poland), formal decisions unfavourable to strategic groups may result in social protest. Of course, social protests take place in Western democracies, too; what makes them particularly important in the Polish case is that they are perceived here as the only feasible form of popular participation in policy-making and the "final" argument in situations of social conflict.

Prospects for the recognition of the uncertainty of institutional outcomes as a natural element of democratic competition also seem rather slight. First of all, the "natural" social strategy under the communist regime was "take-and-keep" rather than "give-and-take". The defensive character of public-oriented attitudes resulted in perceiving others as rivals and not partners in bargaining processes. The orientation to the certainty of institutional outcomes was also facilitated by the development of the Solidarity movement, in both its legal and illegal phases; one should remember that the unity of Polish society formed in the 1980s was, after all, based on the premise that "society as a whole" deserves a better or "normal" life. This has been further reinforced by the rhetoric of post-communist political elites, who have appealed and still do to popular consensus and moral rather than interest-based aspirations of the society. It is not surprising, therefore, that growing financial differentiation of the population is now perceived more as a betrayal of "Solidarity" ideals than as a natural consequence of economic mechanisms triggered by institutional reform. It means, however, that chances for the recognition of uncertainty of outcomes as a natural characteristic of economic political processes are still very low, whereas the risk of social protests is constantly increasing.

To sum up this line of argument, I would say that although Poles are competing all the time and in all spheres of social life, they can hardly be described as part of a democratic, competitive society. Both their patterns of socializing individual behaviour as well as habitual expectations, attitudes, and beliefs make them into competitors for a share of the pie distributed by the state. Disintegrated, fixed on its expectations and interests shaped by the former statist system, and living on the dream of a strong leader who would resolve all the problems accumulated over the years of communist and post-communist experiments, Polish society might seem well prepared for an authoritarian dictatorship.

In any case, the temptation of an authoritarian solution is quite strong on the side of the new political elite. At least some of its leaders, confronted, on the one hand, with social demands that cannot be satisfied because of the desperate condition of the post-communist economy, and on the other, with the necessity to fight against other parties for survival on the political scene,

THE TRANSITION TO WHAT?

would see in some authoritarian measures a means of disciplining both society and their own political rivals.

However, the same social habits that are now postponing the transition to a liberal democracy also make prospects for the introduction of an authoritarian model rather remote. None of the political parties is able to mobilize the support of a significant social group that would allow it to take over and to keep state power for any length of time. With the communist economy already collapsed and the market economy not yet established, they can offer their potential supporters only hope for the future and some substitute satisfactions for the vast economic and psychological hardships; and that is not enough for people who are longing for actual solutions to their present concrete problems.

We can, therefore, expect a continuation of the present political situation that resembles neither a democratic nor an authoritarian model. Political declarations apart, this situation is strongly conditioned by the policy of a state that seems now to be being shaped by two opposing tendencies. The first arises from a dogmatic attitude towards liberal economic principles adopted by present political elites and takes the form of a belief that the state should not influence processes of social self-organization and that society itself is able to generate such institutions as it needs. The second tendency arises from habitual expectations of the society towards the state. It takes the form of constant social demands, the basis for which is the belief that nobody but the state is responsible for the well-being of its citizens. Both partners of the state–society relation ascribe to each other competences and possibilities that do not actually exist.

Nevertheless, the first tendency relieves the government of the necessity to outline any programme for social reconstruction; the existence of the second forces it at least to satisfy the demands of some groups. In practice, state funds are being intercepted by those whose protests might be more dangerous for systemic stability and those with higher institutional competence, instead of being used as the tool for structural reforms. Thus, the attempt to reconcile a liberal doctrine with political necessities leads, paradoxically, to reinforcing those habits that have developed under the conditions of quite contrary systemic rationality.

The process of systemic transformation aimed at establishing a liberal democratic order that started in June 1989 in Poland is irreversible. That does not mean, however, that it is simple, easy, and dependent only on institutional changes. The functioning of society as a *system* is, after all, a complex effect of individuals' everyday activity, aimed not so much at the crea-

185

STATE AND SOCIETY IN POLAND

tion of a new social order as at creating a decent life for themselves and their families. Since this activity is strongly influenced by habitual expectations, dispositions, and perceptions that are regarded as obvious and natural, and are, therefore, out of the individuals' control, it may produce social results quite different from those assumed by the reformers. Being aware of such a possibility is the necessary (although still not the sufficient) condition for being able to prevent it.

Note

1. Cargo cult is a religious movement in the southwest Pacific islands that holds that the spirits of ancestors will return and bring with them large cargoes of modern goods for distribution among its adherents. I borrow this comparison from Berger (1986), who used it in relation to the rôle that modernization ideology plays in third world countries.

References

Berger, P. L. 1986. Trzeci swiat jako idea religijna. *Pismo Literacko-Artystyczne* 6–7.

Bielasiak, J. 1992. The dilemma of political interests in post-communist transition. In *Escape from socialism: the Polish route*, W. D. Connor & P. Ploszajski (eds), 199–216. Warsaw: IFiS.

Bounce, V. 1990. The struggle for liberal democracy in eastern Europe. *World Policy Journal* 7, 395–430.

Jasinska-Kania, A. 1988. *Osobowosc, orientacje moralne i postawy polityczne*. Warsaw: IS UW.

Marody, M., J. Kolbowski, C. Labanowska, K. Nowak, A. Tyszkiewicz 1981. *Polacy 1980*. Warsaw: IS UW.

Marody, M. 1987. Social stability and the concept of collective sense. In *Crisis and transition: Polish society in the 1980s*, J. Koralewicz, I. Bialecki, M. Watson (eds), 130–58. Oxford: Berg.

Marody, M. 1988. Antinomies of collective subconsciousness. *Social Research* **55**(1–2), 97–110.

Marody, M. 1990. Perception of politics in Polish society. *Social Research* **57**, 257–74.

Marody, M. 1991a. New possibilities and old habits. *Sysyphus* **7**, 33–40.

Marody, M. 1991b. From social idea to real world. In *Constructing capitalism*, K. Poznanski (ed.). Boulder & Oxford: Westview Press.

Mokrzycki, E. 1992. The legacy of real socialism, group interests, and search for a new utopia. In *Escape from socialism. the Polish route*, W. D. Connor & P. Ploszajski (eds). Warwas: IFiS.

Narojek, W. 1986. *Perspektywy pluralizmu w upanstwowionym spoleczenstwie*. Unpublished manuscript. Warsaw.

REFERENCES

Ost, D. 1990. Interests and politics in post-communist society: problems in the transition in eastern Europe. Paper presented at Annual Meeting of the American Political Science Association, San Francisco.

Rychard, A. & J. Szymanderski 1986. Kryzys w perspektywie legitymizacji. In *Polacy '84. Dynamika konfliktu i konsensusu*, W. Adamski & A. Rychard (eds), 123–47. Warsaw: IFiS PAN.

Chapter 11

Some thoughts on trust, collective identity, and the transition from state socialism

Adam Seligman

General perspectives on trust in society

The existence of trust is an essential component of all human relationships. As such it has found a place as one of the fundamental concepts of sociological analysis; from the 19th century and the theoretical insights of Emile Durkheim on the existence of a "pre-contractual" element in all social arrangements onwards, the importance of trust to the existence of society has been almost universally recognized.

On the most general and abstract level it can be stated that the need for enduring, stable, and universally recognized structures of trust is rooted in the fundamental indeterminacy of social interaction. This indeterminacy, between social actors, between social actors and their goals, and between social actors and resources, results in a basic unpredictability in social life, notwithstanding the universality of human interdependence.[1] Consequently, any long-range attempt at constructing a social order and continuity of social frameworks of interaction must be predicated on the development of stable relations of mutual trust between social actors. Clearly, however, different ways of organizing society (on the macrosociological level) will bring in their wake different ways of establishing trust in society.

In this context one of the major arenas where the study of trust – on the interpersonal as well as institutional level – has been central, has been in the study of modernization.[2] Here, studies in the 1950s and 1960s concentrated on the establishment of new bases of trust in society, centring on new terms of solidarity, of citizenship and what were in fact new parameters defining the boundaries of trust in modernizing social structures.

This focus on the changing nature of trust in modernizing societies is indeed not surprising given the extraordinary importance of a universal ba-

GENERAL PERSPECTIVES ON TRUST IN SOCIETY

sis of trust in modern, democratic societies. The emphasis in modern societies on consensus, the ideology of pragmatism, problem-solving and technocratic expertise as well as conflict management (as opposed to ideological fission) are all founded on an image of society based on interconnected networks of trust – between citizens, families, voluntary organizations, religious denominations, civic associations, and the like.[3] Similarly the very "legitimation" of modern societies is founded on the "trust" of authority and of governments as generalizations of trust on the primary, interpersonal level. In fact the primary vehicles of socialization, whether they be the educational system or the mass media, are oriented to the continuing inculcation of this value and what is in fact an "ideology" of trust in society. Finally, and perhaps most importantly, the definitions of trust in Western, industrialized and "modern" societies are rooted in the idea of the individual as final repository of rights and values. In these societies, it is the individual social actor, the citizen of the nation-state, and not any collectively defined primordial or corporate entity, who is seen as the foundation of the social order and around whom the terms of social trust are oriented.

On the institutional level the workings of trust in society can be viewed as limitations placed on the free exchange of resources. Such limitations include the very definition of public goods (those that if provided to one member of the collective must be provided to all), or the public distribution of private goods.[4] In this reading, such phenomena as welfare entitlements or progressive income tax are limitations placed on the free exchange of goods based on the overall definitions of trust and solidarity in society, definitions that in modern societies (and as Durkheim noted 100 years ago) are based on the idea of the autonomous individual as the centre and moral foundation of the social order. The derivatives of this idea in terms of the equality of citizens and the extension of this equality in different realms that require such limitations should be clear from the continued struggles over the definition (and redefinition) of the terms of "social citizenship", i.e. social entitlements, in western European and north Atlantic societies, from the early decades of this century until today.[5]

In this context the problem of trust in east central Europe takes on a special dimension. Here, the reigning definitions of individual identity are still to a large extent collective and rooted in the solidarity of particular ethnic or religious groups. What is lacking is precisely those ideas of individual autonomy and integrity – freed from ascriptive criteria – upon which civic selfhood and citizenship (in its formal, institutional, and universal guise) is, in the West, seen to rest, and around which "modern" definitions of trust are oriented.

189

TRUST, IDENTITY, AND TRANSITION FROM STATE SOCIALISM

Here, interpersonal trust, as well as trust in the formal, institutional structures of society, is still characterized by markedly "pre-modern", *gemeinschaftlich* criteria. The basic networks of trust are woven around ethnic relations, local communities, shared religious faith, and traditions. Not surprisingly, it has often been remarked upon that in east central Europe the dividing line between private and public life is more salient than in the West. This insight – into what is essentially the status of civility in east central Europe – is immediately connected to the foundations of trust in society, to the most basic terms of interpersonal solidarity and modes of communication. Civility, the mutual recognition of each individual's innate human dignity and membership in the political community is, as Edward Shils has argued, at the heart of civil society and, in his words "at bottom the collective consciousness of civil society". This very Durkheimian formula presumes, however, the (equally Durkheimian) idea of pre-contractual trust, which in modern, democratic societies is based on the liberal idea of the moral individual freed from particular, communal identities and what we may term ethical solidarities.

Trust in state-socialist societies

It is within this broad theoretical context that we must situate the contemporary terms of trust existing in those east central European societies now in the middle of a crucial transition from state socialism to a market-regulated and democratic regime. This transition, as is often noted, affects all elements of social life, not least the nature of trust, both between individuals as well as between individuals and the major institutions in society. More concretely, the transition to a market economy implies a fundamental reorientation of those structural arenas where trust is essential for the workings of the social order. One of the primary areas where this can be seen is in the reorganization of the public and private realms. The emergence of a market economy implies a redefinition of the terms of public and private realms and of the relative rôle of each in the constitution of new "ground-rules" for social interaction (as for instance in the agreed-upon rules of distributive justice). On an abstract and institutional level these can be subsumed under three central headings:
- The re-structuring of access to major markets
- The construction of new definitions of public goods
- New rules and definitions for the public redistribution of private goods.
  A reorientation of the nature of trust in society is a central component of

THE HISTORICAL BACKGROUND

the restructuring of these spheres in line with the workings of a market economy. We must furthermore recall that under state socialism there existed an historically unique configuration of trust characterized by:

- An almost total lack of trust on the general societal (that is to say institutional) level concomitant with closely articulated networks of trust on the interpersonal level; in more formal terms, there was a failure to generalize trust from the particular to the social level
- The continuation of structures of trust based on what may be described as a neo-feudal heritage of patron-client relationships; these existed, however, without the necessary legitimizing ideology
- The existence of an almost schizophrenic situation in times of shortages where conflicting interests (the need to maximize resources but also the need for others to accomplish this) led to a constantly unfolding dialectic of trust and mistrust; the best example is perhaps the perennial housing shortage and the strategies of what were called in Hungarian "death contracts", where trust and mistrust were interwoven on a personal and pathological level
- A basic grid through which interpersonal trust could be articulated based on an absolute dichotomy between "us" and "them", between the citizens of the country on the one hand and the party bureaucracy on the other.

It must however be added that in the pre-transition era there already existed some degree of generalized trust (on the societal level) that took different forms in different eastern-central European countries. In this context it would be useful to think of the rôle of the media in Hungary, of the Catholic Church in Poland, and of outstanding cultural elites or charismatic personalities in Czechoslovakia. All cases present examples of the continuity of culturally traditional forms of generalized trust that were not totally destroyed during the period of state socialism. In all three cases during the mid-1980s, culturally specific and politically autonomous modes of generalized trust, rooted in each country's pre-state-socialist political culture, re-emerged with a new saliency and came to play a critical rôle in the transition to a democratic polity and market-oriented economy.

The historical background

In spite of such loci of trust, contemporary east central European societies are characterized by a general lack of trust in the public sphere. The sources of the phenomenon lie not only in the anomalies of state socialism but, perhaps more importantly, in the continuity of pre-capitalist forms of social organization that characterized these societies into the 20th century. Indeed, to some extent, the problems of constructing in these countries general forms of social trust that would cut across the existence of strong ethnic solidarities and identities were already recognized at the end of the First World War with the National Minorities Treaty. This, we recall, was meant to guarantee full protection under law, full legal and civil citizenship to those ethnic minorities included in the "successor states" formed with the break-up of the Austro-Hungarian empire.

The historical trajectory of nation-building and state formation, which was markedly different from that of western Europe, is thus of major importance to any understanding of the unique structuring of trust in contemporary east central Europe. Thus, for example, the long, drawn-out process of state-making and nation-building in western Europe was characterized by the only gradual integration of different *ethnicity* into one national identity, each characterized by its own territory, economy, legal, educational and cultural systems, and historical memories. Central to this process were linguistic assimilation, social mobilization and, at a much later date, mass education and the effects of mass media.[6] In this process, as Daniel Lerner noted more than 30 years ago, the formation of "psychologically mobile personalities" enabled the establishment of "empathy" between individuals of different ethnic and religious traditions (Lerner 1985). In terms of our analysis, this empathy rested on the replacement of traditional criteria of solidarity and collective membership and participation with the "modern" values of individual rights, universal citizenship and the idea of the morally autonomous person upon which modern notions of social trust are based.

What took place, to different extents in the different countries of western Europe, was (a) the crystallization of a national identity out of different ethnic groups (sometimes, as in England, France, and Spain, around an ethnic core group and sometimes, as, for example, in Greece or Switzerland, without such core groups), and (b) the formalization and universalization of the criteria for membership and participation within this national entity on the principles of citizenship and mass participation in the social and political life of the nation (Smith 1986, 228–63). In eastern and east central Europe the situation was very different.

There, and in a marked reversal of the historical development of Western societies, the nation-state (or more precisely, the administrative-bureaucratic structures of state rule) emerged, after the First World War, before the

192

THE HISTORICAL BACKGROUND

nation itself. Contributing to this was the oft-noted "gentry" character of political elites who, in the 19th century, while leading the nationalist movements in east central Europe, did not identify national independence with more than their own corporate interests. Social reforms were minimal, and the democratic component of national movements was submerged in the corporate interests of the political elite. Indeed, the very ethnic fragmentation of these societies led to the view that the state itself produces national sentiment and not the other way around. By the mid-19th century all of the ruling elites agreed that the nation stemmed from the state, and the question was solely about the state's rôle as a cultural, administrative or coercive producer of nationalism (Janos 1982, 69). Thus, the type of mass mobilization around social reforms that characterized Western nationalism and, indeed, united diverse communities into one national identity, did not occur.

Without any prior crystallization of national identities, the period of nation-state formation proper (following the First World War) saw the establishment of new states that were either multinational or contained significant national minorities. The disastrous results of this situation were complicated by the appeal of ruling elites in the inter-war years to an ideology of national exclusion in a bid to retain legitimacy. Even in Czechoslovakia, non-Czechs were not fully integrated into the civil polity, and consequently viewed it with suspicion (Schöpflin 1990, 71).

Consequently, and to quote Gyorgy Csepeli, "the concept of 'the nation' came before the establishment of the proper national institutions and the emerging national ideology therefore had to refer more actively to elements of the ethnocentric heritage such as descent, cultural values and norms" (1991, 328). The "prisonhouse of nations", in east central Europe as well as in Russia, was caught first under protracted absolutist regimes and then under semi-autocratic or dictatorial regimes rooted in one ethnic majority. They never emerged in national frameworks of freely associating citizens. What emerged in their stead was the continuity of ethnic identities and solidarities into the 20th century, outlasting not only the Hapsburgs, Romanoffs, and Hohenzollerns, but state socialism as well.

The implications of this pattern of development for the problem of social trust in contemporary east central Europe should be clear. The necessary "pre-conditions" for modern forms of social trust based on the autonomous individual (freed from communal identities) as moral agent cannot be taken for granted. Rather, the historical development of this region has seen the continued existence of strong ethnic and group solidarities that have continu-

193

TRUST, IDENTITY, AND TRANSITION FROM STATE SOCIALISM

ally thwarted the emergence of those legal, economic and moral individual identities upon which modern, democratic forms of social trust are founded.

In the most general of terms, the existence of the individual social actor freed from ascriptive identities, as at the foundation of Western democratic models of social trust, was itself based on the two-fold historical moment of (a) national integration and (b) the universalization of citizenship within the nation-state. In east central Europe, the former process took place only in a partial and mediated manner. The latter – the universalization of citizenship – was never realized and achieved only a caricature of itself under state socialism, which Elemer Hankiss (1989) has appropriately termed "negative modernity". Indeed, as the crises of state-socialist ideology deepened, as "negative modernity" turned in on itself, the "bureaucratic nationalism" of state-socialist regimes was transformed as the older national identities and solidarities re-emerged, with a saliency we are only now beginning to appreciate (Banac 1990).

Preliminary evidence on trust in contemporary Hungary

The implications of this form of historical development for the emergence of modern, Western, and democratic ideas of trust and mutual co-operation between social actors, cutting across local, particular and ethnic solidarities, are of great importance. It is difficult to isolate concrete information on such ideas and on the existence of trust beyond the local, private and particular realm, but one possible source is the European Values Survey, conducted in 1981 and 1990 in 12 European countries. Unfortunately, we have a representative sample from only one east central European country – Hungary. Hungary is, however, as a result of the legacy of Kádár's "goulash communism" and the workings of the "second economy", seen as the most Western and market-oriented of the east central European countries, both today and over the past two decades. It should therefore be the most similar case to those of the West.

Responses to the questions most relevant to the issue of trust and its generalization and abstraction are presented in Tables 11.1–11.3.[7]

Table 11.1 provides an important longitudinal view (from 1982 to 1990) of trust in precisely those civic institutions, trade unions, media, even parliament, that we identity with the workings of modern democratic polities.[8] There is in fact a decline in trust in such institutions over the decade of the 1980s. We see here that the most "trusted" institutions of national life are not

194

Table 11.1 Trust in institutions (percentages).

How much do you trust . . .	very much		rather much		not very much		not at all		don't know		no answer	
	1982	1990	1982	1990	1982	1990	1982	1990	1982	1990	1982	1990
trade unions	20.1	6.0	36.1	22.3	19.7	38.4	7.8	25.6	–	6.7	16.3	1.1
parliament	49.0	8.3	35.4	35.9	6.1	36.5	1.2	13.5	–	4.8	8.3	0.9
legal system	39.4	13.6	44.9	40.3	9.0	32.0	1.8	8.9	–	4.3	4.8	0.9
press, mass media	28.5	6.8	50.5	35.6	16.3	42.3	1.9	10.4	–	3.6	2.8	1.1
church	14.8	23.0	22.0	26.2	25.9	29.2	33.9	17.4	–	3.3	3.3	0.8
public administration	27.6	8.5	42.3	38.7	19.7	38.4	4.8	8.0	–	5.2	5.5	1.2
educational system	28.9	13.5	48.9	41.0	14.2	32.7	2.1	7.7	–	4.1	5.9	1.0

Sample: 1982 N = 1226–1423; 1990 N = 1301–1314.

Source: European Values Surveys 1982 and 1990. Hungarian Academy of Science, Institute of Sociology.

TRUST, IDENTITY, AND TRANSITION FROM STATE SOCIALISM

Table 11.2 Trust in certain social groups in Hungary in 1990 (percentages).

	Totally	A certain amount	Yes/no	Not much	Not at all	Don't know /no answer
How much do you trust . . .?						
your family	89.5	5.6	2.8	0.5	0.4	1.2
Hungarian people	23.0	45.8	20.4	8.7	1.1	1.0
Gypsies	2.3	10.8	14.6	28.3	42.4	1.6
Slovaks	6.2	14.9	30.5	18.3	11.3	18.9
Romanians	3.9	10.8	26.1	23.2	22.2	13.8
Jews	13.9	23.6	31.1	11.3	7.7	12.5
Swabs	11.8	22.7	32.2	10.5	7.4	15.5

N = 1301–1314

Source: European Values Survey 1990. Data set of the Hungarian Academy of Science Institute of Sociology.

Table 11.3 Individualism and privatism in ten European countries in 1982 (percentages).

	GB	IRL	F	B	WG	NL	S	DK	I	HU
You may trust people	43	40	22	25	26	38	32	46	25	32
There is nothing I would sacrifice myself for, outside my family	60	55	64	61	53	54	38	49	45	85
Parents have their own lives: they should not sacrifice themselves for their children	18	15	17	21	28	15	13	39	27	44
Child-rearing principles:										
– respect for other people	62	56	59	45	52	53	44	58	43	31
– loyalty, faithfulness	36	19	36	23	22	24	29	24	43	10
With whom do you prefer to spend your leisure time?										
– alone	11	12	10	9	8	18	7	8	20	10
– with your family	48	39	47	51	52	49	53	53	36	72
– with friends	27	27	22	18	27	15	23	12	29	10
– going out, seeing people	11	12	8	7	5	12	4	4	8	3

Note: All samples were representative national samples

Source: European Value Systems Study 1982.

GB = Great Britain; IRL = Ireland; F = France; B = Belgium; WG = West Germany; NL = Netherlands; S = Spain; DK = Denmark; I = Italy; HU = Hungary.

PRELIMINARY EVIDENCE ON TRUST IN CONTEMPORARY HUNGARY

those based on the general and universal criteria of citizenship but rather those based on more particular identities, the Church and the family. Table 11.2 provides data collected in Hungary in the 1990 Survey on the existence of "trust" in different ethnic and national minorities. Table 11.3 presents comparative results on the 1982 Survey on trust in different countries.[9]

The general picture that emerges from these tables is the failure both in absolute and, more importantly, in comparative terms, of extended, abstract, or generalized trust in society and its institutions. Rather, we find the continuing articulation of trust along more private and restricted lines.[10]

These findings in the case of Hungary can be supplemented by the social-psychological research carried out by Gyorgy Csepeli on the terms and definitions of Hungarian national identity. Csepeli distinguished between what he termed *Gesellschaft* and *Gemeinschaft* types of national identity. In the *Gesellschaft* pattern, national identity is perceived as membership in a democratic political community and, in the *Gemeinschaft* pattern, by the presence of attitudes and beliefs turning on the idea of ethnic purity and distinctiveness, folklore and cultural traditions (Csepeli 1991, 334–8). When Csepeli correlated these types of national identity with religious affiliations, he found that "modern" or at least "liberal" definitions of the political community and the nation were articulated by one culturally salient minority – Jews – while members of other religious groups maintain more *gemeinschaftlich*, or premodern, but not liberal-individualist definitions of the political community.

These survey results and the corresponding questions they raise as to the existence of the necessary preconditions for any civil society are reinforced by the research carried out by Andras Sajó on rights-awareness in Hungary (Sajó 1989, 27–38). What Sajó found, in a study of 1650 respondents carried out between December 1986 and January 1987, was a very "limited, accidental, cursory and contradictory" awareness of rights, an awareness, moreover, that interpreted rights in a pragmatic manner, where "arguments on human dignity are scarce and because of prejudice some people are not willing to extend human dignity to all members of the society", where "submissiveness and primitive rebellion work hand in hand without questioning seriously the authoritarian legitimation of public administration" and where "there is little respect among the citizens towards each other" (ibid., 50). Again, what is lacking are precisely those universal notions of human dignity and moral individualism, rooted in the natural law tradition, that serve as the inclusive basis of citizenship, of membership and participation in the national community, and without which generalized, institutionalized channels of trust in society cannot properly take root.

TRUST, IDENTITY, AND TRANSITION FROM STATE SOCIALISM

If we put together all three surveys, on values, national identity, and rights, we find a perfectly consistent correlation of restricted definitions of trust, with restricted definitions of membership in the political community and a lack of any universal recognition of individual integrity (at least in its legal sense). All raise serious questions as to the viability of democratic political life oriented around those abstract and universal terms of trust that, in the western European and north Atlantic contexts, were the legacy of their particular historical development and the concomitant ideology of "individualism".

The transformation of trust with the move to a market-economy

The politically central and sociologically fascinating question remains: what will happen now? How will the generalization of trust on the societal level progress, and what forms will trust on the interpersonal level take in post-communist societies? An interesting example of the problems involved is presented by the Hungarian taxi- and lorry-drivers strike of October 26–28 1990. In this case we witnessed, on the one hand, continuing distrust of government, not only by the strikers, but indeed, in the early hours of the strike, by the general public, who feared military intervention and a repeat of 1956. On the other hand, there did evolve over a three-day period an institutional framework for presenting and discussing grievances, a consensual agreement and, crucially, through the televised arbitration (one of the strikers' chief demands), a new form of mutuality, participation, and trust, not only among the actors, but in society at large. From this case and others it is clear that a number of crucial changes must evolve in the present configuration of trust for a democratic and market-oriented society to be viable.

First, there must be a dramatic leap in the extension of trust to the institutional level to facilitate the progressive realization of market economics. (Here we recall Durkheim's famous strictures on the necessity, as the *sine qua non* of modern economic life, of rules regulating the market contract that are not themselves the subject of contract.)

Secondly, there will, of necessity, be a reorientation of the almost "feudal" nature of interpersonal trust based on particular, circumscribed, and ethnic solidarities and often turning on strong non-market ties of reciprocity and mutuality. However, the form this will take is an open question.

Thirdly, the basic grid of "us" and "them" that defined social solidarity and the boundaries of trust within state-socialist societies has already been

NOTES

dismantled. What is taking its place at present is a redefinition of the basic terms of social solidarity, of "us-ness" in society. We are witness to this process in a number of different areas, primarily in the rising ethnic and national consciousness of eastern European societies. This "revival" (if that is what it is) of primordial and ethno-centric bases of trust is of course fraught with danger for the emergence of a true civic polity. It does not, however, in itself rule out the establishment of mutual co-operation between different social groups. Whether that will be the rule or whether there will be a heightening of inter-group tensions and mistrust will depend precisely on the new terms of trust evolving in society.

In sum, any successful transition from state socialism and the command economy will be accomplished only if the terms of trust in the societies of east central Europe are universalized and generalized beyond local, circumscribed and, perforce, ethnically specific arenas to society as a whole. The relative rôle to be played by ethnic solidarities and identities in the restructuring of the boundaries of public and private life, of access to major markets in society, and the construction of new definitions of public goods (as well as criteria for public redistribution of private goods) will be central in determining the new terms of trust that will emerge in these societies.

Notes

1. For some recent perspectives on social trust, see Eisenstadt & Roniger (1984, especially 1–42); Giddens (1990); and Luhmann (1988).
2. On these aspects of modernization, see Deutsch (1961); Eisenstadt (1966); Huntington (1968); Inkeles & Smith (1974).
3. One of the few studies carried out into the concrete workings of this image of trust (and which throws important light on its limits) is that of Bernard Barber (1988).
4. For an explication of this view of trust, see Eisenstadt & Roniger (1984, esp. 1–42).
5. On the meaning of social citizenship, see Marshall (1973).
6. On this process, in the European context, see Rokkan (1975).
7. I am grateful to Elemer Hankiss for allowing me access to the as yet unpublished sources of this data and to the staff of TARKI for their technical assistance.
8. It is of some interest to note that the Hungarian responses to the 1982 questions regarding confidence in those institutions listed here were not too dissimilar from those of their western European neighbours. Comparative western European data for 1990 was not available, but one would assume that they did not register the same change as noted in the Hungarian case.
9. This data was originally published in Hankiss (1989).
10. Not surprisingly, this severely mediated expression of trust on the broader societal level echoes the findings of Almond and Verba's now classic study, *The Civic Culture*

TRUST, IDENTITY, AND TRANSITION FROM STATE SOCIALISM

(1963). There, the levels of trust in the USA and Britain were higher than in Germany, Italy and Mexico. Though Almond and Verba were studying the stability of democratic regimes and not democracy *per se* (or the pre-conditions for its existence), the results of both studies corroborate one another. (In Germany, it should be noted, the level of social trust rose from 1948 to 1959 – the year of the study – and again from 1959 to the 1970s as the polity stabilized. See Conradt 1989.)

References

Almond, G. & S. Verba. 1963. *The civic culture*. Princeton, New Jersey: Princeton University Press.

Banac, I. 1990. Political change and national diversity. *Daedalus,* special issue on Eastern Europe, Central Europe, Europe. Winter, 141–60.

Barber, B. 1988. *The logic and limits of trust.* New Brunswick, New Jersey: Rutgers University Press.

Conradt, D. 1989. Changing German political culture. In *The civic culture revisited*, G. Almond & S. Verba (eds), 212–72. London: Sage.

Csepeli, G. 1991. Competing patterns of national identity in post-communist Hungary. *Media, Culture and Society* **13**, 325–39.

Deutsch, K. 1961. Social mobilisation and political development. *American Political Science Review* **55**(3), 493–514.

Eisenstadt, S. N. 1966. *Modernisation, protest and change*. Englewood Cliffs, New Jersey: Prentice-Hall.

Eisenstadt, S. N. & L. Roniger 1984. *Patrons, clients and friends*. Cambridge: Cambridge University Press.

Giddens, A. 1990. *The consequences of modernity.* Palo Alto, California: Stanford University Press.

Hankiss, E. 1989. Between two worlds. In *Changing values in Hungarian society*, P. Somlai (ed.), 39–58. Budapest: CCP-Ts3.

Huntington, S. P. 1968. *Political order and changing societies*. New Haven, Connecticut: Yale University Press.

Inkeles, A. & D. H. Smith 1974. *Becoming modern: individual change in six developing countries.* Cambridge, Mass.: Harvard University Press.

Janos, A. 1982. *Politics of backwardness in Hungary 1825–1945*. Princeton, New Jersey: Princeton University Press.

Lerner, D. 1985. *The passing of traditional societies*. New York: The Free Press.

Luhmann, N. 1988. Familiarity, confidence, trust: problems and perspectives. In *Trust: making and breaking cooperative relations*, D. Gambetta (ed.). Oxford: Basil Blackwell.

Marshall, T. H. 1973. *Class, citizenship and social development*. Westport, Connecticut: Greenwood Press.

Rokkan, S. 1975. Dimensions of state-formation and nation-building: a possible paradigm for research on variations within western Europe. In *The formation of nation-states in western Europe*, C. Tilly (ed.), 562–600. Princeton, New Jersey: Princeton University Press.

REFERENCES

Sajó, A. 1989. Rights awareness in Hungary. In *Changing values in Hungarian society*, P. Somlai (ed.), 27–38. Budapest: CCP-TS3.

Schöpflin, G. 1990. The political traditions of eastern Europe. *Daedalus*, special issue on eastern Europe, central Europe, Europe. Winter, 55–90.

Smith, A. 1986. State making and nation building. In *States in history*, J. Hall (ed.), 228–63. Oxford: Basil Blackwell.

Index

Advisory Council on Applied Research and Development (ACARD) 47, 52
activism 88, 92, 106, 115, 140, 145
Alliance of Free Democrats (SZDSZ) 158, 159, 166–8, 173
  liberal intelligentsia 171, 172
Alsace 119, 122
anti-apartheid movement 78, 79, 98
anti-nuclear movement 88, 91, 93, 95–7, 99–101, 103–106
armament culture 67, 68
Armenia 60, 69
armies 58, 63–6, 70, 75
atomic energy 98
attitudes 81, 87–91, 95–98, 106, 107, 117, 130, 131, 137, 158, 164, 171, 173, 176, 178–82, 184, 189, 197
  anti-statism 124
  anti-militarism 66, 68
  anti-politicians 154
  anti-war 68, 91, 105
  pro and anti European 15, 16, 21, 83, 84
  social movements 87–91
Australia 61
Austria 69, 118, 119, 121, 122, 125, 127, 128, 130
Austro-Hungarian empire 192
authoritarianism 62, 138, 184
authoritarian solution, Poland 184
authority 17, 73, 75, 76, 84, 146,

149–51, 159, 166, 189
Azerbaijan 60, 69

Baltic states 65, 115, 116
Belgium 14, 60, 68, 73, 80, 118, 119, 121, 122, 128, 130
Bohemia 16, 126, 128
Bosnia 60, 67
bourgeois values 156, 165
Brezhnev, L. 150
Britain 29, 41
  attitudes towards environmental issues 120, 122, 123, 126, 129
  attitudes towards immigration 21
  mobilization potential, support for new social movements 94–105
  nation state 14, 18
  post-war militarism 56, 65, 66, 68
  social change 73, 78–80, 83, 87, 91, 93
  technology 46, 47
budget 14, 39, 50
Bulgaria 125, 129, 130

Canada 28, 61
capitalism 30, 47, 51, 53, 55, 57, 70, 121, 147, 153, 156, 158, 186
cargo cult 179, 186
central Europe 59, 125, 131, 137, 147, 173, 189, 190, 192–4, 199–201
Chernobyl disaster 51, 95, 115

203

INDEX

children and individualism 74, 81
Christian Democratic People's party
(KDNP) 157, 166, 173
Christianity 15, 121, 131
and environmentalism 121–3
citizenship 14, 55, 61, 63, 194
and state socialism 188, 189, 192, 197
civic culture 199, 200
civil society 24, 67, 69, 71, 140, 141,
145–7, 156, 172, 190, 197
civilization 55, 71, 114
Cold War 13, 55, 56, 58–63, 65–7,
70, 71
Common Agricultural Policy (CAP) 39,
50
common market 31–5
communication 16, 17, 19, 22–4, 37,
44, 45, 49, 52, 72, 190
communism 56, 62, 64, 66–9, 112,
114–16, 118, 124, 125, 134, 149–
75, 176–87, 194, 198, 200
collapse 56, 62, 69
see also socialism
Conference on Security and Co-
operation in Europe (CSCE) 28, 64
conscientious objection 61, 62
conscription 55, 61–63, 66
Council of Ministers 32, 33, 35, 39
convergence 81, 84
crisis theory 135
Croatia 16, 60, 67, 69, 129
cultural change 73
cultural identity 31, 72
cultural specificity 19
culture 13, 17, 18, 21, 23, 30, 36, 40,
55, 60, 64, 65, 113, 156
Czechoslovakia 60, 68, 115, 123, 125–
30, 191, 193
as a nation-state 191, 193
environmentalism/Green party 115,
123, 125–90

decentralization 119, 124, 128, 166
Delors, J. 14, 49, 51, 52, 53
democracy 20, 21, 23–5, 33, 35, 115,
124, 130, 142, 146, 149–73, 185,
186, 200
Democratic Charter, Hungary 161,
165, 171–3
democratic socialism 152, 161
Denmark 29, 118, 120
Durkheim, E. 72, 85, 188, 189

East Germany 115
eastern Europe 27, 36, 56, 58, 62
environmental concern 124–8
transition from state socialism 132–
48, 176–87, 188–201
ecology movement 88–91, 93, 95–
100, 103, 104, 106
mobilization potential 89–107
economic deprivation and environmentalism 120, 122
economic development 28, 35, 113,
121, 122, 129, 145, 146
economic growth 52, 136
economic rationalization 37
economic unification 35
economists 41, 151, 152, 154, 158–
60, 163
efficiency 19, 20, 23, 29, 34, 37, 44,
135, 160
elite collapse 138, 139
England 27, 42, 53, 123, 126, 128,
130, 192
environmental degradation 112, 115,
120, 121, 129
environmental movement 51, 114–17,
120, 127, 131, 134, 141, 142, 146
environmental politics 117, 125, 131
environmental protection 89, 91, 93,
112, 140
environmentalism 112–14, 116–25,
127–31
concern 114–18, 120–29
declining interest in eastern Europe 127–9
historical evolution 121
equality 24, 63, 79, 83, 177, 189
Estonia 132, 140, 143, 146, 147

INDEX

Law of Citizen Associations 140
singing revolution 143
ethnonationalism 116, 123, 129
Eurobarometer data/surveys 87, 90,
  102, 105, 118
Europe
  becoming postmodern 15, 19
  convergence/divergence 81, 84
  military service in 61–3
  state social interventionism 24
  post-military 55, 71
  Gulf War 67, 68
European Central Bank 28
European Commission 21, 32–5, 39,
  40, 48–52
  budget of 50
  central position 33
  decision making capacity 33
European Community 14, 15, 23, 27–
  38, 39, 40, 48, 50, 52, 53, 60, 61,
  63, 64, 69, 72–85, 107, 112, 113,
  114, 116, 118–21, 129, 130
  institutionalization of criteria of
    rationality 29, 31–37
  integration of members by legal
    norms 32
  political union 29, 34
  regime building 27, 28, 36
  security 28, 31, 45, 58, 63
  supra-national integration of 61
  weakness of Yugoslav interven-
    tion 67
European Court 32, 33
European currency union 28, 34
European integration 13, 15, 18, 21–9
European militarism 64, 65, 68
European Parliament 34, 35, 39, 50,
  72
European Values Study Surveys 72,
  73, 75, 76, 83, 194
expansion 73, 102, 135

familial privatism 13–26, 176–187,
  188–201
family life 74, 75, 81

FIDESZ (party of urban youth) 157,
  158, 166, 169, 173, 174
First World War 192, 193
FKGP *see* Independent Smallholders'
  party
Foucault, M. 18, 41–4, 52, 53
France 14, 17–21, 42, 46, 47, 53, 62,
  65, 68, 73, 79, 83, 87, 90, 93, 95–7,
  101–108, 118, 120–22, 128, 131,
  192
  anti-nuclear power movement 93,
    95–7, 101–106
  conscription in 62
  consistent mobilization poten-
    tial 101, 104
  freedom 19–24, 26, 31, 75, 79, 81, 83,
    84, 153, 161, 177
  functionalist 136, 142
Fund Supporting the Poor
  (SZETA) 154

G7 meetings 28
GATT (General Agreement on Tariffs
  and Trade) 15
Gemeinschaft 170, 190, 197
gender equality 63, 84
"geopolitical privacy" 57, 58
Germany 14, 16, 28, 36, 46, 62, 65,
  68–70, 73, 78, 79, 87–90, 93, 96,
  97, 99–104, 106–108, 115–23, 128,
  130, 174, 200
  anti-militarism 68
  conscription in 66
  Green parties/voters 117–20
  reunified, problems of 21
  see also East Germany; West Germany
Gesellschaft 106, 197
glasnost 62, 115, 155
global policing, European states 61
goods, public and private 15, 25, 31,
  135, 136, 178, 179, 186, 189, 190,
  199
government, liberal 41, 42
governmentality 41, 52, 53
Great Britain *see* Britain

INDEX

Greece 14, 29, 55, 62, 70, 73, 113, 118, 120, 121, 123, 127, 130, 192
Green electorate/groups/parties 114, 117–20, 123, 125–8, 130, 131
  politics 117, 119, 130
  vote 122, 123, 131
grievances 139, 144
Gulf War 67, 68

Habermas, J. 50, 53, 136–8, 140, 141, 147
harmonization 39–42, 44–6, 48–52, 152
  scientization of politics 50
  of technical procedures and standards 42, 46, 47
Havel, V. 62, 144
homogenization of politics 35
housing movements 142, 146
human rights 78, 79, 154
  Kis model 154, 159, 169, 174
Hungarian Democratic Forum (MDF) 159, 166, 167, 168, 169, 173, 174
  movementism/professionalism conflict 166
Hungarian Social Democratic Party (MSZDP) 157, 173
Hungarian Socialist Party (MSZP) 161, 162, 166, 173
Hungarian Socialist Worker's Party (MSZMP) 160, 161, 163, 168, 172, 173
Hungary 69, 125, 126, 128, 129, 132, 134, 140, 146–50, 153–5, 165, 167, 168, 174, 191, 194, 197, 200, 201
  Budapest taxi-drivers' blockade 168
  Green parties in 125, 126, 128
  intellectuals and democratization in 134, 140, 147–50, 153–5, 167, 168, 174
  liberal intelligentsia 171, 172
  opposition parties 167–72, 174
  pluralization of politics 156, 159

Iceland 61, 118
identity 14, 19–26, 31, 36, 49, 72, 84, 116, 141, 145, 153, 162, 188, 189, 192–4, 197–200
immigration 14, 21, 25
imperialism 66, 67
Independent Lawyers' Forum 152, 159
Independent Smallholder's Party (FKGP) 157, 166, 169, 173
individual behaviour, informal socializing of, Poland 180, 184
individualism 18, 20, 21, 24, 71, 73–5, 78, 84, 197, 198
  and family life 74, 75
industrial society/industrialism 17, 20, 21, 24, 55–7, 73, 85, 107, 123
  logic of 2
industrial standards 46
institutionalization 19, 27, 31, 36, 37, 56
intellectuals 133, 134, 140, 142–4, 147, 149, 150, 152–8, 160–74
  and democracy 9, 142, 147, 152, 154, 156, 157, 161, 163–5, 170–74
  in eastern Europe 133, 134, 143, 144, 147, 174
  people of rapid retreat 164, 165, 169
  as politicians 143, 152, 154, 157, 158, 160–71
  urban intellectual opposition 153
  with a sense of mission 164, 165, 167, 169
intelligentsia 124, 149–63, 167, 169–74
  liberal, Hungary 171, 172
  mediacracy 155, 156, 172
  retreat to political society 171–3
  and revolution 150, 155, 156
  in state socialism 149
  technocrats and meritocrats 150, 151, 160, 163
internal markets and international trade 16
International Telephone and Telegraph

206

INDEX

Consultative Committee (CCITT) 47

interpersonal trust 190, 191, 198

Ireland 61, 63, 73, 78–81, 83, 113, 118–21, 129

Italy 21, 22, 60, 68, 73, 78, 79, 83, 87, 91, 93, 95–7, 100–106, 114, 118–22, 129, 130, 200
  Green parties 114, 118–20
  mobilization potential, new social movements 87, 93, 95–106

Japan 15, 16, 23, 28, 61

journalism, mediacray in Hungary 155

justice 41, 147, 177, 183, 190

Kádár, J. 152, 153, 157, 163, 167–71

Kis, J. 154, 159, 169, 174

Konrád, G. 144, 147, 149, 150, 156, 171, 172, 174

KISZ see Young Communist League

language 14, 15, 30, 116, 155, 156, 168, 170

left-libertarian parties 118

legitimation 16, 32, 34, 136–8, 150, 162, 164, 171, 189, 197
  crises 9, 63, 138, 141, 147

Liberal government 41, 42

liberalism 23, 57, 121, 153, 154

Liechtenstein 61

lifestyle 144, 154

logic of system/actor, conflict between 18

Luxembourg 52, 118–21

Maastricht Treaty 1, 15, 25, 29, 34, 50

manufacturing technology 46

marginal movements 97, 98, 104

market socialism 151

marriage 74, 81

Marx, K. 57

marxism 57, 150, 152

mass communication 16, 23, 24, 156

mass consumption 16, 17, 20–24

mass culture 13, 16–18, 20–25

mass mobilization 56, 142, 143, 193

MDF see Hungarian Democratic Forum

media 40, 50, 67–9, 71, 88, 114, 132, 156, 168, 169, 175, 189, 191, 192, 194, 200
  the press 138, 155, 161, 169, 170, 171

mediacracy 155, 156, 172

mediation 25, 32, 35–7, 69, 86

metric system 42

militarism 55, 57, 59, 62, 64–6, 68–71

military conflict 37, 55, 57, 62, 65, 67, 69

military integration 25

military power 60, 64

military service 61–3

minorities 20, 23, 24, 67, 68, 192, 193, 197

mobilization cycle 102

mobilization potential 86, 87, 89–107
  total 99, 100, 105

modernity 13, 17, 53, 65, 107, 170, 194, 200

modernization 73, 87, 102, 103, 153, 154, 170, 186, 188, 199

Monaco 61

movements see anti-apartheid; anti-nuclear; ecology; environmental; Green parties; housing; mobilization potential; peace; polarizing; provocative; social; valence; women's

MSZDP see Social Democratic Party

MSZP see Hungarian Socialist Party

MZSMP see Hungarian Socialist Workers' party

nation-building 192, 200

nation-state 13–16, 18, 19, 23, 24, 29, 32, 35, 37, 42, 50, 53, 56, 57, 59, 60, 63, 69, 70, 71
  emergent, eastern and central Europe 189, 192–4, 200

INDEX

national destiny, issues 153, 160
national governments 33, 35, 51
national identity 14, 22–5, 83, 116,
192–4, 197–200; *see also Gesellschaft;
Gemeinschaft*
National Minorities Treaty 192
national pride 68, 77, 78
national society 16, 17, 19, 20, 22, 23
nationalism 1, 5, 9, 15, 22, 24, 59, 60,
70, 116, 123, 124, 129–31, 193, 194
nature protection organization 91, 115
natural resources 44, 113
nature protection 91, 115
Netherlands 73, 80, 87, 90, 93, 96–8,
102, 103, 106, 107, 116, 118, 120,
121, 128
 ecology movement 93, 96–8, 103
Network of Free Initiatives 166, 168
New March Front 161
New Zealand 61
nomenklatura 155, 167, 172
North Atlantic Treaty Organization
(NATO) 31, 60, 61, 103
Northern Ireland 73, 79, 81, 83
Norway 118
nuclear power 39, 48, 88, 91, 93, 95–7,
99–101, 103–106

obey/rebel alternative, Poland 181
opportunities 22, 34, 107, 139, 142,
143
Opposition Round Table (EKA) 152,
162, 163
output tensions 137

particularism 22, 24
peace movement 58, 69, 88, 93, 95–
100, 103–106, 115
 mobilization potential 93–106
peacekeeping 28, 63, 66
people of rapid retreat 164, 165, 169
personal complaint *vs* general concern 118, 120, 127
personal relationships 74, 75, 81, 84
pluralist interest groups 133

pluralization 156, 159
Poland 125, 126, 129, 134, 137, 174,
176, 178, 181–3, 185, 191
 Green parties 125, 126
 post-communist transition to democracy 181–5
polarizing movement 97, 98, 103
political culture 61, 119, 120, 147, 163,
171, 174, 191, 200
political elites 148, 167, 168, 171, 184,
185, 193
political integration 15, 22, 25, 48
political opportunity 103, 107, 139,
143, 144
political participation 84, 105, 124, 131
political science 138, 151
political society 145, 168, 171–3
political subsystems 136–8
political systems 15, 16, 22, 23, 25, 27,
32, 60, 80, 86, 115, 137, 176, 181
political transition 139, 170
political union 29, 34
politician-intellectuals 169
politicians 62, 63, 113, 115, 125, 135,
143, 151, 152, 154, 157–67, 169–71
pollution 51, 113–15, 120, 121, 126,
128–30, 141
Portugal 14, 29, 113, 118, 120, 121,
127, 129
post-Cold War 58, 65, 67, 70, 71
post-communist societies 173, 174,
178, 187, 198
post-military society 55, 71
post-national society 16, 17, 26
post-transition phase 143, 145
post-war society 47, 65, 68, 125, 163,
177
post-war Europe 138
postmaterialism 102, 116, 124
postmodern world 15, 19
Pozsgay, I. 152, 161, 162, 163
Prague Spring 150
pressure groups 114, 127, 152
private enterprise, Poland 182
productivity 17, 31, 102, 135

INDEX

provocative movements 97, 98, 104

rationality 17, 20, 41, 53, 137, 138, 150, 152, 176, 177–80, 183, 185
  criteria 29, 31, 32, 34–6, 37
rationalization 20, 23, 29, 30, 37
reform 35, 62, 108, 128, 148, 150–54, 158–63, 174, 184
Reform Alliance 162
reform circle 161, 162
reformers 151, 161, 177, 186
regime-building 27, 28, 36
religion and religious belief 74–6, 81, 120, 121, 130
  Catholic 79, 121, 122, 126, 129, 157, 191
  non-Protestant 121
  Protestant 115, 121, 122, 129, 159
representative democracy 23, 25, 152, 171
re-regulation 31
resources 113, 114
revival 59, 60, 199
revolution 52, 108, 135, 143, 148, 150, 155, 156, 170, 173, 174
Riesman 17
Romania 125, 129
rulers–ruled relations 178
Russia 62, 63, 129, 132, 140, 146, 193
nation-states 193

Scandinavia 123, 129, 146
science and technology, significance 17, 41, 47, 121
Second World War 56, 65, 68, 69
security 31, 45, 58, 63
security council 28
self-domestication, of humankind 36, 37
self-legitimation 162, 164
Serbia 60, 69, 129
singing revolution 143
Single European Act (1987) 39
Single European Market 27–9, 31, 34, 39, 40, 41, 51, 52

Slovakia 60, 123, 126, 128, 129
Slovenia 60
social and political conflict 32, 72, 102, 142, 144, 146, 166, 167, 182–4, 189, 191
social change 55, 70, 71, 73, 78, 84, 147
Social Charter 41
social citizenship 189, 199
social demands 23, 25, 184, 185
social democracy 24, 161
Social Democratic Party (MSZDP) 157, 162, 173
social development 121, 181, 182, 200
social expectations 18
social habits, Poland 177, 183, 185
social integration 24, 25, 179
social interaction, ground rules 188, 190
social movement 25, 58, 59, 86–93, 95, 96, 99–103, 105–108, 131–4, 138–42, 144–8
social order 132, 135, 141, 144, 186, 188–90
social organization 17, 22, 55, 192
social protest 180, 182, 184
social security 14, 23, 34
social solidarity, definition of basic terms 198, 199
social system 19, 132, 176
socialism 51, 53, 64, 88, 112, 115, 118, 132, 134, 135, 147–53, 156, 160–62, 173, 179, 186, 188–94, 198, 199; *see also* communism
socialization 18, 19, 61, 163, 189
socio-political outlook, Europe 77
sociological theory 57, 85
sociology 13, 29, 41, 53, 57, 58, 67, 70, 71, 73, 106, 107, 148
Solidarity 134, 137, 184
Soviet bloc (former) 27, 28
Soviet Union (former) 59, 69, 115, 116, 123–5, 133, 137, 138, 147, 160
Spain 14, 29, 63, 73, 78, 113, 114, 118, 120, 121, 123, 127, 129, 192

INDEX

Stalin, J. 133, 138, 145
standardization 43–51
standards 30, 31, 34, 42, 44–9, 51, 52, 116, 180
state bureaucracy 56, 59, 141, 191
 Hungary 149–60
state formation 59, 192, 193
state social interventionism 24
state socialism 132, 135, 149, 188–94, 199
surveillance, mutual 42, 53, 56–9
Sweden 118
Switzerland 16, 102, 118, 119, 128, 130, 192
SZDSZ *see* Alliance of Free Democrats
Szelényi 144, 147, 149–51, 156, 171, 174, 175
SZETA *see* Fund Supporting the Poor

technical standard 42, 46, 47
technocrats 150, 151, 160, 163
technology 17, 23, 39, 41, 44, 46–9, 51–3, 56, 61, 63, 67, 121
tolerance 75, 150, 155
totalitarianism 132
tradition 13, 20, 22, 23, 119, 137, 156, 197
transformation 25, 84, 132, 134, 145, 152, 171, 176, 185, 198
Treaty of Rome 4, 49
trilateral talks, Hungary 162, 164
trust 13, 88, 129, 188, 189, 190, 191, 192, 193, 194, 197, 198, 199, 200
 in Europe 191, 193
 in Hungary 191, 194, 197, 200
 in society 188–190
 in state-socialist society 188, 190–194, 199

transformation with move to market economy 199, 200
TUC 41

Ukraine 60, 129
united Europe 69, 83, 84
United Kingdom 40, 47, 50, 61, 63, 68, 118, 120, 126
United Nations 28, 66
United States 15, 16, 23, 28, 35, 46, 47, 60, 61, 67, 68, 69, 108, 200
universalism 22, 24

valence movement 97, 98
values study 73, 75, 76, 83

war 91, 105
Warsaw Pact 61
way of life 23, 168
Weber, M. 29, 30, 36, 45, 53, 55, 71, 137, 148
West Germany 70, 73, 78, 79, 87–90, 93, 96, 97, 99–104, 106–108, 118–20, 122
western Europe 27–8, 50, 57–71, 72, 84, 107, 108, 113–31, 189, 198, 199, 200
 social heterogeneity 14, 88
 state-making and nation-building 192
women's movement 79

xenophobia 22, 116

Yeltsin, B. 62
Young Communist League (KISZ) 160
Yugoslavia 59, 60, 65, 67, 69, 125
 EC response to conflict 5